PLUTARCH'S LIVES
FOR BOYS AND GIRLS

PELOPIDAS SETTING OUT FOR THEBES

PLUTARCH'S LIVES
FOR BOYS AND GIRLS
BEING SELECTED LIVES
FREELY RETOLD BY
W. H. WESTON
AND ILLUSTRATED BY
W. RAINEY

YESTERDAY'S CLASSICS
CHAPEL HILL, NORTH CAROLINA

Cover and arrangement © 2008 Yesterday's Classics, LLC.

This edition, first published in 2008 by Yesterday's Classics, an imprint of Yesterday's Classics, LLC, is an unabridged republication of the text originally published by Thomas Nelson and Sons in 1900. For the complete listing of the books that are published by Yesterday's Classics, please visit www.yesterdaysclassics.com. Yesterday's Classics is the publishing arm of the Baldwin Online Children's Literature Project which presents the complete text of hundreds of classic books for children at www.mainlesson.com.

ISBN-10: 1-59915-293-2

ISBN-13: 978-1-59915-293-6

Yesterday's Classics, LLC
PO Box 3418
Chapel Hill, NC 27515

PREFACE

This book aims at presenting, for the reading of boys and girls, a version of certain selected narratives from the immortal Lives of Plutarch.

In making the selection, the writer has been guided by the wish to choose those lives which appear to him to be most likely to interest young readers, and which also exhibit most clearly, either by example or contrast, the beauty of patriotism and the nobility of the manly virtues of justice, courage, fortitude, and temperance.

The selected lives have been freely retold. The discursive reflections, in which Plutarch frequently indulges, have been generally omitted; so also have many proper names not necessary to the full understanding of the stories. But, while much has been omitted, the writer has not presumed to add matter, other than seemed necessary to explain the importance or bearing of events, or to make the narrative clear to young readers. He trusts, therefore, that the version here presented retains much of the manner and method of Plutarch, and especially that the distinctive quality of that author which, to many readers throughout the ages, has given form and substance and a living reality to the heroes of ancient story, otherwise but the shadows of great names, has not been sacrificed.

He trusts, too, that his young readers may realise from Plutarch how little the essential things of life have changed during twenty centuries and more of the world's history; that, though trireme has given place to ironclad, and javelin-flight to bullet-hail, Salamis and Marathon called for the same wisdom, foresight, and courage as Trafalgar and Waterloo; and that to-day our country may demand from us, according to the measure of our abilities, service as unselfish and self-sacrificing as that which the noblest heroes of ancient Greece and Rome rendered to the lands whose history their deeds illumine for all time.

W. H. W.

CONTENTS

ARISTIDES 1
THEMISTOCLES 25
PELOPIDAS 53
TIMOLEON 80
ALEXANDER 113
PHILOPŒMEN 171
CORIOLANUS 193
THE GRACCHI 229
   TIBERIUS GRACCHUS 231
   CAIUS GRACCHUS 250
CAIUS MARIUS 268
JULIUS CÆSAR 319
BRUTUS 372

ARISTIDES

ARISTIDES *lived during the earlier part of the fifth century before Christ, a time when the liberties of the Greek states and cities in Europe were threatened by the vast hosts of the Persian Empire. The Persians had already conquered and enslaved the Greek cities of Ionia, that is, the coast districts and adjacent islands of western Asia Minor. Moreover, the Greeks in Europe were by no means united in opposition to the Persians. Hence it appeared almost certain that the vast forces at the disposal of the Persian king would speedily overrun the Greek states, and that their liberties and their civilisation would be destroyed, or at any rate profoundly altered, by the rule of a despotic foreign king. Had such been the event of the war, the whole subsequent history of Europe through all the ages would have been changed, since our civilisation has its roots in the glorious achievements of Ancient Greece. For this reason the great victories in which the Greeks overthrew the vast Persian armies have a direct personal meaning for every one of us to this day.*

In the three great battles by which Greece was saved, Marathon, Salamis and Platæa, Aristides played a distinguished part. The first of these, the battle fought in the plain between the mountains and the sea, where

> "The mountains look on Marathon
> And Marathon looks on the sea,"

showed that the Persians, who had never before been beaten by any army of Greeks, were not invincible. It proved indeed that their vast hosts could be conquered by a small number of Greeks who were inspired by staunch patriotism and dauntless courage.

The chief credit for the second of the great victories belongs to Themistocles, the great rival of Aristides. Not least among the glories of Aristides, however, is the lofty patriotism with which he put aside all feelings of personal enmity, and devoted himself to second the plans of his rival by which the sea-fight at Salamis was won, the Persian navy destroyed, and King Xerxes himself driven from Europe.

In the battle of Platæa the army which Xerxes had left behind was utterly destroyed and the dread of Persian conquest removed. In this battle the Spartan, Pausanias, was in chief command, but Aristides shared in the glory of the day, though, in truth, the victory was won by the valour of the Greek soldiers rather than by the skill of their generals.

ARISTIDES was an Athenian by birth, but accounts vary as to his station in life. For while some say that he was always very poor, another writer contradicts this view, and endeavours to prove that his family possessed a fair estate.

ARISTIDES

Some writers say that Aristides was from infancy brought up with Themistocles, who was destined to be his chief rival in the leadership of affairs at Athens. They tell us also that even in childhood the two were always at variance, not only in affairs of some importance but even in their sports and games, and that in their opposition they showed the differences in character which distinguished them throughout their careers. Themistocles was plausible, bold and artful, changeable in mood and yet impetuous in action. Aristides, on the other hand, was plain and straightforward, absolutely just and incapable of any falseness or deceit even in play.

When both had grown up, Themistocles proved himself a pleasant and agreeable companion. He made many friends, and his strength in public affairs depended largely upon his popularity. He did not hesitate to favour his friends, and when some one remarked of him that he would govern the Athenians very well if he would do so without respect of persons, he exclaimed, 'May I never sit upon the seat of judgment where my friends shall not receive more favour from me than strangers.'

Aristides, on the other hand, pursued an entirely different course in public affairs. He could not be persuaded to any act of injustice in order to oblige his friends, though he was willing to help them when what they requested was right and proper. He saw indeed that many, relying upon their interest with people in power, did things which could not be justified, but he, for his part, held that a good citizen should trust for his safety solely to the justice and rectitude of his actions.

But, as Themistocles made many rash and dangerous proposals and always endeavoured to thwart him in every way, Aristides was, in his turn, obliged to oppose his rival similarly, partly in self-defence and partly to lessen the power of Themistocles, which was daily growing through his popularity. Indeed, with the latter purpose, he was sometimes induced to oppose proposals of Themistocles which were good in themselves. Thus, on one occasion, he strenuously and successfully opposed a motion of Themistocles which he nevertheless felt to be of advantage to the public. Conscious of the evil of this rivalry between them, he could not forbear saying as he went out of the assembly, 'Athenian affairs cannot prosper unless both Themistocles and myself are put to death.' Very often Aristides put forward his proposals by means of a third person, in order that the public welfare should not suffer through the opposition of Themistocles to him. His steadfastness amid the frequent changes of political affairs was wonderful. Honours did not elate him nor was he cast down by ill success; in either case he pursued his course, convinced that his country had a claim to the services which he rendered without thought of advantage to himself. Not only was he able to resist the promptings of favour and affection, but also the temptation to let enmity and revenge sway the scales of justice.

It is said that, on one occasion, when he was prosecuting an enemy and had brought his charge against him, the people were about to give sentence against the accused without waiting to hear his defence.

Thereupon Aristides came to the assistance of his enemy, and entreated that he might be heard in accordance with the laws. Another time, when Aristides was himself the judge between two private persons, one of them observed that his opponent had injured Aristides many times. 'Tell me not,' said Aristides, 'what injury he has done to me, but what harm you have suffered from him, for I am trying your cause and not my own.'

Now about this time, when Aristides was in high reputation with his fellow-citizens, the Persian King Darius sent one of his generals to invade Greece. His pretext was the punishment of the Athenians for burning the city of Sardis in Asia Minor, but the real object of the invasion was the conquest of the whole of Greece. The Persian fleet arrived in the Bay of Marathon, and the invaders began to ravage the country round.

The Athenians now appointed a number of generals to command their army against the Persians. Of these Miltiades was the first in dignity, while in reputation and authority with the people Aristides stood next. Miltiades, in a council of war which was held, was in favour of attacking the enemy, and Aristides by seconding him added no little weight to his advice. Now it was the custom for the generals to command in turn, each for a day. But when it came to the turn of Aristides, he surrendered his right to Miltiades. Thus he stilled the spirit of contention, and induced the other generals to follow his example, so that Miltiades had supreme and continued command, and the other generals readily submitted to his orders.

In the battle of Marathon the main body of the Athenian army was the hardest pressed, for the Persians made their fiercest attacks upon the tribes which were stationed there. Themistocles and Aristides belonged to these tribes, and fought at the head of them. In the spirit of emulation which inspired them, they fought with such fury that the Persians were put to flight, and sought refuge on board their ships. The Greeks, however, saw with alarm that these vessels of the enemy, instead of sailing by way of the isles to return to Asia, were being driven in by the winds and currents towards Attica. They feared, therefore, lest Athens, left undefended in their absence, might fall an easy prey to the Persians. Nine of the tribes marched homewards at once to defend their city, and such speed did they make that they reached Athens in one day.

Aristides was left behind at Marathon with his own tribe to guard the spoils and prisoners. He did not disappoint the general opinion of his probity, for though there was much treasure of gold and silver scattered about, and rich garments and other spoil of great price in the tents and in the ships which had been taken, he was neither inclined to take anything himself nor would he suffer others to do so. Notwithstanding his watchfulness, however, some enriched themselves with stolen plunder unknown to him. Among them was Callias, the torch-bearer. One of the defeated barbarians, happening to meet him in a quiet place, prostrated himself before him and, taking him by the hand, showed him a great quantity of gold that lay hidden in a well. Callias, not less cruel than unjust, took the gold, and then slew the barbarian lest he should tell others of the matter.

Of all the virtues of Aristides, the people were most impressed by his justice, because that merit was of most advantage to the commonwealth. Hence, though he was a poor man and a commoner, he was given the royal and divine title of *the Just*. The name at first brought him love and respect, but, as time went on, envy began to arise. Themistocles was chiefly the cause of this, for he insinuated that Aristides, by drawing all cases to himself for decision, was practically abolishing the courts of law, and that he was thus insensibly gaining sovereign power, even though he was without the guards and outside show of royalty. The victory of Marathon, too, had greatly swollen the pride of the individual citizens, and they resented the fact that one of their number had risen to such extraordinary honour above them. They assembled, therefore, at Athens from all the towns of Attica, and pronounced the banishment of Aristides by the Ostracism, disguising their envy of his virtue under the pretence of guarding against tyranny.

The Ostracism was wont to be conducted in the following manner. Each citizen wrote the name of the man he wanted to be banished upon a shell or a piece of a broken pot. This he deposited in a part of the market-place enclosed with a wooden rail. Afterwards the magistrates counted the shells, and if the number did not amount to six thousand the Ostracism stood for nothing. If there were that number, however, or more, the shells were sorted, and he whose name was found on the greatest number was banished for ten years, but was allowed to retain his property.

It is said that while the people were writing the names on their shells a certain citizen, who could not write, came up to Aristides, whom he did not know by sight. Handing him the shell, the citizen requested that he would write the name of Aristides upon it. His hearer was greatly surprised at this, and inquired whether Aristides had ever injured him. 'No,' said the fellow, 'and I don't even know him, but it wearies me to hear everybody call him "the Just."' Aristides made no answer, but taking the shell, wrote his own name upon it and returned it to the man.

When, in obedience to the decree of banishment, Aristides quitted Athens, he lifted his hands to heaven and prayed that the people of his native city might never see the day when trouble would force them to remember him.

That day, however, came three years afterwards when King Xerxes with his vast host was advancing by long marches upon Attica. The Athenians then reversed the decree and recalled all the exiles. Their chief inducement to do so, however, was their fear lest Aristides would join the enemy and by his influence persuade many of the citizens to side with the Persians. Those who feared this little knew the man. Before the order for his recall was issued, Aristides was already busily engaged in stirring up the Greeks to defend their liberty. And afterwards, when Themistocles was appointed to the command of the Athenian forces,

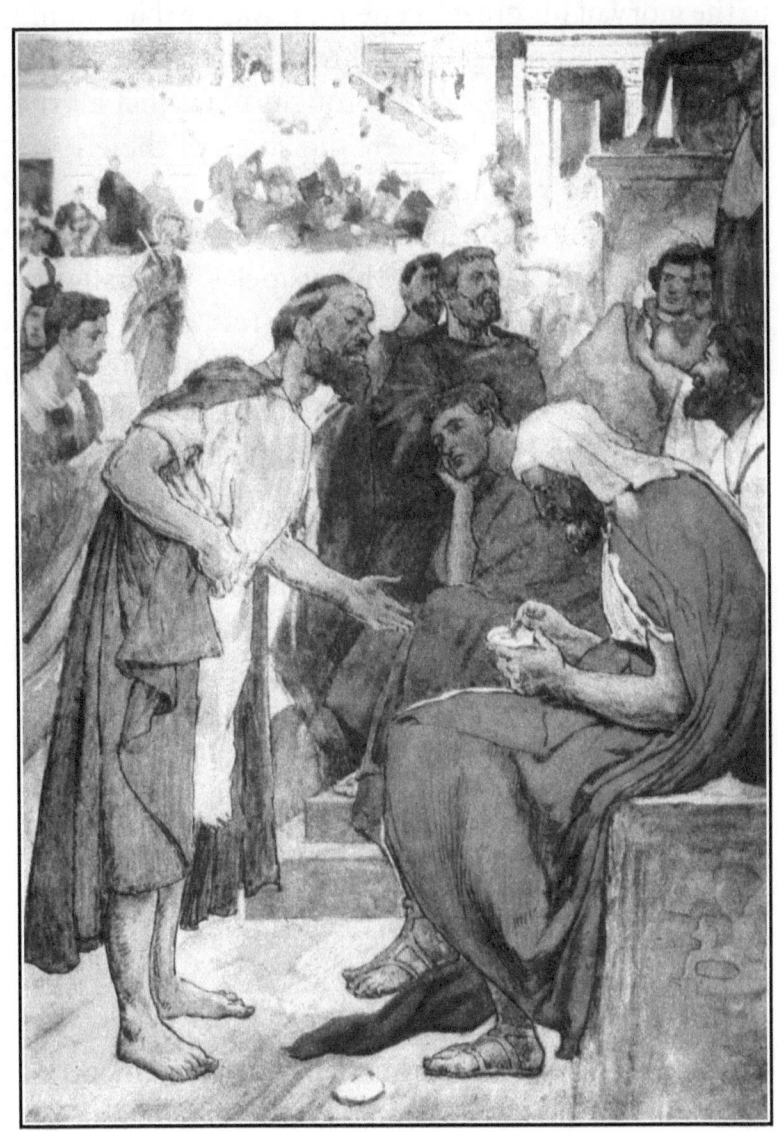
ARISTIDES AND THE CITIZEN

Aristides supported him both in person and by his counsel, being ready in the public welfare to contribute to the glory of his greatest enemy. It was he that, sailing by night with great danger through the Persian fleet to Themistocles at Salamis, brought news that all the narrow straits were beset by the ships of the enemy. As soon as he reached the tent of Themistocles he desired to see him in private, and spoke thus to his rival: 'If you and I are wise, Themistocles, we shall now lay aside our vain and childish quarrels, and contend only as to which of us shall do most for the safety and preservation of Greece.' He approved also of the plans of Themistocles, and set himself to further them. His former rival especially begged his support in impressing upon the Spartan Eurybiades the necessity of fighting the Persian fleet at once in the narrow seas, for he knew that Aristides had more influence with the Spartan leader than he himself had. In the council of war which assembled on this occasion, a Corinthian officer who was present said to Themistocles, 'Aristides does not agree with your opinion, for he says nothing.' 'You are mistaken,' said Aristides, 'for I should not have been silent had I not considered the counsels of Themistocles the best for our situation.' Hence, it was determined to fight in accordance with this advice. Aristides then, seeing that a small island which lies in the straits over against Salamis was full of the enemy's troops, embarked a number of the bravest and most determined of his countrymen on board some small transports. With these troops he attacked the enemy upon the island so fiercely that they were all cut to pieces, except a few of the most important persons, who were made prisoners. Aristides then placed a strong guard round the island, so that, of those who were driven ashore there, none of the Greeks should perish and none of the Persians escape. For it was round about this island that the battle raged most fiercely.

After the battle Xerxes, alarmed at the report that the Greeks intended to break down the bridge of boats across the Hellespont and thus cut off his retreat, hastened thither with all speed. However, he left behind him three hundred thousand of his best troops under Mardonius.

With so great an army the Persians were still very formidable, and Mardonius wrote menacing letters to the Greeks in such terms as these: 'You have indeed at sea defeated landsmen unused to naval war. There remain, however, the wide plains of the mainland, where we shall meet you with horse and foot.'

He wrote particularly to the Athenians, stating that he was empowered by King Xerxes to promise that their city should be rebuilt, that large sums of money should be paid the citizens, and that they should be given the sovereignty of Greece, if they would refrain from taking any further part in the war. When the Spartans heard of these proposals, they were very much alarmed lest the Athenians should accept them. They therefore sent ambassadors to offer shelter for the wives and children of the men of Athens and provision for the aged. Certainly the Athenians were in great distress, for they had lost both their city and their country. Nevertheless, by the influence of Aristides, they returned such an answer as can never be too much admired. They declared that they could forgive their enemies for thinking that they could be bought for silver and gold, since the barbarians knew of nothing more excellent. But they could not altogether forgive the Spartans for having so poor an opinion of them, as to think it was necessary to bribe them to fight in the cause of Greece by the offer of a paltry supply of provisions.

Aristides, having drawn up the answer in the form of a decree, summoned the ambassadors, both of the Spartans and of Mardonius, to an audience. To the Spartans he gave this message: 'The people of Athens would not barter the liberties of Greece for all the gold that exists above or under the ground.' Then, turning to the envoys of Mardonius, he pointed to the sun and said. 'So long as the sun shines, so long will the Athenians wage war against the Persians, to avenge their country which has been laid waste, and their temples which have been profaned.'

After this failure to win over the Athenians, Mardonius invaded Attica a second time, and the Athenians again retired to Salamis. Aristides was then despatched as ambassador to hasten the sending of the Spartan levies to their assistance. Afterwards he was appointed general of the Athenian forces, and, with eight thousand foot, marched to Platæa. There he was joined by the Spartans under Pausanias, who was commander-in-chief of all the allies, and by the troops of the other Greek states, who daily arrived in large numbers. The Persian army, which occupied an immense tract of ground, was encamped along the river Asopus. Within the camp they had fortified a space ten furlongs square, in which were stored their baggage and other things of value.

When the posts of the allies in the order of battle came to be assigned, a great dispute arose between the Athenians and the people of another town, for both claimed to be placed upon the left wing. Aristides, however, sought to compose the quarrel. 'This is no time,' said he, 'to dispute with our allies as to our relative bravery. Let us say to the Spartans and to the rest of the Greeks, that we are ready to do honour to any position by our actions. For we are here, not to quarrel with friends, but to fight our enemies, not to boast of the courage of our ancestors, but to show forth our own valour in the cause of Greece.' The council of war, however, decided in favour of the Athenians, and gave them the command upon the left wing, the Spartans being stationed on the right. When the armies were thus encamped near one another, Mardonius, in order to test the courage of the Greeks, ordered his cavalry, in which lay his chief strength, to skirmish with the enemy. Nearly all the Greeks were encamped on the slopes of a mountain on steep and stony ground, and could not therefore be well attacked by the enemy's cavalry. The Megarensians, however, three thousand in number, were posted in the plain. They were thus exposed alone to the attack of the horsemen, who charged them on every side. The greatly superior numbers of the Persians threatened to crush them, and they were obliged to send a messenger to Pausanias beseeching assistance.

Pausanias was at a loss what to do. He saw that relief was needed at once, for the camp of the Megarensians was darkened by the shower of darts and arrows rained upon it. He knew, however, that his own heavily armed Spartans were not fitted to act against cavalry. He therefore endeavoured to get the other generals and officers to volunteer to go to the aid of their distressed comrades. All declined with the exception of Aristides, who offered the services of his Athenians, and at once gave orders to one of the most active of his officers to advance to the rescue with a chosen band of three hundred men and some archers.

The Athenians were ready in a moment, and hastened to the attack. The general of the Persian cavalry, a man remarkable for his strength and graceful carriage, saw them approaching, and immediately spurred his horse and charged them. The Athenians received the attack of the Persian leader and his followers firmly, and a sharp conflict ensued. At length, however, the Persian general's horse threw his rider, who was so heavily armed that he could not recover himself. Indeed, for the same reason, he could not easily be slain by the Athenians, so thickly was he covered all over with plates of gold, brass, and iron. At last, however, the visor of his helmet leaving part of his face exposed, he was despatched by a spear-thrust in the eye. The fall of their leader decided the combat, and the Persians broke and fled.

Not many of the enemy were slain in this action. Nevertheless, the fight appeared important to the Greeks, for the general who was killed was second only to Mardonius himself in courage and in authority with the Persians, who loudly mourned his loss.

After this engagement with the cavalry, both sides forbore from fighting for a long time, for Greeks and Persians were alike assured by their diviners that victory would rest with the side which stood upon the defensive. At last, however, Mardonius, finding that he had only a few days' provisions left, and seeing also that the Greek army was daily increased by the arrival of fresh troops, grew uneasy at the delay. He resolved to cross the river at daybreak the next day and fall upon the Greeks, whom he hoped to find unprepared.

But at midnight a horseman quietly approached the Greek camp, and addressing the sentinels bade them call Aristides to him. The Athenian general came at once, and the stranger said to him: 'I am the King of Macedon, who out of friendship to you have come through great dangers to prevent your fighting under the disadvantage of a surprise. Mardonius will attack you to-morrow, for scarcity of provisions forces him to risk a battle or see his army perish with hunger. He must fight, therefore, though the soothsayers seek to prevent him from doing so.' Aristides promised that if the Greeks were victorious, the whole army should be acquainted with the generous daring of the King of Macedon in coming to give the warning. At present, however, it was decided that only Pausanias should be given the intelligence of the enemy's intention.

Aristides therefore went immediately to the tent of the commander-in-chief and laid the whole matter before him. At once the other chief officers were sent for, and were ordered to get their troops under arms and drawn up in order of battle. At the same time, Pausanias, it is said, informed Aristides that he intended to change the position of the Athenians from the left wing to the right. His object was to bring the Athenians against the Persians, because they had already had experience in fighting them, and would on this occasion fight with the more confidence because of their previous success.

All the Athenian officers, except Aristides, thought that Pausanias was acting in a very high-handed manner in thus moving them up and down without consulting them, while he left the other allies in their allotted posts. Aristides, however, reproved them. 'You contended,' said he, 'for the command of the left wing, and now, when the Spartans of their own free will offer you the right wing, which is in effect the leadership of the whole army, you are dissatisfied.'

Influenced by these words, the Athenians readily agreed to change places with the Spartans, and nothing was now heard among them but words of encouragement and confident anticipations of victory. 'The Persians,' said they, 'bring neither bolder hearts nor stouter bodies to battle than at Marathon. We recognise the same gay clothes and the display of gold, the same effeminate bodies and unmanly souls. And, for our part, we bring against them the same weapons and the same strength that have conquered them before. Bold in the memory of our victories, we fight them again for the trophies of Marathon and Salamis, and for the glory of the people of Athens.' But, while the change of posts was being carried out, the movement was perceived by the Thebans, who were serving with the Persians, and intelligence of it was given to Mardonius. The Persian general thereupon immediately changed the position of his wings, and this was followed by yet another change on the part of Pausanias. Thus the day passed in marchings, backwards and forwards, without the two armies coming to action at all.

In the evening the Greeks held a council of war, and determined, because their water supply in the position they now occupied was disturbed and fouled by the enemy's horse, to move their camp during the night. Accordingly, when darkness had fallen, the officers began to march off their men to the new position which had been chosen. The movement, however, led to great confusion, for the men followed unwillingly, and many regardless of discipline made off to the city of Platæa. The Spartans, too, were left behind, for one of their officers, a man of undaunted courage, bluntly called the retirement a disgraceful flight, and declared that for his part he would not quit his post, but would remain where he was with his troops, and fight it out alone with Mardonius.

In vain Pausanias urged that the retirement was made in agreement with the decision of all the allies. Taking up a large stone, the officer cast it at the feet of his general. 'There,' cried he, 'is my vote for battle, and I despise the timorous counsels of others.' The commander was at a loss what to do, but at length sent word to the

Athenians, who by this time were advancing, to halt a while. He then set off to join them with the other troops, hoping that by doing so he should in the end induce the stubborn Spartan officer to follow him.

By this time day had dawned, and Mardonius, who was aware of the movement of the Greeks, set his army in order of battle and bore down upon the unsupported Spartans. The Persians and their allies rushed to the fight with loud shouts of triumph and clanging of arms, as if they expected rather the plundering of a mob of fugitives than a battle. And indeed it seemed like to be so, for though Pausanias halted and ordered every one to his post, yet for some reason he did not give the order for battle, and hence the Greeks did not engage readily. Moreover, even after the battle was begun, the Greek forces remained scattered in small bodies.

Meanwhile, Pausanias sacrificed to the gods. The omens, however, were unfavourable, and he therefore ordered his Spartans to lay down their shields at their feet and await his order. Then, while the Persian cavalry was still advancing, he offered other sacrifices. At last the enemy came within bowshot, and a number of the Spartans were wounded by their arrows. Among them was one who was held to be the tallest and finest man in the whole army. As he was on the point of dying this brave soldier exclaimed, 'I do not lament dying for Greece, but bitter it is to die without sword-stroke at the enemy.' In this trying ordeal the firmness and steadiness of the Spartans were wonderful. They stood as marks for the enemy's archers calmly awaiting the orders of their general.

At length the omens for which Pausanias had waited and prayed appeared, and the diviners promised him victory. Then at once his orders to charge rang out, and the Spartan phalanx leapt into life, like some fierce animal erecting his bristles and preparing to put forth his mighty strength. Then did the barbarians see that they had to deal with men who were ready to shed their last drop of blood, and covering themselves with their targets, they shot their arrows thickly upon the advancing Spartans. Steadily, in a close compact body, the phalanx bore down upon them, their targets were thrust aside, and pike-thrusts at faces and breasts brought many of them to the ground. But even when overthrown they fought desperately, breaking the pikes with their naked hands, and leaping to their feet again they stood the quarrel out with sword and battle-axe.

Meanwhile, the Athenians at a distance remained at the halt, as they had been ordered. But the tumult of battle reached them and, moreover, an officer sent by Pausanias informed them of the position of affairs. At once they hurried to the assistance of the Spartans, and as they were crossing the plain, the Greeks who fought on the Persian side came up to attack them. As soon as he saw them, Aristides advanced a long way in front of his own troops, and with a loud voice called upon them to give up this unnatural war and not to oppose their fellow-Greeks, who were risking their lives for the common country of all their race. But he found that the foe paid no heed to his words, but continued their hostile advance. He had therefore to await the attack of this body of Greeks, who were about five thousand in number, instead of going to the assistance of the Spartans as he had intended.

Thus the battle resolved itself into two actions, the Spartans against the Persians, and the Athenians against the traitor Greeks, of whom the Thebans made up the chief part. The former of these two actions was the first decided, for the Persians were broken and routed and their general slain by a blow on the head with a stone, as the oracles had foretold. The barbarians then fled before the Spartans to their camp, which they had beforehand fortified with wooden walls. Soon after the Athenians routed the Thebans, killing some three hundred of their most distinguished men on the spot. Just at this time the news came that the Persians were shut up in their wooden fortifications, and the Athenians, leaving the defeated Greeks to escape, hastened to join in the siege.

Their assistance was timely, for the Spartans were unskilled in the storming of walls, and therefore made but slow progress. The Athenians, however, soon took the camp, and there was made great slaughter of the enemy. It is said that out of three hundred thousand men barely forty thousand escaped. On the other hand, only one thousand three hundred and sixty of those who fought in the cause of Greece were killed. Of these fifty-two were Athenians, while the Spartans lost ninety-one.

This great victory at Platæa went near to being the ruin of Greece, for the Athenians and the Spartans began to contend as to which of the two had gained the chief glory of the day, and to which should be given the honour of erecting the trophy for the victory. Indeed, it is likely that the quarrel would have been decided by arms had not Aristides exerted himself to pacify the other Athenian generals, and to persuade them to leave the matter to be decided by the general body of the allies. Accordingly a general council was called, and, in order to avoid civil war, it was decided to award the palm of valour to neither of the disputants, but to a third place. In the end Platæa, the scene of the battle, was pitched upon for this purpose, it being a place which could not excite the envy of either Athens or Sparta. To this proposal Aristides first agreed on behalf of Athens, and was followed by Pausanias, who accepted it for Sparta.

Thus the allies were reconciled. Eighty talents were then set aside for the Platæans, and with it they built a temple and set up a statue of the goddess Athene. There annually they celebrated the victory with solemn services and sacrifices, and with a libation to the memory of the men who died for the liberties of Greece.

Some time after these events Aristides was sent, with Cimon as a colleague, in command of the Athenians, to continue the war against the Persians. He found that the pride and insolence of Pausanias and the other Spartan generals were making them very unpopular with the allies. For Pausanias scarcely even spoke to the officers of the forces of the other states without anger and bitterness, and he punished many of the men severely, flogging some, and ordering others to stand all day with an iron anchor upon their shoulders.

In all things he gave first place to Spartans, and would not allow any of the allies to supply themselves with forage, or sleeping-straw, or drinking-water, until the Spartans had first been supplied. Indeed, he stationed servants with rods to drive off any who should attempt to take these things before it suited his pleasure. Aristides went in vain to remonstrate with him. The only answer of Pausanias was to knit his brows and say that he had no leisure to hear such complaints.

Aristides, on the other hand, treated all with courtesy and kindness, and prevailed on his colleague Cimon to behave with equal affability. Hence the sea-captains and officers of the allies, particularly those from the islands, tired of the harshness and severity of the Spartans, besought Aristides to take the chief command. Two of the officers indeed boldly attacked Pausanias's galley at the head of the fleet. They told him that the best thing he could do was to retire, and that nothing but the memory of the great victory which fortune had permitted him to win at Platæa, prevented the Greeks from wreaking upon him a just vengeance for his treatment.

The end of the matter was that the allies left the standards of the Spartans and ranged themselves under the ensigns of Athens. The people of Sparta took the matter in a noble and wise spirit. They saw that power had spoiled their generals, and they therefore sent no more in their place, for they thought it more important that a lesson in moderation and regard for right and justice should be given than that they should retain the chief command of the Greek forces.

The allies now further begged that the Athenians would allow Aristides to fix the amounts which each state and each city should be called upon to provide for the purposes of the war. This power, which in a way made him master of Greece, was given to him. But in his hands authority was not abused. He went forth to his task poor and returned from it poor, having arranged matters with such equal justice that the allies blessed the settlement as 'the happy fortune of Greece.'

Indeed, though Aristides had extended the influence of Athens over so many allied cities and states, he continued poor to the end, and gloried in his noble poverty no less than in the laurels he had won. This was clearly proved in the case of Callias, the torch-bearer, his near relation, who was prosecuted by certain enemies. When the accusers had alleged what they had to bring against him, which was nothing very serious, they brought in other matters which had nothing to do with the case, and thus addressed the judges: 'You know Aristides, who is justly the admiration of all Greece. You have seen how mean his garb is, and that his home is almost bare of necessaries. Yet this Callias, the richest man in Athens, is his own cousin. He, nevertheless, allows his noble relative, of whose influence he has availed himself, to live in utter wretchedness.'

Callias perceived that the charge thus dragged into the case was likely to prejudice the judges against him. He therefore called upon Aristides, who testified in the court that Callias had many times offered him considerable sums of money, but that he had always refused the proffered gifts, with some such words as these: 'Aristides has more glory in his poverty than Callias in his riches. We see every day many who spend freely for good or ill, but it is hard to find one who bears poverty with a noble spirit. And he only is ashamed of poverty who is poor against his will.' When he had thus given evidence, there was not a man in court who did not feel that it was indeed better to be poor with Aristides than rich with Callias.

His conduct with regard to Themistocles furnishes a striking instance of his uprightness. For when Themistocles was accused of crimes against the state, Aristides had the opportunity of revenging himself upon the man who had been his constant opponent and the chief cause of his banishment. But, while many others of the leading men in Athens joined in the outcry against Themistocles and aided in driving him into exile, Aristides alone made no accusation against him. As he had not envied his rival in his prosperity, so neither did he rejoice at his misfortunes.

Aristides died in the year of the banishment of Themistocles. It is said that his funeral was conducted at the public charge, since he did not leave behind him enough money to defray the cost, and that the city of Athens further gave marriage portions to his daughters, and a gift of land and money to his son.

THEMISTOCLES

PLUTARCH, *who loved comparisons and contrasts, is careful to bring out into strong relief the difference in character between Themistocles and his great rival Aristides. But, however much inferior Themistocles may have been to Aristides in the virtues of justice and simplicity, he was undoubtedly the greatest man of his age in foresight and in fertility of resource; possibly a worse man than Aristides, but certainly a greater statesman. To British boys and girls, justly proud of the great deeds of those heroes of our own race, who*

> *"Left us a kingdom none can take,*
> *The realm of the circling sea,"*

it should be especially interesting to find how clearly this old Greek statesman, sailor, and soldier realised the value of sea-power, how steadfastly he pursued his object of making Athens a great naval power, and how skilfully he used the weapon he had forged to shatter the Persian fleet at Salamis. This battle, the crowning achievement of Themistocles, ranks among the very greatest sea-fights in history, both in the importance of its results and the completeness of the triumph. Salamis shattered the naval power of Persia as completely as Trafalgar ruined the

French at sea, and Salamis made the final victory at Platæa possible, just as Trafalgar prepared the way for the victories of Wellington. The completeness of the triumph is well expressed by Byron in one stanza of the **Isles of Greece:**

> "A king sat on the rocky brow
>   Which looks o'er sea-born Salamis;
> And ships, by thousands, lay below,
>   And men in nations; all were his!
> He counted them at break of day,—
>   And when the sun set where were they?"

The banishment of Themistocles on unproved charges was a bitter reward for his unexampled services to Athens. But it at least served to show that, however great his arrogance and pride may have been, his resentment did not so far overcome his patriotism as to lead him, like another Coriolanus, to avenge himself actively upon his native city.

In the words of one of the greatest of the Greek historians, Themistocles was 'of all men the best able to decide upon the spur of the moment the right thing to be done.'

THE lofty honours which Themistocles attained were in nowise due to the advantages of birth. On his father's side he sprang from an Athenian family which was but of the middle class, while on his mother's side he is said by some to have been of alien blood. But be that as it may, he early showed his ingenuity in overcoming difficulties. For it was a rule of the city of Athens that the base-born lads should assemble for their sports at a separate wrestling place outside the city walls. But Themistocles induced some of the noble Athenian youths of his acquaintance to join him in the wrestling at this place. Thus he contrived to break down one of the distinctions between himself and those of pure Athenian descent.

He was indeed a lad of lively spirit, quick of apprehension, and keenly interested in affairs of state. Even his holidays and times of leisure he spent, not as other boys are wont to do, in idleness or play, but in composing speeches and practising the delivery of these orations. Hence his schoolmaster was wont to say, 'You, Themistocles, are destined to be something out of the ordinary. Great you will be one way or the other, either for good or for evil.'

But though he applied himself eagerly to subjects which appeared to him to be of real importance, he paid but slight attention to merely graceful or pleasing studies. This neglect of the lighter accomplishments brought upon him, in later years, ridicule, which called from Themistocles a proud retort. 'True it is,' said he, 'that I cannot play upon the lute or tune a harp. This only can I do—make a small and obscure city great and glorious.'

The story is told that his father wished to dissuade him from taking part in politics, and to this end took the youth down to the seashore. There he pointed out to his son the old galleys lying forsaken and rotting on the beach, and told him that thus did political parties treat their leaders when they had no further use for them. But the youth, fired with a passion for renown, was not to be persuaded, and very early in life began to take the keenest interest in political affairs. From the outset he was determined to become the greatest man in the state, and, full of ambition and of confidence in himself, he eagerly joined in schemes to oust those who were then the leaders in the state.

Themistocles especially opposed and attacked Aristides, and the breach between them was widened by the difference between their characters. For Aristides was of a gentle and honourable nature, caring much for the interest and safety of the state, but little for his own profit and glory. Themistocles, on the other hand, was at this time madly inflamed with a craving for personal renown, so that the great deeds of others filled him with envy. It is said that after Miltiades had defeated the Persians in the great battle of Marathon, Themistocles withdrew himself from the society of his friends, and lay sleepless at night for envy of the glory which Miltiades had won.

But unworthy envy did not diminish his wisdom nor cloud his foresight. For, while others thought that the victory of Marathon had put an end to the war, Themistocles saw that it was but the beginning of a still greater struggle. Fully impressed by this opinion, he set himself to prepare for the conflict, so that he might stand forth as the champion of the whole of Greece. And he sought by all means in his power to make his city ready for the day of trial.

THEMISTOCLES

Not only did Themistocles foresee the coming struggle with the mighty power of Persia, he saw also the means by which the invasion could be defeated. To him alone was given the foresight to perceive that the fate of Athens, and indeed of the whole of Greece, would be decided upon the sea. He found his city so weak in her land forces that they were unable to contend even with the troops of the neighbouring states. Small, therefore, was the hope that they could successfully resist the vast armies of the Persian king. But Themistocles saw that by building a powerful Athenian fleet the means would be provided of foiling the Persian invasion, and of making his native city the mistress of Greece. Thenceforth, by slow but unswerving steps, he laboured unceasingly to turn the thoughts of his fellow-citizens towards the sea.

In the first measures which he took towards this end, Themistocles showed great wisdom. For it happened that the Athenians were at war with the Æginetans, and that the latter, by reason of the number of their ships, held sway upon the waters. Now it was the custom at this time for the Athenians to divide among themselves the money which was derived from the produce of certain silver mines. In this position of affairs, Themistocles came forward with the proposal that the people should forgo the distribution among themselves, and should, out of patriotism, devote the money to the building of ships to be used against the Æginetans. In urging this course upon them he made no mention of the Persians, whose coming invasion was ever in his mind, for he well knew that men are more ready to provide against an immediate, though smaller, danger than against a greater peril which is still remote. And since the minds of the Athenians were inflamed with anger against the Æginetans, Themistocles had his way. The citizens consented to the sacrifice, and with the money thus provided, a hundred ships were built which afterwards did good service against the Persian fleet.

Thenceforward, step by step, the sea-power of Athens was built up under the influence of Themistocles, so that, as Plato says, he changed the Athenians from steady land-soldiers to storm-tossed mariners. Some there were who reproached him with the change, saying that he took from his countrymen the spear and the shield, and bound them, as in servitude, to the rowing-bench and the oar. But the wisdom of Themistocles is sufficiently shown by events. For it was from the sea that deliverance came unto the Greeks, and the city of Athens, after it had been destroyed, was reestablished by the galleys which the foresight of Themistocles had provided.

Meanwhile, Themistocles sought by all means the favour of the people. He is said to have been eager to acquire riches, in order that he might be liberal in giving to others and in providing splendid entertainments. He was able to salute each citizen by name, and this proof of his notice greatly pleased the common people. Moreover, in disputes between private persons, he showed himself a just and upright judge. Thus his favour with the people increased, and his party, having gained the upper hand over the faction of Aristides, procured the banishment of his rival from Athens.

At length the time of danger which Themistocles had long foreseen and for which he had long prepared arrived. The vast hosts of the King of Persia were set in motion and advanced upon Greece. Meanwhile, the Athenians were eagerly discussing the choice of a commander, and there appeared a danger lest the popular choice should fall upon one who was indeed a man of eloquent tongue, but who was faint-hearted and a slave to the love of riches. Under such leadership all must have been lost, but Themistocles, it is said, averted the danger by buying off the orator's claims by the payment of a sum of money.

During the advance of the Persian host, Themistocles in many ways gave evidence of the resolute spirit with which he faced the danger. Thus, when the Persian King Xerxes sent messengers and an interpreter into Greece demanding from the Greeks earth and water in token of subjection, Themistocles caused the interpreter to be seized and put to death for daring to utter the barbarian orders in the Greek tongue. And when another came, bearing gold with which to bribe the Greeks to espouse the Persian cause, Themistocles issued an order by which the agent of Xerxes and all his descendants were declared infamous. But most of all to the credit of Themistocles was his success in persuading the Grecian states to lay aside their quarrels among themselves during the Persian war, and to present a united front against the common foe.

When the command of the forces of Athens had been given to Themistocles, he at once endeavoured to persuade the citizens to leave the city and to take to their ships, in order that they might fight the enemy as far as might be from Greece. But, as many opposed this plan, he led a large land force into Thessaly. The army, however, returned without accomplishing anything of importance; and when it was known that Thessaly and the states even to the very borders of Attica were going over to the Persians, the Athenians were more ready to listen to the advice of Themistocles, and to fight the matter out at sea.

They therefore sent him with the ships to guard the straits of Artemisium against the advance of the Persian fleet, and there the Athenians were joined by the ships of the allied Greek states. The majority of the allies wished that Eurybiades should have the supreme command, and begin the fight with his Spartans. To this the Athenians were loath to consent. For, as the number of their ships exceeded that of all the other allies together, they considered the post of honour their rightful due. Themistocles, however, seeing the danger of any division among the allies at this time, persuaded his fellow-citizens to submit, telling them that, if they acquitted themselves manfully in the war, their allies would of their own free will award them the post of honour in the future. Thus the moderation of Themistocles upon this occasion prevented disunion among the Greeks, and contributed to the deliverance of his country. Moreover, through him the Athenians gained the lofty glory of alike surpassing their enemies in valour and their allies in wisdom.

But, when the vast armada of Persia appeared in sight, Eurybiades was astonished at the prodigious number of vessels, the more so as he learnt that two hundred other ships of the enemy were hidden from view by an island which lay between them and the Grecian fleet. He despaired of conquering so vast a navy, and was anxious to retreat to the coasts of the southern peninsula of Greece, where he might have the support of his land forces. Against this timorous policy Themistocles exerted all his arguments, and it was only by his urgent advice and his stratagems that the fleet of the Greeks was kept together to face the foe.

No decisive result arose from the battles of Artemisium which followed. But from them the Athenians drew this great advantage. They learnt in the press of actual battle that neither the numbers of the foe, nor the splendour of their arms and ornaments, nor their boastful barbaric shoutings were terrible to men of resolute courage. Such things they learnt to despise, and they learnt, too, to come to close grips with their foes and fight them hand-to-hand. Therefore the poet Pindar rightly says of the fights at Artemisium, that in those conflicts with the invaders Athens laid the foundation-stones of liberty.

Soon, however, there came to the fleet at Artemisium the news that Leonidas and his three hundred Spartans had fallen in heroic fight in the Pass of Thermopylæ, and that the Persian king was master of all the passes into Greece by land. Thereupon the Grecian fleet retreated, and to the Athenians, elated by the valour they had displayed, was given the command of the rear, as the post of most danger and honour. As the fleet sailed along Themistocles caused to be set up, at all likely places along the coast, stones bearing inscriptions calling upon the Ionians, who were serving with the Persians, to come to the aid of the Greeks from whom they were descended. This he did hoping that the Ionians would indeed come to the succour of their kinsmen, or that, at the least, the Persians might be made to doubt the fidelity of the Ionians, and thus dissension be spread in the ranks of the enemy.

By this time Xerxes had advanced some distance southward, devastating the country and destroying the cities, and daily the danger to Athens became more imminent as he approached the borders of Attica. The Athenians urgently, but in vain, implored the allies to join them in opposing the Persian host beyond the northern borders of their state. For the thoughts of all the allies were engrossed with the defence of the Peloponnesus, the southern peninsula of Greece, which they hoped to secure by building a rampart across the narrow Isthmus of Corinth.

Thus the Athenians, enraged by their betrayal and cast down by their desertion, were left to their own resources. To fight alone against such a host was hopeless; one course only remained to them—to abandon their beloved city and to take to their ships. But this the common people were very unwilling to do, not seeing how even victory in the future would profit them, if their homes were left desolate, and the temples of their gods and the tombs of their forefathers abandoned to the fury of the barbarians.

In this position of affairs Themistocles, being at a loss how to persuade the people by any use of human reason, had recourse to signs and wonders. The serpent of Athene, patron goddess of Athens, disappeared mysteriously from the inner sanctuary of her temple. Acting upon the suggestion of Themistocles, the priests declared that the disappearance signified that the goddess herself had departed from the city and had gone down before them to the sea. Moreover, Themistocles made use of an oracle, which declared that when 'all else was captured the wall of wood alone should remain.' He urged upon the citizens that by 'walls of wood' the oracle could mean nothing but ships; moreover that, in speaking further of 'divine Salamis,' the oracle revealed that the island of Salamis should one day be the scene of some great good fortune to the Greeks. So at length Themistocles prevailed upon the Athenians to leave their beloved city and set sail for Salamis.

A decree was therefore passed that Athens should be left to the protection of its patron goddess, and that all citizens able to bear arms, having first sent away their dependents to some place of safety, should embark on board the ships. In accordance with this decree, most of the Athenians sent their parents, wives and children to Trœzen, where they were received with ready goodwill and hospitality.

Thus the whole city of Athens was embarked

upon board ship. It was indeed a sight to awaken both pity and admiration, to see the citizens thus send away their beloved ones, and, without yielding to their tears and embraces, themselves man the fleet and pass over to the island of Salamis. Especially was compassion stirred on account of the many old men who, by reason of their great age and infirmity, were left behind in the abandoned city. Nor, indeed, could even the dogs and other tame animals be seen without pity. For they ran piteously along the shore, when the ships put off, as if imploring their masters to take them. One dog, so it is said, leaped into the sea and swam beside his master's galley even until the fleet came to Salamis, where the faithful creature lay down exhausted and died.

The recall of Aristides was not the least of the great actions of Themistocles at this time. Perceiving that the people regretted the absence of their former leader in this crisis of their affairs, he procured the passing of a decree to the effect that those Athenians who had been banished might return to aid the cause of Greece. Thus Aristides, who had formerly been banished through the party of Themistocles, was now restored by his influence.

On account of the greatness of Sparta, its admiral Eurybiades was given the command of the whole of the Greek fleet which assembled off Salamis. He was, however, unfitted for the command, for he was faint-hearted in the presence of danger. And at this juncture he wished to weigh anchor and to set sail for the Isthmus of Corinth, near which the army of the Greeks was encamped. Themistocles exerted all his influence in opposition to this proposal. He saw that the only hope of the Greeks was to fight the battle in the narrow straits, where the Persians would largely lose the advantage of their vast numbers. On one occasion Eurybiades, to check the eagerness of the Athenian commander to engage the enemy, reminded him that, in the Olympic sports, those who started before the signal for the race was given, received the lash. 'True,' replied Themistocles, 'but those who lag behind at the start do not win the race.' On another occasion, Eurybiades, whose patience was tried by the persistent arguments of Themistocles, lifted his staff as if to strike the Athenian. Thereupon Themistocles said calmly, 'Strike if you will, but at least hear me.' The Spartan could not but admire such self-command, and in spite of himself listened to the Athenian's further arguments against retreat. But one of the officers who stood by broke in with the taunting words: 'It ill becomes you Athenians, who have no city of your own, to advise us to give up our homes and abandon our countries.' Themistocles sharply retorted: 'Base fellow art thou to use such a taunt! True it is that we have left our houses and our walls, for we will not endure to be made slaves for the sake of such things. But in these two hundred ships here ready to defend you all, we still possess the finest city in Greece.'

 While Themistocles, standing upon the deck of one of the ships, reasoned thus, it is said that an owl, a bird sacred to the goddess Athene, the protectress of Athens, came and perched upon the mast. By this fortunate omen the Greeks were encouraged to prepare for the fight.

But presently the Persian ships appeared in such numbers that they hid the neighbouring coasts from view. At the same time Xerxes himself was seen marching his land forces down to the shore. Amazed at the sight of such vast armaments the Greeks forgot the counsels of Themistocles. Once again the Peloponnesians, despairing of present victory, bent their thoughts upon the defence of the Isthmus. They resolved to retreat that very night, and gave orders to that effect to the pilots.

Thus Themistocles at the last moment was faced by the prospect of the failure of his plans, and of the loss of the advantage of position in the narrow straits upon which his hopes of victory were based. He therefore had recourse to craft. There was with him an attendant who, though he was a Persian captive, was nevertheless devoted to his master. Themistocles secretly sent this servant to the Persian king with a message saying that the Athenian leader intended to betray his country, and to go over to the Persians. Further, to persuade the king that he really intended to play the traitor, Themistocles informed him of the intention of the Greeks, and besought him to prevent their escape. Xerxes fell into the trap thus artfully prepared for him. Overjoyed at the news, he did as Themistocles had desired and foreseen, and gave orders that all the passages to the open sea should be beset to prevent the escape of the enemy.

Aristides, who was then in a neighbouring island, was the first to perceive that the Grecian fleet was thus surrounded. At great risk he sailed by night through the midst of the Persian ships and bore the news to Themistocles. The Athenian commander took his former enemy into his confidence and told him of the measures he had taken. Aristides approved the wisdom of his action, and supported him in advising the Greeks that their only hope of safety lay in engaging the enemy. The allies, however, would scarcely believe that they were surrounded, until the crew of a galley which deserted from the Persians confirmed the truth of the report. Then indeed they saw that there remained for them nothing but to fight, and anger and necessity alike fired them for the combat.

At daybreak the Persian king seated himself upon a rocky height overlooking the narrow waters below. He sat, confident of victory, upon a throne of gold, while around him were many scribes whose business it was to write down the events of the battle. Beneath him he saw his fleet of twelve hundred great ships, and a vast number of smaller vessels, blocking up the entrances to the narrow strait between the island of Salamis and the mainland.

The wisdom which Themistocles had displayed in the choice of a place for the battle was no less shown in his choice of the most favourable time for the combat. For, at a certain time in each day, it usually happened that a brisk wind blew in from the open sea, and raised high waves in the narrow channel. The rough water was no inconvenience to the Grecian ships, which lay low in the water and were solidly built. But the Persian ships, which had lofty sterns and decks and were clumsy and unwieldy, were with difficulty managed in the high waves. Until this wind arose Themistocles shunned an engagement, but when the Persian ships, pitching violently in the heavy sea, exposed their sides to attack, the Greeks fell upon them furiously.

Throughout the fight all paid special attention to the actions of Themistocles, as being the most skilful of the Greek leaders. Against him, too, the Persian admiral, by far the bravest of the brothers of Xerxes, chiefly directed his efforts. The Persian's ship was very lofty, and from her decks darts and arrows were rained as from the walls of a castle. But a Grecian ship bore down upon her, and the vessels meeting prow to prow, the brazen ram of each transfixed the timbers of its opponent. Thus the two ships were firmly fixed together, and across the bridge thus formed the Persian admiral leapt to board the Grecian galley. But the Greek pikes were ready to receive him: he was transfixed and his dead body thrust into the sea. As it floated among others it was recognised by a follower of the Persians, and was carried to his brother the king.

So the fight raged furiously. And, on account of the narrowness of the straits, but few of the Persian ships could come against the Greeks at any one time. Indeed, their very numbers often threw the Persian fleet into confusion, since the ships interfered with the movements of one another. Thus the Greeks equalled them in the fighting line, and fought with them all through the day. When evening fell the Persian fleet was utterly broken, and great numbers of its ships were sunken or captured. Thus was won the battle of Salamis, the greatest naval victory of ancient days, and one of the most wonderful sea-fights of all time. The victory was

DEATH OF THE PERSIAN ADMIRAL AT SALAMIS

gained, of course, by the valour of all the Greeks, but especially by the wisdom and skill of Themistocles.

After the battle, Xerxes, full of rage at the unexpected defeat of his fleet, tried to build a great dam across the narrow strait between the mainland and the island of Salamis, so as to shut in the Greeks completely. Meanwhile Themistocles, in order to test the opinion of Aristides, proposed to him that they should set sail to the Hellespont and destroy the bridge of boats across that strait by which Xerxes had crossed from Asia into Europe and by which he could alone retreat. Aristides by no means agreed with this plan. 'Hitherto,' said he, 'we have had to do with a slothful foe steeped in luxury, but if we shut him up in Europe necessity will drive him to fight desperately. So, awakened by danger, and taught by his past errors, he may yet win victory with his vast land forces. Therefore, instead of breaking down that bridge, we should rather build him another one, if by so doing we may hasten his departure.' This indeed was the real opinion of Themistocles, and he set about to contrive means to hasten the Persian king's retreat.

He therefore sent one of Xerxes' servants, who had been taken prisoner, with a message to the king saying that the Greeks intended to sail to the Hellespont to break down the bridge, and that Themistocles, who was really his friend, advised him to hasten into Asia with all speed before they could do so. Further, the message said that Themistocles, in order to provide time for the safe passage of the Hellespont, would by every means seek to delay the pursuit by the Grecian fleet.

THEMISTOCLES

This message filled Xerxes with terror at his own danger, and he retired from Europe with the greatest possible speed.

Not even envy could refuse to admit that the chief credit for the wonderful success at Salamis was due to Themistocles. The Spartans indeed awarded the prize of valour to their own admiral, Eurybiades, but to Themistocles they assigned the award of wisdom. Both they crowned with the olive wreath. Moreover, they presented the Athenian with the finest chariot in their city, and when he departed ordered three hundred of their youths to attend him to the borders of their state.

At the next Olympic games the attention of the spectators was distracted from the sports and the champions when Themistocles entered the ring. All had eyes but for him, greeted him with loud applause, and pointed him out to strangers with admiration.

All this praise was very grateful to Themistocles, who was by nature greedy of fame and glory, as is shown by some of his memorable acts and sayings. For example, when he was elected admiral by the Athenians, he put off all manner of business, public and private, until the day upon which he was to embark, so that the multitude of affairs he then had to transact might impress the people with a great idea of his importance.

On one occasion, walking on the seashore with a friend, he came upon a number of dead bodies washed up by the sea, and upon them were chains and ornaments of gold. 'You,' said he to his companion, 'may take these things, for you are not Themistocles.'

He was accustomed to say that the Athenians did not pay him any sincere respect, but that they sheltered themselves under him in times of danger, as men take refuge from a storm beneath a spreading plane-tree which, when fair weather came again, they would strip of leaves and branches.

A certain officer, who considered that he had done the state worthy service, ventured to set up a comparison between himself and Themistocles. Thereupon the latter answered him with this fable:

'Once upon a time there happened a dispute between the *Feast-Day* and the *Day after the Feast*. The latter claimed to be the most important as being a day of bustle and commotion, whereas the *Feast-Day* was a day of easy enjoyment. "You are right," said the *Feast-Day*, "but if I had not been before you, you would not have been at all."

'In like manner,' said Themistocles to the officer, 'if it had not been for me, where would you have been?'

It chanced that his son was able to get his own way with his mother. 'This child,' said Themistocles, laughing, 'is greater than any man in Greece, for he rules his mother, his mother rules me, I rule the Athenians, and the Athenians rule Greece.'

When two citizens sought his daughter in marriage, he preferred the one who was a man of worth to the other, whose chief merit was his wealth, for, said he, 'I prefer that she should marry a man without money rather than money without a man.'

In this pointed way he often expressed himself. The next enterprise of Themistocles, after the great actions which have been related, was the rebuilding and fortifying of the city of Athens. When that was completed, he proceeded to construct and fortify the Piræus as the harbour of the town. Further, he joined Athens and the Piræus by a line of communication. Thus he strengthened the city as a naval and maritime power.

He had indeed a design in his mind, after the retreat of Xerxes, to make Athens the sole naval power in Greece. The fleet of the allies having gone into winter quarters, Themistocles announced to his fellow-citizens in full assembly that he had hit upon a plan which would be greatly to the advantage of the state, but which he could not communicate to the whole body of citizens. The Athenians therefore told him to inform Aristides alone of his project, and to abide by his decision as to whether it should be put into practice. To him, accordingly, Themistocles disclosed his plan of treacherously burning the allied fleet in its winter quarters. Such a plan was repugnant to the noble spirit of Aristides, and he informed the citizens that the plan was indeed to their advantage, but that no proposal could be more unjust. The Athenians therefore commanded Themistocles to think no more about it.

But about this time Themistocles stirred up powerful enemies. He displeased the Spartans by opposing their plans, and they therefore gave their support to those Athenians who were opposed to his party. Moreover, he offended the allies by sailing round the Grecian islands, and exacting contributions of money from them.

In Athens, too, envy readily gave ear to evil reports, and the displeasure of many was increased by the arrogance of Themistocles and by his insistence upon his own services to the state. 'Are you weary,' he would say when this displeasure was expressed, 'of so often receiving benefits from the same man?'

At length the Athenians, unable any longer to tolerate the high distinction which Themistocles had attained, pronounced against him the Ostracism, or ten years' banishment, as they had done to other great men whose power had become a burden to them.

For some time the fallen leader sheltered himself in other Grecian cities. But it chanced that Pausanias, who had rendered great services to Greece, was now nevertheless plotting to go over to the Persians. Seeing that Themistocles was driven into exile, Pausanias conceived that he would be filled with anger against the Athenians, and ventured to tell him of the intended treason. Themistocles refused to have any share in it, but nevertheless kept the secret which had been entrusted to him and gave no information to the Greeks. Hence, when the plot was discovered and writings concerning it were found, great suspicion fell upon Themistocles. The charge being brought against him, he answered by letter saying, 'I, Themistocles, who was born to command and not to serve others, could not sell myself, and Greece with me, into servitude to the enemy.' Nevertheless, his enemies prevailed, and messengers were sent to seize him and bring him before the states of Greece. For some time he was forced to wander from place to place in Greece and the neighbouring countries, always pursued by the hatred of his fellow-countrymen. At length he was driven to seek refuge in Asia within the domains of the Persian king.

There he was in great peril, for the king had by proclamation offered a reward of two hundred talents to any one who should capture him. For a few days he lay hid in a little town where he was known to none save his host. But, being warned in a dream, he determined to take the risk of setting out to the court of the Persian king. Now the Persians are very jealous to keep their women folk from the gaze of other men, and for this reason their wives and daughters are kept closely shut up at home, and, when they travel, are borne along in carriages covered in on all sides. To provide for his safety, Themistocles was carried in such a conveyance, and the attendants were told to give out that they were carrying an Ionian lady to a gentleman at court.

Arrived thither, Themistocles prepared for the dangerous experiment of presenting himself before the Persian king. He applied first to an officer of the court, whom he told that he was a Greek desirous of having audience with the king on matters of high importance. He was informed that he could only come before the king if he bore himself, not according to the manner of the Greeks, who loved liberty and equality above all things, but according to the manner of the Persians, who were accustomed to prostrate themselves before the king as before the very image of the deity that rules all things. Themistocles having professed himself ready to adopt the Persian custom, the officer asked him, 'Who shall we say that you are? By your conversation you seem to be no ordinary man.' 'That,' replied Themistocles, 'no man must know before the king himself.'

So the Athenian was brought before the king, prostrated himself and stood silent. Then the king commanded an interpreter to ask the Greek who he was, and the question being put, Themistocles answered:

'I, who now come to address myself unto you, O king, am Themistocles the Athenian, an exile driven from Greece. The Persians have suffered much from me, but, after I had delivered Greece and saved Athens, I did them a great service in preventing the pursuit of their army. And as my present misfortunes are, so is my attitude of mind. If you will favour me, I will welcome your favour; if you cherish anger against me, I will submit to it.'

The king admired his courage, but gave him no answer. But privately among his friends he rejoiced at the submission of Themistocles as the most fortunate of all events, and prayed to the gods that his enemies might ever be smitten with the madness of driving away into exile their greatest men. So much was he filled with joy that, it is said, even in his sleep he cried out thrice, 'Themistocles the Athenian is mine.'

As soon as it was day the king gave orders

THEMISTOCLES AT THE PERSIAN COURT

that Themistocles should be brought before him. The Athenian expected no favour, for the guards when they heard his name reviled him, and one of the officers as he passed said, 'The king's good fortune has brought thee hither, thou wily serpent of Greece.' But when he had come into the presence and had prostrated himself, the king spoke graciously to him, saying that since Themistocles had given himself up, the two hundred talents offered for his taking were due to him. Further, the king assured the Athenian of protection, and commanded him to utter all that he had to propose with regard to Greece. Themistocles answering said, 'A man's conversation is like a piece of tapestry, which, when spread open displays the figures upon it, but when folded, the designs are lost to view.' Therefore he besought the king to give him time that he might learn the Persian tongue, in order to unfold his mind freely to the king without the help of an interpreter.

The king, pleased with the answer, gave him a year as he desired. Moreover, the monarch honoured him beyond all other strangers, taking him a-hunting and conversing freely with him. For his support there were granted to him three, as some say, or, as others have it, five cities. For these reasons Themistocles incurred the envy of some of the Persian nobles, the more so as about this time a number of them who attended upon the king were dismissed from their posts, and it was suspected that the conversations of Themistocles with the monarch were the cause.

It happened that during this time Themistocles had occasion to travel to the seacoast. A certain Persian noble, who had long designed to kill him and had prepared murderers for the purpose, determined to carry out his plan when Themistocles should reach a certain place, the name of which, being interpreted, signifies the Lion's Head. But, as Themistocles lay asleep one day at noon-tide, he dreamt that the mother of the gods appeared unto him and said, 'Beware, Themistocles, of the Lion's Head, lest the Lion crush you.' Themistocles awoke much disturbed in mind, and having returned thanks to the goddess, left the highroad so as to avoid the place of danger, and took up his quarters for the night at a place beyond it. It chanced that on the way one of the horses which carried his tent fell into a river. A party of servants were therefore left behind to spread out the hangings to dry. In the darkness the murderers approached with drawn swords, and taking the hangings to be the tent wherein Themistocles was sleeping, lifted them up with the intention of slaying him. While they were doing this, the servants who had been left behind fell upon them and secured them. Thus the danger was avoided, and Themistocles in gratitude to the goddess built a temple in her honour, and made his daughter the priestess of it.

Warned by this and other occurrences of the envy of the Persians, Themistocles settled down in the city of Magnesia. There he long abode in riches and honour, for the king, engaged in the affairs of other parts of his domains, gave but little attention to the concerns of Greece. But when Egypt revolted from his rule, the Athenians came to the help of the Egyptians, and the fleet of Athens rode triumphant as mistress of the seas.

Then the Persian king felt himself forced to take active measures against the Greeks and to prevent the further growth of their power. He therefore set his armies in motion, and sent forth his generals, and despatched messengers to Themistocles, commanding him to take the field against his countrymen.

But neither resentment against his fellow-citizens who had banished him, nor the honours and dignities which the Persians had showered upon him, could persuade Themistocles to take command of an expedition against his native land. Possibly he may have doubted the result of the war, but above all he was unwilling to tarnish the glory of his achievements for Athens and the whole of Greece. Therefore, having sacrificed to the gods and taken leave of his friends, he took poison, and so died in the city of his exile.

PELOPIDAS

THE great events of the life of Pelopidas fall within the earlier half of the fourth century before Christ. The life, as told by Plutarch, is a good example of our author's frequent neglect of regular order in telling his stories, for he begins with reflections upon the duty of a general to safeguard his own life; reflections which naturally arise out of the death of Pelopidas, and which most authors would therefore have placed at the end of the story of his life.

In the youth of Pelopidas, Sparta exercised a selfish ascendency over the whole of Greece. It was the life-work of Pelopidas and of his friend Epaminondas to break down that supremacy and to make their city of Thebes for a time the greatest power in Greece. Unfortunately the life which Plutarch wrote of the noble Epaminondas has been lost.

The friendship of that great general and statesman with Pelopidas forms one of the most beautiful stories in Greek history. Their deeds made them the two most famous men in Greece, but no shadow of distrust or unworthy rivalry ever disturbed their friendship. Epaminondas was the greater general, Pelopidas the more impetuous and daring officer. Plutarch indeed, rightly enough no doubt, *blames Pelopidas for the too reckless exposure of himself by which he lost his life. But it was this very quality of almost desperate courage, which remained uncooled even when Pelopidas had become a famous and experienced general, which alone made his early exploits successful. Seldom or never in the history of the world has a more apparently hopeless adventure than the retaking of Thebes by the handful of exiles, and their defiance of the crushing power of Sparta, been undertaken and carried through to a successful issue.*

CATO the elder, when he heard a man praised for foolish and reckless daring in war, justly observed that there is a great difference between a reasonable valour and a contempt for life. And, bearing upon this matter, there is a story of a soldier who was astonishingly brave, but unhealthy in appearance and of a bad habit of body. The king, his commander, questioned him as to the cause of his pallor, and the soldier confessed that he was secretly suffering from a dire disease. Thereupon the king commanded that his physicians should attend to the soldier, and he was cured. It was then noticed that he no longer courted danger, and did not risk his life as before. The king questioned him to find out why his character was thus changed. The soldier answered: 'You, sire, are the cause why I am less bold, for you have delivered me from the misery which formerly made life of no account to me.' Arguing in the same way, a certain lover of luxury and pleasure said of the Spartans: 'No wonder they venture their lives freely in battle, since death releases them from the severe labours they undergo, and the wretched food to which they limit themselves.' It was natural that lovers of ease and pleasure should think thus of the Spartans, but in truth that people thought neither death nor life the happier state, for they accounted a noble life or a glorious death equally fortunate.

A commander, above all other soldiers, should be careful not to expose himself to needless hazards, since upon his safety, if he be a man of experience and valour, depends the safety of the whole army. Therefore the general spoke wisely who, when another officer exhibited his wounds and his shield pierced with a spear, said: 'I, for my part, was ashamed when at the siege of Samos a javelin fell near me, inasmuch as it showed that I had acted like a venturesome youth, and not like the commander of a great array.' When, however, the whole issue of the fight depends upon the general's risking his life, then must he stand the combat and brave all dangers. But when the advantage to be gained by his personal bravery is small and his death likely to ruin everything, the general must not be endangered by playing the part of the private soldier.

Pelopidas sprang from a distinguished family in the city of Thebes, and his friend Epaminondas was also of noble descent. Early in life Pelopidas, who had been brought up in affluence, succeeded to a great estate. He showed, however, that he was a master of his riches and not their slave. He freely gave to such needy persons as deserved his bounty, and the Thebans rejoiced in his liberality.

Epaminondas alone could not be induced to share in his friend's bounty. He had been brought up in poverty, and he made its burden light by a cheerful spirit and the utmost simplicity of life. Indeed, as regards his manner of living, Pelopidas shared the poverty of his friend. He gloried in plainness of dress, frugality in food, and tireless industry in labour. While he occupied the highest posts, his life and conduct were simple and open.

The little store which Pelopidas set upon money, and the time he devoted to the affairs of the state, impaired his great estate. His friends remonstrated with him, and reminded him that money is a very necessary thing. 'True,' replied Pelopidas, 'it is very necessary for that poor fellow there, who is both lame and blind.'

Epaminondas and he were equally inclined to all noble things, but Pelopidas delighted especially in bodily exercises, Epaminondas in the cultivation of the mind; so that the first found pleasure in wrestling and hunting, the second in the sayings and writings of philosophers. Many things reflected honour on both, but nothing was more admirable than the close and firm friendship which existed between them from first to last, and in all the high offices which they held. Often enough the welfare of the state is injured by the envy and jealousy which great men bear towards one another. Pelopidas and Epaminondas, however, sought not how one might get the better of the other, but how they might best help one another in the service of the state.

Some are of opinion that the extraordinary friendship between the two men had its origin in a campaign in which they fought. They served together in a Theban force which had been sent to help the Spartans, with whom the Thebans were, as yet, in alliance. In a battle which took place during this campaign, the wing in which the Thebans were stationed gave way and was broken. Thereupon Pelopidas and Epaminondas locked their shields together and drove back the enemies who attacked them. But, at last, Pelopidas, bleeding from seven great wounds, sank exhausted upon a heap of friends and enemies who lay dead together. Epaminondas believed his friend to be dead, but nevertheless stood forward to defend his body and his arms, being determined to die himself rather than allow the armour of Pelopidas to be taken as spoil by the enemy. As he fought with many foes at once, he was in extreme danger, and was wounded in the breast with a spear and in the arm with a sword. But just when it seemed that he must be overpowered by numbers, help came unexpectedly from the other wing of the army, and both the friends were, at the last moment, rescued from the enemy.

After these events the Spartans for some time made an outward show of treating the Thebans as friends and allies. In reality, however, they were suspicious of the spirit and the power of Thebes. Moreover, they hated the party to which Pelopidas belonged, because it favoured government by the people.

Now there were in Thebes certain rich men who were also opposed to popular government, and sought

EPAMINONDAS DEFENDING PELOPIDAS

to get the rule of the city into their own hands. These men proposed to a Spartan general, who came with troops to Thebes as an ally, that he should seize the citadel of the town and drive out the leaders of the popular party. The Spartan listened to the proposal, seized the citadel called Cadmea, and drove Pelopidas and others into exile. Epaminondas, however, was allowed to remain in the town, for he was looked upon as a man who, from his poverty and quiet disposition, was unlikely to give trouble.

All Greece was astonished at the action of Sparta in regard to this treacherous seizure. The government, indeed, degraded and fined the officer who had carried it out, but kept the fruits of his treachery and maintained a Spartan garrison in the citadel. Thebes was now ruled, not according to its ancient form of government, but by tyrants, from whom there seemed to be little hope of deliverance, since they were supported by the great power of Sparta. Nevertheless, those who had seized upon the rule of Thebes, learning that the exiles had taken shelter in Athens, sent assassins thither to murder them. One of the Theban patriots was slain by these murderers, but the others fortunately escaped. Letters were also sent to Athens from Sparta, demanding that no shelter should be given to the exiled Thebans. The Athenians, however, mindful of help they had received from Thebes in their own struggles, would by no means suffer any injury to be done to them.

In this state of affairs Pelopidas busied himself continually in persuading his comrades to attempt the desperate adventure of freeing their city from the rule of the tyrants and their Spartan allies. 'It is dishonourable,' argued he, 'that we, meanly contented with our own safety, should live here, dependent upon the Athenians, while our city is enslaved and garrisoned by an enemy. We ought, in a cause so glorious as ours, to be ready to face any danger.' At last he succeeded in prevailing upon them to make the attempt, and the exiles therefore sent secretly to such friends as were left behind in Thebes to inform them of their resolution. These men entered eagerly into the project. One of them, named Charon, offered his house as a hiding-place for the exiles when they should succeed in re-entering the city. Another, Philidas, contrived to get himself made secretary to two of the tyrants. As for Epaminondas, he had all along been seeking to stir up the youth of the city against their masters. He used to incite them to try their strength in wrestling against the Spartans at the public games. When he saw them elated by success he would say, 'You should rather be ashamed at the meanness of spirit which allows you to remain subject to your inferiors in strength.'

A day was fixed for carrying out the plan. The exiles agreed that most of them should wait behind at a certain place, while a few of the youngest should first attempt to enter the city. Pelopidas was the first to volunteer to be of this party, and he was joined by eleven others. All were men of noble blood, all were united in the closest friendship, and the only contest among them was as to which should be first in the race for honour and glory.

The twelve adventurers, having sent on a message

PELOPIDAS

in advance to Charon, set out. They went without armour, and in their hands they carried hunting-poles, while their dogs ran beside them, so that they might seem to be merely a hunting party beating about for game.

Meanwhile, their messenger came to Charon, and he, being a man of courage and resolution, made ready to receive them. But another who was in the secret was made dizzy, as it were, by the nearness of the danger. He sent one of his friends to beg the exiles to desist from the enterprise for a time, and to await a more favourable opportunity. The friend went off in haste, took his horse out of the stable, and called for the bridle. His wife was unable to find it, and at last said that she had lent it to a friend. Thereupon a quarrel arose between husband and wife, and finally the man went out of the house in a huff, and gave up all thought of taking the message. Such was the trivial matter by which the carrying of the message, which might have stopped the glorious enterprise of Pelopidas and his companions, was prevented.

Towards the close of the day the exiles, now disguised as peasants, entered the city at different places. Fortunately the cold weather was setting in at the time. There happened to be a bitter wind and a fall of snow, so that few people were abroad in the city. Friends who were in the secret awaited the exiles, and at once led them to Charon's house, where the conspirators all assembled to the number of forty-eight.

Meanwhile Philidas, the secretary, who was a

party to the plot, had invited two of the tyrants to his house that very night, intending to ply them freely with wine. But before they had drunk at all deeply, a confused and uncertain rumour reached them that the exiles had entered the city. Philidas endeavoured to put the matter aside as of no importance. Nevertheless, an officer was sent to Charon commanding him to attend upon the tyrants immediately. By this time it had become dark and Pelopidas and his friends were preparing for action. They had put on their breast-plates and girt on their swords, when there came a sudden knocking at the door. One of those present ran to the door, and learning the officer's business, came back in great alarm with the news. All believed that the plot was discovered, and that every man of them was lost without having had the chance to strike a blow. Nevertheless, they thought it well that Charon should obey the order and go boldly to the tyrants.

Charon was a man of great courage in dangers which threatened only himself, but he was now greatly concerned for the safety of his friends. Moreover, he feared that if harm befell them some suspicion of treachery would rest upon him. Therefore, when he was ready to depart, he brought out his son, who was but a child, but of a strength beyond his years, and placed him in the hands of Pelopidas. 'If,' said he, 'you find me a traitor, treat this child as an enemy and spare not his life.' His friends, however, assured him that they were not so much disturbed by their present danger as to be capable of suspecting or blaming him in the least. They therefore besought him to take his son away to some place of safety. But Charon refused to do so. 'What life or what death,' said he, 'could I wish for him more glorious than to fall in this enterprise with his father and his friends?'

Having prayed to the gods and embraced his associates, Charon set out, endeavouring to compose his mind, and to keep his agitation from appearing on his countenance or in his speech. When he reached the door of the house the tyrants came forth and questioned him. At first Charon was somewhat confused, but he soon found that his questioners had no certain information. He therefore advised them not to be disturbed by idle rumours, but, said he, 'However, perhaps no matter of this kind ought to be disregarded, and I will therefore go and make the closest inquiry I can.' Philidas, who stood by, applauded this as a prudent course. So Charon returned home, while the tyrants resumed their carouse and the secretary plied them freely with wine.

The first storm which threatened the exiles had scarcely blown over before fortune raised a second. There arrived a messenger, who had travelled in haste from Athens, bearing a letter from the high priest at that city to one of the tyrants. This letter, as it was afterwards found, contained not mere idle rumours, but an exact account of the whole affair. However, by this time, the tyrant was almost intoxicated. Although the messenger told him that the letter was to be read at once, he put it on one side, saying with a smile, 'Business to-morrow,' and resumed his talk with Philidas. This saying, 'Business to-morrow,' passed into a proverb among the Greeks to signify the folly of delay.

The friends of liberty now took the opportunity of carrying out their project. They divided their little party into two bands. One, in which was Charon, went against the two tyrants who were revelling in the house of Philidas. The other, in which was Pelopidas, went against the two other tyrants, who happened to dwell near one another.

Charon and his party disguised themselves by putting women's clothes over their armour, and by wearing thick wreaths of pine and poplar upon their heads so as to throw their faces into shadow. Thus attired, the pretended women came into the guest-chamber. Having looked round to make sure of their prey, they drew their swords and made at the two tyrants across the table. Some of the guests endeavoured to defend their masters, but all being confused with wine, the tyrants and those who drew in their defence were easily despatched.

The party of Pelopidas had a more difficult task, for their first adversary was a sober and valiant man. When the friends arrived at his house they found the door fast, for he had gone to bed. For a long time they knocked without awakening anybody. At length a servant came down and removed the bar. Immediately Pelopidas and his friends burst into the house, threw the servant down, and rushed to the bedchamber. The tyrant, guessing his danger from the noise and trampling, leapt from his bed and seized his sword, but neglected to put out the lamps. Had he done so, the friends might well have fallen foul of one another in the darkness. The tyrant then, fully exposed to view, took his stand in the doorway, and with one stroke slew the first man who attempted to enter. He was next engaged by Pelopidas, and, in the narrow way encumbered by the body of the fallen man, the combat between the two was long and doubtful. At length Pelopidas prevailed and slew his adversary.

The little band then proceeded against the fourth tyrant. He quickly perceived them and escaped into a neighbour's house, whither, however, they followed and slew him.

The two parties now united and sent a message to bring up the exiles whom they had left behind. They also proclaimed liberty to the Thebans, and armed such as joined them with weapons from the shops of the armourers and other places. Among those who joined them was Epaminondas with a body of men whom he had collected and armed.

The whole city was now in a state of alarm and confusion. Lights shone in all the houses, and the streets were full of men hurrying hither and thither. The people, however, did not assemble, for they had no certain knowledge of what had happened, and waited impatiently for daylight to dawn. It seems, therefore, that the Spartan officers made a great mistake in not sallying out during the night from the citadel, for they had a garrison of fifteen hundred men. However, disturbed by the tumult and the lights and the shouting, they contented themselves with holding the citadel.

As soon as it was day, the exiles who had been sent for marched into the city armed. The people, too, assembled, and Pelopidas and his companions were presented to them. Greatly excited, the whole assembly acclaimed them as the benefactors and deliverers of the city. Pelopidas, being chosen, together with two companions, governor of the state, immediately formed the blockade of the citadel, being in haste to take it before succour could come from Sparta. In this he narrowly succeeded, for the garrison had but just surrendered, and was marching away, when they met a great army coming to their rescue. Of the three Spartan officers who signed the capitulation, two were executed and the third ruinously fined.

It is difficult to find an instance so remarkable as the exploit of Pelopidas of the few overcoming the many, the weak the strong. For the war, which humbled the pride of the Spartans and deprived them of their rule by sea and land, began that night when Pelopidas, being but one of twelve men, entered Thebes and burst asunder the chains of Sparta, until that time deemed unbreakable.

The Spartans soon entered Bœotia, the state of Thebes, with so powerful an army that the Athenians were terrified and renounced their alliance with the Thebans. Thus the latter, left alone to face the power of Sparta, seemed to be in the most desperate straits. Pelopidas, however, found means to embroil Athens again with Sparta. He secretly sent a merchant to one of the Spartan generals, whom he knew to be a brave soldier but not a man of sound judgment. The merchant suggested to him that it would be a splendid enterprise, and one very agreeable to the Spartan government, if he made some sudden stroke against Athens, such, for instance, as the seizure of the Piræus. The general suffered himself to be persuaded, and invaded the territories of Athens. But, when he had advanced some distance, the hearts of his soldiers failed them, and his army retreated. Angered at the invasion, the Athenians readily joined the Thebans again, and fitted out a great fleet to act against the Spartans.

Meanwhile, the Thebans by themselves frequently fought the Spartans in Bœotia, not in set battles, but in minor actions, in which they gained both experience and courage in warfare. The prudent Theban generals made choice of fit occasions to let loose their soldiers, like so many young hounds in training, upon the enemy, and when they had tasted of victory brought them off again in safety. The credit for this policy is mainly due to Pelopidas, who, from the time of being first appointed general until the day of his death, was constantly in employment either as governor of Bœotia, or as captain of the Sacred Band, the flower of the Theban army. In one of these lesser fights Pelopidas with his own hand slew the Spartan general opposed to him.

One battle fought at Tegyræ brought especial honour to Pelopidas. He had long kept a strict watch upon a certain town which favoured the enemy, and which had admitted a Spartan garrison. Learning that the garrison had gone away upon an expedition, Pelopidas made a dash upon the place with a small force consisting of the Sacred Band and a few horsemen. When he came near the town, however, he found that other Spartan troops were marching to take the place of those who had left town. He therefore led his troops back by way of Tegyræ, keeping along the sides of the mountains, because all the low-lying land was covered by flood-water from the river which flowed through the valley. In this place they suddenly perceived the Spartan troops returning from their expedition. One of his men thereupon ran and told Pelopidas, saying, 'We are fallen into the enemy's hands.' 'Why not rather,' said the general, 'they into ours?'

He then ordered his cavalry to the front and drew up the Sacred Band, who numbered but three hundred men, in close order, trusting that they would force a way through the enemy, who were greatly superior in numbers. The shock of battle began in that part of the field where the commanders fought in person. The two Spartan leaders were among the first to fall, and their army was so broken that the Thebans might, had they so chosen, have passed through their disordered ranks. Pelopidas, however, turned to attack those who still stood firm, and made such havoc among them that they fled in great disorder. The Thebans, having erected a trophy and gathered the spoils of the slain, returned home not a little elated with their victory. The success was the more notable, since it seems that in all their former wars, either with Greeks or foreigners, the Spartans had never been defeated in a pitched battle by an army smaller than their own, nor indeed by one equal in numbers. This battle, therefore, first taught the Greeks that there was no special virtue in the Spartan soil, and that, wherever the youth fear disgrace more than danger and scorn everything base, there will be found men terrible to their enemies. From the time of this battle Pelopidas would never split up the Sacred Band, but kept them in one body, and frequently charged at their head in battle.

But the time came when the Spartans, having made peace with the other Greeks, continued the war against the Thebans alone, and invaded their land with an army of ten thousand foot and a thousand horse. The Thebans were now threatened not merely with the ordinary dangers of war, but with utter destruction. At this time, on an occasion when Pelopidas was leaving home to join the army, his wife with tears in her eyes besought him to take care of himself. 'My dear,' replied the Theban, 'it is rather the duty of a man in my position to take care of others.' When he came to the army, he found the generals differing in opinion. He at once advocated the advice of Epaminondas that battle should be given to the enemy. He was not at the time one of the generals-in-chief, but only captain of the Sacred Band. Nevertheless, his opinion had great weight, and the resolution was taken to risk a battle.

The two armies came in sight of one another at Leuctra. Epaminondas, who was in chief command, drew up the foot-soldiers of his left living in an oblique formation, so that the right wing of the Spartans in order to meet him might be obliged to divide from the other Greeks, their allies. The Theban general intended after this manœuvre to fall upon the Spartans with his whole forces and to crush them. The enemy, however, perceived his intention, and began to change his order of battle and to extend the right wing, with the object of surrounding Epaminondas. But while the movement was yet incomplete and the Spartans consequently in some disorder, Pelopidas dashed upon them with the Sacred Band, while at the same time Epaminondas, neglecting other opponents, furiously attacked their right wing. Though the Spartans were masters of the art of war and most excellent in discipline, the incredible speed and fury of the attack broke their resolution, and they suffered such a defeat and slaughter as had never been known before. Since the attack of Pelopidas had so much to do with the issue of the battle, he gained as much honour by the day's success, though only captain of his three hundred, as did his friend Epaminondas, who was governor of Bœotia and commander of the whole army.

Soon after the two friends were appointed joint-governors, and together led an army into the Peloponnesus. They caused several cities to revolt from the Spartans, and brought a number of states into alliance with Thebes. By this time it was mid-winter, and but a few days of office remained to them, for, by the law of their state, the office of governor had, on penalty of death, to be surrendered at the close of the year to those who had been appointed for the next year. This law Epaminondas and Pelopidas disregarded, in order to carry their successes further. With an army of seventy thousand Greeks, of whom not one-twelfth were Thebans, they laid waste the Spartan territories. Upon their return they were tried for the breach of the law, but were acquitted, in spite of some ignoble men who looked with envy upon the honour and glory which their great deeds had won.

Some time after, there came messengers from the people of Thessaly imploring the Thebans to furnish them with a general and some troops to aid them against a certain tyrant named Alexander, who had attacked some of their cities and who sought to bring the whole country into subjection. Epaminondas was at the time in the Peloponnesus. Pelopidas therefore offered himself for this new service, for he well knew that, where Epaminondas commanded, there was no need for another general. He therefore marched into Thessaly and forced the tyrant to make submission. Having settled affairs there he marched into Macedonia to compose disturbances which had broken out in that kingdom.

Some time after, there came further complaints from the people of Thessaly, to the effect that the tyrant Alexander was again disturbing the peace. Pelopidas and a companion were therefore chosen to attend upon the Thessalians, but, having no expectation of war, they took no troops with them. At the same time fresh disturbances broke out in Macedonia, where the king was slain and his throne usurped by the murderer. The friends of the dead king besought aid from Pelopidas, who, having no troops of his own, marched against the usurper with an army of hired soldiers. These, however, were bribed by the usurper and went over to his side. Nevertheless, though Pelopidas was thus left without support, such was the terror of his very name and reputation that the usurper came to him as to a superior. He promised to hold the kingdom for the brothers of the dead king, and to regard the friends and enemies of Thebes as his own. These terms Pelopidas was induced to accept. He was, however, deeply incensed at the treachery of the hired troops, and resolved to avenge it by the capture of the town in which they had lodged most of their goods, together with their wives and children. Having collected some Thessalian troops, he therefore marched against the town, but no sooner had he arrived before it than the tyrant Alexander also appeared with an army. Pelopidas supposed that he had come thither to explain his conduct, and, suspecting no treachery, went to meet him with but one companion. But the tyrant, seeing them thus alone and unarmed, at once seized them and bore them off prisoners to his stronghold.

When the Thebans heard of this outrage they were filled with indignation, and at once gave orders to their army to march into Thessaly. Meanwhile the tyrant, imagining that the spirit of Pelopidas was broken by misfortune, at first allowed his captive to speak with those who came to see him. The Theban, seeing the people crushed with misery under the rule of Alexander, sought to comfort them by assuring them that vengeance would soon fall upon their oppressor. Moreover, he sent a message to Alexander telling him that he acted foolishly in torturing and slaying his innocent subjects while he spared him, Pelopidas, who was determined to punish him as soon as he was free. The tyrant, surprised at the boldness of the message, sent to ask, 'Why is Pelopidas in such a hurry to die?' To this question the prisoner replied, 'In order that thou, being more hated by the gods than ever, mayest the sooner be brought to a shameful end.'

From that time forth Alexander allowed none but his gaolers to visit the captive. The wife of the tyrant, however, was the daughter of an old friend of Pelopidas. The keepers told her of the noble and courageous bearing of the prisoner, and she felt a strong desire to see him and to speak with him. She came therefore to the prison, and, seeing by the disorder and meanness of his dress and the wretchedness of his provisions that he was treated in a manner unworthy of his rank and character, she could not forbear from weeping. At this Pelopidas was at first much surprised, but, learning who his visitor was, he addressed her by the name of her father, whom he had known well. In the course of their conversation she happened to say, 'I pity your wife, Pelopidas.' Thereupon the prisoner answered, 'For my part I pity you, for you are free, and nevertheless endure to live with such a man as this Alexander.' This remark affected her much, for the cruelty and pride of the tyrant were hateful to her.

The generals who were at first sent to Thessaly by the Thebans were unable, either through lack of ability or through ill-fortune, to accomplish anything. They therefore returned in disgrace, and the command was given to Epaminondas.

The fame of the new general raised the spirits of the people of Thessaly. In many places insurrections broke out among the tyrant's subjects, and his affairs seemed desperate. Epaminondas, however, made the safety of his friend his first consideration. He knew full well the savage disposition of the tyrant and his numerous acts of cruelty; how, for example, he buried some persons alive, how others were dressed in the skins of bears or wild boars and then baited with dogs or hunted with darts, and how he had treacherously put to the sword the peoples of two towns in alliance with him. Epaminondas therefore did not drive matters to an extremity, lest the tyrant, being rendered desperate, should kill his prisoner. The Theban general contrived, however, to keep Alexander in suspense, and succeeded in terrifying him so much that he sent to make submission, and delivered up Pelopidas and his companion.

Soon after his release the Thebans learnt that the Spartans and Athenians had sent ambassadors to the king of Persia, in order to gain his aid. The Thebans therefore, on their part, despatched Pelopidas to the court of the king. From this embassy he received great honour, for the fame of his deeds had spread throughout Asia, and he was greeted with admiration as the conqueror of Sparta. The Persian king himself loaded him with honours, and fully granted his demands for the freedom and independence of Greece. The honour which Pelopidas thus gained was increased by the fact that, whereas other Greeks accepted costly gifts from the Persian king, the Theban ambassador declined to enrich himself thus, and would accept only some small tokens of the king's regard.

While Pelopidas was absent upon this embassy, the tyrant Alexander returned to his evil ways. When, therefore, his oppressed people learnt that Pelopidas had returned out of Asia, they again sent to Thebes, begging that he should be allowed to lead an army to their relief. The request was readily granted, and an army was soon got ready. But when the forces were on the point of marching, there happened an eclipse of the sun, and darkness fell upon the city in the day-time. Thereupon terror came upon all, for the people looked upon the eclipse as a sign from heaven foretelling some great disaster. On this account Pelopidas did not think it right to compel the army to move, since the soldiers shared in the general terror at the eclipse. He himself, however, with only three hundred volunteers, set out for Thessaly. He was moved to this partly by resentment against the tyrant, but especially by the honour of the thing. For he esteemed it greatly to the glory of Thebes that her people should take the field in defence of liberty and in aid of the oppressed at the very time when Sparta and Athens were in alliance with tyrants.

Having arrived in Thessaly, Pelopidas assembled his forces and marched against Alexander. The tyrant was emboldened by the knowledge that but few Thebans accompanied their general, and that he himself had twice as many Thessalian infantry as marched in the army of Pelopidas. He therefore advanced boldly against the deliverer, who, being informed of the approach of an army so much larger than his own, remarked, 'So much the better, for now we shall beat so many the more.'

The armies came in sight of one another in a place where two steep hills rise up out of a plain. Both sides pressed forward to get possession of these hills. Meanwhile Pelopidas, who had a numerous and excellent body of horse, fell upon the enemy's cavalry and routed them. But, while he was pursuing them over the plain, Alexander gained the hills in advance of his antagonists.

The Thessalian foot vainly attempted to force these strong heights. The foremost were slain and many were wounded, so that the attack accomplished nothing. Seeing this, Pelopidas recalled his cavalry from the pursuit, and ordered them to fall upon such of the enemy as still stood their ground upon the plain. Then, seizing his buckler, he himself ran to join those who were engaged upon the hills. He forced his way to the front, and his presence so inspired his men that their valour seemed redoubled. The enemy stood two or three charges, but finding the attack still hotly pressed, and seeing the cavalry returning from the pursuit, they began to give ground. They retreated, however, slowly, step by step. Pelopidas then, from a height, surveyed the whole field of battle, wherein the enemy, though broken and disordered, did not yet take to flight. As he looked, he saw upon the right the tyrant Alexander rallying and encouraging his troops. Thereupon Pelopidas lost control of himself. Forgetting that it was his duty as general to have a proper regard for his own safety, he rushed forward a great way in advance of his own troops. Loudly he called upon the tyrant and challenged him to combat. But Alexander dared not to meet him. The craven slunk back and hid himself in the midst of his guards. The foremost ranks with whom Pelopidas came into hand-to-hand fight were broken by him, and a number of them were slain. But others, fighting at a distance, hurled their javelins at him and pierced his armour. Meanwhile his Thessalians, sorely anxious for his safety, rushed down the hill to his assistance, but when they came to the place, they found him lying dead upon the ground. Both horse and foot, filled with fury, then dashed against the enemy's main body, completely routed it, and slew above three thousand. For a long way they pursued the flying enemy, so that the fields were covered with the carcases of the slain.

Those Thebans who were present at the battle were deeply afflicted at the death of Pelopidas, whom they called their father, their saviour, their instructor in all great and honourable things. Nor were the Thessalians and allies behind them in testifying their regard for him by the deepest sorrow. It is said that those who were in the action neither took off their armour, nor unbridled their horses, nor bound up their wounds after they had heard the news. Notwithstanding their heat and weariness, they made their way to the body of the hero and piled around it the spoils taken from the enemy. Then in token of mourning they cut off their hair and the manes of their horses. Many, when they had withdrawn to their tents, neither kindled a fire nor partook of food. The silence of sorrow hung over their camp as if, instead of being gloriously victorious, they had been defeated and enslaved.

When the news of the death of Pelopidas was carried to the towns of Thessaly, the rulers, the priests, and the people came forth to meet the body with trophies and crowns and golden armour. Further, they besought the Thebans that they might have the honour of burying the dead hero. Surely no funeral was ever more magnificent, at least in the judgment of those who do not place magnificence in mere display. For the body of Pelopidas, who was but one of the subjects of a republic and who died in a strange land far from kindred and friends, was attended and conducted to the grave and crowned by many cities and tribes. Indeed, in his life and death Pelopidas was most fortunate, for his life was occupied by many great enterprises, all of which were successful, and he died in a great exploit from which resulted the freedom of Thessaly and the destruction of the tyrant.

For when the Thebans heard of his death they were filled with a burning desire for revenge. They therefore sent forth a great army into Thessaly and broke down the power of the tyrant Alexander. Him, too, the gods punished soon after for his treatment of Pelopidas. It was, as has been said, by that hero that the tyrant's wife was first taught to scorn the pomp and splendour of the palace and not to dread the guards by whom it was surrounded. Hating and fearing her husband's cruelty, she plotted with her three brothers to slay him. Their plan was carried out after this manner.

The whole palace, except the tyrant's bedchamber, was full of guards who kept watch throughout the night. The bedchamber was an upper room, and the door of the apartment was guarded by a fierce dog who was chained there, and who would fly at everybody except his master and mistress and a slave who fed him. When the time fixed for the attempt had come, the tyrant's wife concealed her three brothers before nightfall in a room hard by. Then at night she entered the bedchamber as usual and found the tyrant already asleep. Coming out again, she ordered the slave to take away the dog, saying that her husband wished to sleep undisturbed. She then covered the stairs with wool, so that her brothers might approach in silence. They crept stealthily up, but when they had reached the door of the bedchamber they were seized with terror, although their sister brought them the tyrant's sword which hung at the head of his bed, as a proof that he was fast asleep. Thereupon she reproached them with cowardice, and swore that she would awaken Alexander and tell him all. Shame and fear together now steadied the minds of her brothers, and while she held the light they stationed themselves around the bed. One seized the tyrant's feet, another his head, while the third stabbed him to the heart with a dagger. Such a death was perhaps too merciful for so abominable a monster. But seeing that he was murdered by his own wife, and that his body was cast forth to be spurned and trodden under foot by the populace, it will appear that the manner of his death was not altogether out of proportion to his deserts.

TIMOLEON

THE situation of Corinth upon the narrow isthmus joining the mainland of Greece to its southern peninsula, the Peloponnesus, caused the city early to become a place of great commercial importance. All the great roads by land met at Corinth, while for sea traffic the town had two ports, one on either side of the isthmus, across which the small boats of early days were often carried in order to avoid the dangerous passage round the south of Greece.

These advantages of position naturally turned the inclinations of the people of Corinth towards the sea. There the first artificial harbour in Greece was made, and there also the trireme, a vessel with a triple bank of oars, was invented. With the growth of commerce by sea came expansion across its waters. A number of colonies were sent out from Corinth, and, among other places, the town of Syracuse in Sicily was founded, and grew into a wealthy and populous city.

The story of Syracuse, like that of most Greek cities and colonies, is largely made up of the struggles between those who strove to maintain a more or less popular government, and 'tyrants' who aspired to sole rule. It must be noticed that the Greek word from which we derive our word tyrant means an absolute ruler simply,

TIMOLEON

and not necessarily a cruel or unjust one. Dionysius of Syracuse, whom Timoleon overthrew, was, however, a tyrant in both the Greek and the English senses of the word.

It was natural that the Syracusans, suffering bitterly from the oppression of the tyrant, should apply to the mother-city Corinth for assistance. The remarkable series of triumphs won by Timoleon freed not only Syracuse, but the whole of Sicily, from the rule of the tyrants, while in the brilliant victory on the river Crimissus Timoleon with 12,000 men defeated 80,000 Carthaginian foes. The second invasion of the Carthaginians, however, won some successes at first, but on the whole Timoleon had the advantage, and the enemy was glad to accept terms of peace, which settled the boundary between the Greek and Carthaginian territories in Sicily.

Timoleon lived in the fourth century before Christ. The freedom which he had given to Syracuse did not last long, and twenty years after the hero's death the city again came under the rule of a tyrant.

A German writer calls Timoleon the Grecian Garibaldi. Their exploits are certainly not unlike, though the Greek excelled the hero of Italian independence in political wisdom and foresight.

BEFORE Timoleon was sent into Sicily, the affairs of Syracuse, the chief Greek colony in the island, were in a desperate condition. The tyrant Dionysius, who had oppressed the city, had indeed been driven out, but the people of the town were torn by faction; one tyrant succeeded another, and Syracuse was made almost desolate by the miseries it underwent. As for the rest of Sicily, a part of the island was made quite a desert by the wars, and such towns as remained were in a state of utter confusion and turmoil.

Such being the state of affairs, Dionysius, in the tenth year after his expulsion, was able by the aid of a body of foreign soldiers to retake and establish himself once again in his dominions. At the best Dionysius was of a cruel nature, but by this time he had been exasperated, on account of his expulsion and the miseries he had endured, to a state of savage ferocity. All those who remained in Syracuse became, therefore, the abject slaves of the tyrant. The best and most important of the citizens, however, fled from the city, sought shelter in a neighbouring town, and put themselves under the protection of its prince, Icetes. They also chose Icetes as their leader and general, not because he was himself any better than the most avowed tyrants, but because they had no other resource. Moreover, they hoped that they might place some trust and confidence in him, since he came of a Syracusan family. He had the power to help them, too, for he possessed an army capable of encountering the forces of Dionysius.

Meantime the Carthaginians with a great fleet appeared off Sicily, and it appeared likely that the disordered state of the island would afford them the opportunity of reducing the whole of the Greek colonies. The Sicilian Greeks were struck with terror, and determined to send an embassy to the mother-country to beg assistance from the Corinthians. They appealed to them especially, partly because Corinth was their parent city, and had helped them on many former occasions, and partly because they knew that Corinth was ever the friend of liberty and the enemy of tyrants. Icetes pretended to approve of this embassy, but in secret he was treating with the Carthaginians. He hoped to use them either against Dionysius or against the friends of freedom, as might be most to his advantage, and in either case he hoped to establish himself as master of Syracuse by their aid.

The people of Corinth were always accustomed to pay especial attention to the affairs of the colonies, and particularly to such matters as concerned Syracuse. Moreover, it happened that at the time no danger threatened the Corinthians in their own country. Hence, when the ambassadors arrived and stated their business, the people of Corinth readily passed a vote that the succours should be granted. The question of the choice of a general then arose. The magistrates nominated such as had already made some show in the state, when, quite unexpectedly, one of the common people stood up and proposed Timoleon, who up to this time had taken no special part in public business. It seemed as though some god inspired the proposer, so wonderfully did fortune, against all reasonable expectations, secure the election of Timoleon, and so wonderfully did fortune afterwards make that general's deeds and valour illustrious.

Timoleon was of noble birth on both sides, for his father and mother alike were of the greatest families in Corinth. He was remarkable for his deep love of country, and also for a natural kindness of disposition, except that he bore a deep hatred to oppressors and to all evil men. He had great natural talents for war, and these were so happily tempered that, while he showed great prudence in his early years, his old age was distinguished by the boldest courage.

The elder brother of Timoleon, who was named Timophanes, was altogether unlike him. He was rash, indiscreet and wildly ambitious by nature, and his natural tendencies were encouraged by loose acquaintances, and by certain foreign soldiers with whom he habitually consorted. In battle he made a show of great daring, and appeared to court danger. Hence he gained such a reputation among his countrymen that they frequently put him in command of the army.

In a certain battle between the Corinthians and the forces of another Greek state, it happened that Timoleon was serving with the infantry, while his brother Timophanes was in command of the cavalry. During the fight the latter's horse was wounded, and plunging and rearing in pain, threw the rider in the midst of his foes. Timophanes was now in a position of extreme danger. Some of his companions took fright and fled, while such as stood their ground were greatly outnumbered by the enemy. His danger was perceived by Timoleon, who at once rushed to his assistance. He covered the body of his fallen brother with his shield and, though many darts were hurled at him and he received many sword-strokes upon body and armour, he succeeded in driving back the enemy and in saving his brother's life.

TIMOLEON

Some time after this battle, the Corinthians made Timophanes the commander of a body of four hundred hired soldiers who had been engaged to protect the city against any surprise. Timophanes, however, was destitute of the sense of truth and honour. He employed the power, which had been entrusted to him, to subject the city to his own will. A number of the chief citizens were put to death, and Timophanes proclaimed himself absolute prince of Corinth. Timoleon was profoundly vexed and upset by this action. He felt the treachery of his brother as a reproach to himself, and went to reason with him in the hope of inducing him to give up his mad ambition for authority. All he could say was, however, scornfully rejected by the usurper.

A few days later Timoleon again visited his brother for the same purpose, taking with him one of his kinsmen and another friend. The three stood in a group with Timophanes, and earnestly besought him to listen to reason and to change his designs. At first their entreaties were met with laughter, but as they continued to urge him, Timophanes burst into a violent passion. Thereupon Timoleon turned aside and covered his face, for he was weeping at his brother's treachery and violence. At the same time his two companions drew their swords, and in an instant slew Timophanes.

The news of the killing of the usurper was soon noised abroad, and awakened diverse opinions. The best and worthiest of the Corinthians praised Timoleon's greatness of soul, which they believed had led him, in spite of his natural gentleness and family affection, to put the welfare of the state before the interests of his family. 'When his brother,' said these citizens, 'was the valiant soldier of the state, Timoleon saved his life; when, on the other hand, he enslaved his native city, Timoleon stood by at his slaying.' Others, however, while pretending to be glad of the death of the tyrant, spoke with horror of Timoleon as one guilty of an unnatural deed. The opinion of these latter caused Timoleon much uneasiness, and his distress was greatly increased when he learnt with what bitter sorrow his mother heard of the death of Timophanes, and what dreadful curses she called down upon the head of her younger son. Timoleon went to see her, in order if possible to console her and excuse himself, but she refused to see him, and ordered the doors to be shut in his face. He was then overwhelmed with sorrow, so much that he even sought to starve himself to death. His friends, however, did not abandon him, and at length, by entreaties and even by force, they prevailed on him to live. He dwelt, however, in solitude and withdrew from all public affairs. For years he did not even approach the city, but wandered, a prey to melancholy, in the most gloomy recesses of his estate.

When, after his long seclusion from public affairs, which lasted almost twenty years, he was chosen general of the expedition, one of the most powerful and reputable citizens of Corinth besought him to be of good courage and to execute his commission well. 'If,' said he, 'you conduct the expedition well, we shall esteem you the destroyer of a tyrant; but, if ill, the murderer of your brother.' While the forces for the expedition were being assembled and Timoleon was making ready to set sail, letters came from Icetes which plainly revealed his treachery. The prince had indeed openly joined the Carthaginians as soon as the Sicilian ambassadors had set out for Greece, and acted in alliance with them in order to drive out Dionysius, and set himself up as tyrant in his stead.

He now wrote to the Corinthians to tell them that it was useless for them to send their fleet. He told them also that the Carthaginians were watching for them with a great navy, and would oppose them, and that he, for his part, had been obliged to join the Carthaginians by reason of the delay of the Corinthians in sending the succours.

The reading of these letters and the treachery which they revealed greatly incensed the people of Corinth, so that even those who had hitherto been cold or indifferent in the matter now readily joined in supplying whatever was wanted, and in hastening the sailing of the expedition.

When the fleet was fitted out, the priestesses of the goddess Proserpine had a dream in which the goddess and her mother Ceres, habited as for a journey, appeared to them and declared their intention of accompanying the expedition into Sicily. Thereupon the citizens fitted out a sacred galley, and called it the Galley of the Goddesses. Further, when Timoleon went to sacrifice to Apollo, a wreath, ornamented with crowns and other signs of victory, fell down from among the offerings in the temple and rested on his head. Thus

Apollo seemed to send Timoleon forth crowned as to victory.

With ten ships Timoleon set sail in the night time. As the vessels were making their way before a strong favouring wind, it seemed on a sudden as if the heavens opened, and a bright flaming light fell thence upon Timoleon's ship. The flame spread itself out in the form of a torch, and, guiding the ships throughout the whole passage, brought them at last to that part of Italy which they desired to reach. The heavenly light, said the soothsayers, confirmed the dream of the priestesses, and showed that the goddesses were indeed interested in the success of the expedition.

The men in the fleet were much encouraged by these signs of divine favour. But when they reached the coast of Italy discouraging news, which caused much perplexity to Timoleon, met them. They learnt that Icetes had beaten Dionysius in a pitched battle, and, having captured the greater part of the town of Syracuse, had shut up the tyrant in the citadel and a part of the city near it, and was closely besieging him therein. At the same time he had sent the Carthaginian fleet to prevent the landing of the Corinthians in Sicily. He trusted that, once rid of the Corinthians, he and his new allies would have little difficulty in taking the whole island and sharing it between them.

Thus it happened that, when Timoleon's expedition arrived at Rhegium on the Italian side of the Straits of Messina, they found twenty Carthaginian ships riding at anchor in the harbour. With them were

TIMOLEON SETTING SAIL FOR SICILY

ambassadors from Icetes, who bore a message to the effect that Timoleon might, if he liked, go unaccompanied to assist Icetes with his counsel, but that all the ships and troops must be sent back to Corinth, and that, if they attempted to cross over to Sicily, the Carthaginians would oppose them.

The Corinthians were filled with indignation against Icetes and with perplexity at their own position. There seemed little chance of getting the better of the Carthaginians, who lay watching them with twice their number of ships. Even could they do so, it seemed improbable that they could contend successfully with the forces of Icetes, which they had expected to meet as allies, and now found to be foes.

In this state of affairs Timoleon, in an interview with the ambassadors and the Carthaginian commanders, pretended to agree to their proposals. There was, he said, nothing to be gained by opposition, and he must therefore submit, but, for his own security and so that the facts might be generally known, he required that the proposals should be laid before the people of Rhegium in public assembly.

All the while he was intending to steal secretly away from the town. The magistrates of the place, to whom he disclosed his intentions, entered heartily into the scheme, for they favoured the cause of the Greeks in Sicily, and dreaded the power of the Carthaginians. They summoned the people to meet in public assembly, and shut the gates of the town, so that none might leave the place upon any other business. When the people were gathered together, one after another of those who were in the secret stood up and made long speeches, with the object of giving time for the Corinthian galleys to get under sail. Meanwhile the Carthaginians remained in the assembly without any suspicion, for they saw that Timoleon was present, and they expected every moment that he would stand up and make his speech. But when word was privately brought that Timoleon's galley alone remained in the harbour and that all the others had set sail, the Rhegians crowded round Timoleon and hid him from view while he slipped through the crowd. Once clear of the assembly, he hastened down to the harbour and made sail with all speed. When the assembly broke up, the Carthaginians found that Timoleon was gone and that they had been outwitted. They could not conceal their vexation and annoyance, and the Rhegians were greatly amused to find so deceitful a people as the Carthaginians complain of being tricked.

Timoleon soon arrived with all his ships at the town of Tauromenium in Sicily, and was kindly received there. The lord of the town was much the best of the Sicilian princes, a lover of justice and an enemy of tyranny. He therefore readily allowed the Corinthians to use his city as a place of arms, and persuaded his people to aid them.

Thither there soon came one of the Carthaginian galleys with an ambassador to the prince. With much pride and insolence he demanded that the Corinthians should be turned out of the town. Stretching out his hand palm upwards, he turned the palm downwards.

With the same ease, said he, would the Carthaginians overturn the city if their demands were not complied with. The prince only smiled at the threat. Stretching out his hand, and turning it over as the other had done, he made this reply, 'Begone immediately, if you do not choose to have your galley turned upside down in like manner.'

Icetes heard with alarm that Timoleon had made good his footing in Sicily, and at once sent for a large number of the Carthaginian galleys to come to Syracuse. The condition of the people of that town now appeared to be desperate. The Carthaginians held the harbour, Icetes the city, and Dionysius the citadel. Against these forces there seemed small hope of succour from Timoleon, who held but the little town of Tauromenium with a force numbering not more than a thousand men scantily supplied with provisions. Moreover, most of the Sicilian states had no confidence in the Corinthians, and believed that they themselves came not as deliverers, but to establish their own authority. In one town, Adranum, opinions were divided, and while one party called in Icetes, the other applied to Timoleon. Both generals therefore set out for the town, each seeking to get there first, but while Icetes led five thousand men with him, Timoleon had but twelve hundred at the most. Towards evening of the second day after setting out, after a hurried march through rugged country, Timoleon received news that Icetes had just reached the town, and was encamping outside it. Just at that time the officers of Timoleon's vanguard called a halt, so that the men might have some rest and refreshment and be fresh and vigorous for the fight that lay before them. But this plan did not meet with Timoleon's approval. Hurrying to the front, he besought his men to march forward with all speed in order that they might attack the enemy while they were in the disorder of pitching their tents and preparing their supper. Then, seizing his buckler, he put himself at the head of his force, and led them on with the air of one marching to an assured victory. Encouraged by their leader's manner, his men followed him cheerfully over the distance of rather more than three and a half miles which lay between them and Adranum. As soon as they came up with the enemy they fell upon them vigorously. The troops of Icetes, however, were in such confusion and disorder that they fled almost at the first shock. So poor a stand did they make that only about three hundred were killed, but twice as many were taken prisoners, and their camp was captured.

In consequence of this success the people of Adranum opened their gates to Timoleon and allied themselves with him. Moreover, several cities and one of the most warlike and wealthy princes of the island also cast in their lot with Timoleon. Most important of all, Dionysius, who despaired of victory for himself and felt he could not hold out much longer, sent to Timoleon offering to surrender himself and the citadel to the Corinthians, for he despised Icetes on account of his shameful defeat, and admired the courage of Timoleon.

The Corinthian general gladly accepted this good fortune, so greatly in excess of his hopes, and sent two of his officers and four hundred men to take possession of the city. They did not, of course, march in openly, for the enemy were upon their guard, but, a few at a time, they stole through the enemy's lines and entered the citadel. They then took possession of the place and of the stores which the tyrant had provided for carrying on the war. Among them were a good number of horses, all kinds of engines of war, a vast quantity of javelins, and also arms for seventy thousand men, which had been laid up in store for a long time. With these stores Dionysius also delivered up his two thousand soldiers. The tyrant, however, reserved his money to himself, and, having secretly gone on board ship, stole away without being perceived by Icetes, and came to the camp of Timoleon. Thus Dionysius for the first time appeared as a private man, and as such he was sent off to Corinth with only one ship and a moderate sum of money. His life affords a striking instance of the changes of fortune, since he had been born in a splendid court, and had for years held the most absolute monarchy that ever existed. But for many years he had been constantly engaged in wars and troubles, so that the evils of his tyranny were fully avenged in his own sufferings.

When Dionysius arrived at Corinth, nearly every one sought to see him and to talk with him. Some did so for the pleasure of reviling the fallen tyrant whom they hated, but others, when they saw his present condition, were touched with some compassion for him. For he, who had but lately been master of Sicily, now spent his time wholly in trivial and unworthy pursuits: gossiping in a butcher's shop, or spending a whole day with a perfumer, or drinking in the taverns and squabbling in the streets.

The success of Timoleon in Sicily was no less striking than the downfall of Dionysius. Within fifty days of his landing in the island, he was master of the citadel of Syracuse, and had sent off Dionysius to Greece. His success encouraged the Corinthians, and they sent a reinforcement of two thousand infantry and two hundred cavalry to join him. These forces arrived safely in Italy, but for a time were unable to make their way into Sicily, because of the great fleets of Carthage which held the sea.

Meanwhile, Icetes kept up the siege of the citadel, and invested it so closely that no provisions could reach the garrison. He also planned the murder of Timoleon, and, having hired two assassins for the purpose, sent them to Adranum, where the Corinthian general still lay. Timoleon never kept any regular guards about him, and lived among the people of the town without any suspicion or precaution. After their arrival in the city, the assassins learnt that Timoleon was going to offer sacrifice. Concealing their daggers under their clothes, they went into the temple and mixed with the people who stood around the altar. Gradually working their way among the press, they at last came close to the general. But, at the very moment when they were looking to one another for the signal to strike, one of them was struck dead by a blow from the sword of a man in the crowd, who at once fled to the top of a high rock near by. At this the second assassin was seized with terror, for he imagined that his purpose was known. Laying hold of the altar, he implored pardon, and confessed that he and the man who was slain had been sent to murder Timoleon. Meanwhile, the man who had killed the assassin was brought down from the rock. He loudly protested that he was guilty of no injustice, since he had only taken vengeance upon a villain who was the murderer of his father. The truth of this statement was attested by several of those present, and men could not but wonder at the marvellous ways of fortune, which had moved this man to take vengeance at the very moment when his act availed to save the life of Timoleon. So far from being punished, the slayer of the assassin was rewarded by the Corinthians.

Icetes, having failed in this treacherous attempt to compass the death of Timoleon, now resolved to call in the aid of the full forces of the Carthaginians, whom hitherto, as if ashamed of their help, he had only employed in small numbers. In response to his appeal, Mago, the Carthaginian commander-in-chief, entered the harbour of Syracuse with a hundred and fifty ships, and landed an army of sixty thousand men, who encamped in the town. Thus Syracuse, which had never, in the course of the many wars waged by the Carthaginians against the Greeks in Sicily, been taken by them, now became a camp of the barbarians.

The Corinthians still held the citadel, but they found themselves in a position of great difficulty and danger. They were constantly engaged in sharp fights about the walls, and, moreover, they were in want of provisions, which could not be brought in on account of the fleet blockading the harbour. Timoleon, however, managed to bring them relief. He sent a supply of corn in fishing-boats and other small vessels, and these, waiting an opportunity, slipped into the harbour at a time when the enemy's fleet happened to be driven off by a storm. Icetes and Mago now determined to capture the town from which the food had been shipped, in order to prevent further supplies from being sent thence. With this object they took ship with the best of their troops, and sailed from Syracuse. The Corinthian officer in command of the garrison, watching from the top of the citadel, noticed a slackening of vigilance on the part of those who were left behind, and that they were keeping a careless guard. He therefore made a sudden sally from the citadel, fell upon them, killed some, and putting the rest to flight captured an important quarter of the town. There he found plenty of provisions and money. He therefore determined to hold the part of the town he had won, and with that object fortified it and joined it to the citadel by new defences. Meanwhile, Mago and Icetes had almost reached their destination when a horseman dashed up to them with the news of the Corinthian success. Thereupon they hastily returned, having neither succeeded in the object of their expedition nor in retaining what they had before possessed.

Fortune greatly favoured the Corinthians in the next event of importance in the war. The reinforcements which had landed in Italy, and which were prevented from crossing by the Carthaginian fleet, determined at length to march by land to Rhegium. In spite of some resistance they effected their purpose. Meanwhile a storm raged and the sea for many days was very rough and tempestuous. The Carthaginian admiral thought that the Corinthians would never venture to take ship in such a storm. He therefore hit upon the stratagem of sailing to Syracuse with his ships and men decorated as if for victory over the reinforcements, in order to make the defenders of the citadel despair of succour. With his galleys adorned with Greek bucklers and his sailors crowned with garlands, he accordingly entered the harbour with loud cheers and cries of triumph. But, while he was playing this part, the Corinthians got down to the shore at Rhegium and found the coast clear. Moreover, the wind fell as if by a miracle, and the sea became calm. The troops immediately went on board such fishing-boats and other vessels as they could find. They crossed so smoothly and in such a calm that they were even able, by holding the reins, to swim their horses across alongside the ships.

When the reinforcements had joined Timoleon, he captured the town of Messina, and thence, though he had still but four thousand men with him, advanced against Syracuse. His approach greatly disturbed Mago, who felt some suspicion of the troops of Icetes. His doubts were increased by the fact that these allies of his, who were Greeks by race, often met the Corinthians in times of truce and intervals of the fighting. The soldiers of Icetes, too, frequently repeated in camp the words of the Corinthians, who on such occasions expressed their wonder that men of Greek blood should act in concert with the Carthaginians, who were the enemies of the Greeks, and whose success would be to their

TIMOLEON

disadvantage. Hence, though Icetes begged him to stay, and pointed out how few the Corinthians were, Mago weighed anchor on the approach of Timoleon, and shamefully sailed back to Africa. Thus he allowed Sicily to slip from his grasp.

Next day Timoleon drew up his forces in order of battle before Syracuse. When, to their astonishment, they saw the harbour empty of Carthaginian ships, and learnt that Mago had sailed away, they were consumed with laughter at his cowardice. In mockery, they caused a proclamation to be made offering a reward to any one who would reveal the hiding-place of the Carthaginian fleet. Icetes, however, showed a more resolute spirit, and vigorously defended those parts of the town which he held. But Timoleon, dividing his forces into three bodies, delivered an assault upon three different quarters of the city at the same time. He succeeded in overpowering the enemy and in putting their troops to flight. The capture of the town may in itself be fairly ascribed to the genius of the general and the valour of the troops. But the extraordinary fact that not one Corinthian was killed or wounded in the assault can only be put down to the good fortune which assisted Timoleon.

The fame of this achievement spread rapidly through Sicily and Italy. In a few days, indeed, it resounded throughout Greece, so that the city of Corinth, which had been in doubt whether its succours had arrived in Sicily, heard at the same time of their arrival and of their success in attaining the object of the expedition. Thus the glory of the exploit was increased by the rapidity of its execution.

The city being now in the hands of Timoleon, he issued a public order calling upon all who wished to do so to assemble and destroy the ramparts by which the tyrants had maintained their rule. With one consent the citizens obeyed the summons, which they regarded as marking the first day of their liberty. Not only did they destroy the citadel, but they also levelled the palaces and monuments of the tyrants with the ground.

The Corinthians found the town, in comparison with its former flourishing condition, almost destitute of inhabitants. Many of its citizens had perished in the wars and in domestic broils, many more had fled from the savage rule of the tyrants. Grass grew so thickly in the very market-place, that the horses of the troops pastured there, while the grooms reposed on the herbage. With very few exceptions, the other cities of Sicily were deserts, so that deer and wild boars harboured in them. Timoleon and the people of Syracuse therefore wrote to the Corinthians asking them to send a good number of colonists who were required, not only to cultivate the land, which must otherwise lie desolate, but also because a new and more formidable war with Carthage was threatened. The news came that Mago had killed himself and that the Carthaginians, in anger at his conduct of their forces, had crucified his body, and were now collecting great forces with the object of invading Sicily in the following summer.

These letters having been delivered, the Corinthians caused proclamation to be made by the heralds inviting all fugitives from Syracuse and Sicily to return to their native island, and assuring them that they should there enjoy their liberties and privileges, and that the vacant lands should be divided among them. They also sent envoys with a message to this effect into the Greek islands and cities of Asia, and at their own expense provided vessels to bring the refugees safely to Corinth. Hence the Corinthians earned the honour and glory of having delivered a Grecian city from tyrants and the barbarians, and of restoring it to its citizens without seeking their own advantage in the matter.

The fugitives who assembled at Corinth were not sufficient in number to repeople Syracuse, and other new colonists from Corinth and other parts of Greece were therefore added to them. The whole body, fully ten thousand in number, then sailed to Syracuse. Meanwhile great numbers of people had flocked into the town from Italy and from the rest of Sicily. Timoleon divided the lands freely among the settlers, but sold the houses in order to raise a public fund. Thus the fortunes of Syracuse were revived and the city replenished with inhabitants. Timoleon then proceeded to free the other cities of Sicily and to destroy arbitrary rule throughout the island. He compelled Icetes to give up his alliance with Carthage, to pull down his castles, and to live among his people as a private person. Another prince was also forced to surrender and was sent to Corinth. Timoleon then returned to Syracuse in order to settle the government of the place, and to aid in the establishment of necessary laws.

While he himself was engaged in this important work, he sent his hired soldiers to lay waste the

Carthaginian province in Sicily. They succeeded in withdrawing several cities from the interests of Carthage, and also obtained such an amount of plunder as not only supplied themselves abundantly, but also provided money for carrying on the war. While affairs were in this state, a vast Carthaginian expedition arrived in the island. It consisted of two hundred war galleys, with a thousand other vessels laden with engines of war, chariots, provisions and other stores, and bearing seventy thousand land forces. As soon as the invaders learnt that the Carthaginian territories had been laid waste, they marched in great fury against the Corinthians.

The news of the advance of this great force caused such terror to the people of Syracuse that scarce three thousand men, out of ten times that number, were bold enough to take up arms and follow Timoleon. There were, in addition, four thousand hired soldiers, but of these about a thousand gave way to their fears while upon the march, and refused to advance farther. Timoleon, they declared, must be mad to march against seventy thousand men with but five thousand foot and a thousand horse, and still more mad to draw them away eight days' march from Syracuse.

Timoleon considered it a good thing that the cowardice of the deserters had been revealed before the battle. He encouraged the rest of his troops, and led them hastily to the banks of a river, where he understood that the enemy was assembled. As the troops were climbing a hill, from the top of which they would be able to see the camp of the enemy, they met some mules laden with parsley. The soldiers took this to be a bad omen, because the Greeks were accustomed to place parsley upon their sepulchres. To rid them of this superstition and the fear that it was likely to occasion, Timoleon called a halt and made an address to his men. He told them that crowns of victory were brought to them even before the fight; for the Corinthians from the earliest days looked upon garlands of parsley as sacred, and with such garlands were accustomed to crown the victors at the Isthmian games. Timoleon then crowned himself with a wreath of parsley, and next his officers and then the soldiers did the same. At that moment the soothsayers saw two eagles flying towards them, one bearing a serpent transfixed by its claws, the other uttering loud cries. They pointed the birds out to the army, and the soldiers betook themselves to prayer and to the invocation of the gods.

It was now the time of summer, and the Corinthians, when they reached the top of the hill, found that a summer mist lay over the river and the low-lying lands, so that they could see nothing of the enemy, though the confused and indistinct noise which reached them showed that a great army was near. But, after they had laid aside their shields and rested awhile, the mist rose and lay about the summit of the hill, so that it hid the Corinthians from view, while they for their part could see plainly what was happening in the valley below. The river was clearly seen, and crossing it there appeared the Carthaginian army. First came the war-chariots, each drawn by four horses and formidably armed. Next marched ten thousand men with white shields. These the onlookers judged, from the brightness of their armour and the steadiness and good order of their movements, to be native Carthaginians. Behind them, in more confused and disorderly array, marched the troops of other nations who made up the whole great army.

Timoleon saw that while the enemy was crossing the river, he had it in his power, by choosing the moment of attack, to engage with what number of them he pleased. He pointed out to his men how the main body of the enemy was divided by the stream, and ordered his cavalry to press on and attack the Carthaginians before those who had crossed could find time to draw themselves up in order of battle. Descending into the plain, he then arrayed his own army, the men of Syracuse and the best of the hired soldiers being around him in the centre; the other Sicilians with some strangers on the wings. He then stood still awhile to see what success had attended his horsemen. He perceived that they could not deliver their charge upon the Carthaginians because of the chariots which covered the enemy's front. He therefore sent orders to his cavalry to get beyond the line of chariots, and to attack the enemy in flank. Then seizing his shield, he, with a loud shout, called upon his foot-soldiers to follow him. They answered with cheers, and, with ranks closed up and bucklers interlocked, bore down upon their foes to the sound of the trumpet. The Carthaginians bore the first shock stoutly, for, indeed, as they were well armed with iron breastplates and brazen helmets and carried large shields, they sustained little hurt from the spears and javelins. But when the struggle came to a hand-to-hand fight with swords, in which skill is of as much account as strength, a terrible storm burst upon the armies. Dreadful thunders resounded and baleful lightnings flashed among the mountains, and soon the black clouds which swept down upon the valley discharged themselves in a wind-lashed storm of rain and hail. The tempest drove up at the back of the Greeks, and beat full upon the faces of the barbarians, who were almost blinded by the stinging rain and hail and by the almost incessant lightning, while the noise of the thunder prevented them from hearing the orders of their commanders. Moreover, the field of battle was turned into a quagmire by the storm and by the overflowing of the river, which happened partly on account of the rainfall, and partly because the stream was choked by the masses of men crossing. This added to the disadvantages of the Carthaginians, who were very heavily armed, and could neither move readily in the mire nor arise easily if they were overthrown. In short, the storm continuing to beat violently upon them, and some four hundred of the men in the front ranks having been slain by the Greeks, the rest broke and fled. Many were killed in the field itself; others took to the river, where they threw those who were still crossing into confusion, and were swept away and drowned. The majority of the fugitives endeavoured to escape to the hills, but were stopped by the light-armed troops of the Greeks and slain. Ten thousand in all were killed, and of these it is said that three thousand were natives of Carthage, and were, moreover, men of high birth, fortune and character, so that the city sustained a heavy loss in their deaths. Indeed, we have no account of so many native Carthaginians having ever before been slain in one battle, for, as they were accustomed to employ men of other nations in their armies, their defeats were generally at the expense of the blood of strangers.

The spoils of the battle showed the rank and fortune of the slain. So abundant was gold and silver that brass and iron were disregarded, and so busy were the Greeks in collecting the pillage of the battlefield and of the camp that it was not until the third day that the trophy of victory was erected. Many prisoners were secretly sold by the soldiers, but five thousand were delivered up to the public account, and two hundred chariots were also captured. The tent of Timoleon presented a sight of extraordinary wealth and magnificence, for in it were piled all manner of spoils, including a thousand breastplates of the finest workmanship, and ten thousand shields. The best of these arms Timoleon sent, with the news of the victory, to Corinth, in order that the temples of the gods might be adorned with the spoils of the barbarians. The spoils bore this inscription: 'The Corinthians and Timoleon their general, having delivered the Sicilian Greeks from the Carthaginians, make this offering in gratitude to the gods.'

After the victory Timoleon left the hired soldiers to lay waste the Carthaginian province, and himself returned to Syracuse. There he issued a decree banishing the thousand hired soldiers who had refused to follow him to the battle. The cowards passed over into Italy, and were there treacherously slain by one of the peoples of that country. Thus the faithless desertion of their leader met with a just punishment.

In spite of the success of Timoleon, Mamercus, the Prince of Catania, either through envy or dread of the Corinthian general, entered into a league with the Carthaginians, and besought them to send a new army and a new general. In response there came a fleet of seventy ships under Gisco and a body of Greeks whom he had hired. Hitherto the Carthaginians had not employed any Greeks, but now the victories of Timoleon caused them to regard the Greeks as the bravest of men.

About this time a body of foreign soldiers whom Timoleon had sent to Messina were slain by the populace. The hired soldiers who had been left in the Carthaginian province were also cut off by an ambush. The tyrants boasted loudly of these successes, and while Timoleon was laying siege to a town, Icetes ventured to make an inroad into the territories of Syracuse, and audaciously marched back with his booty past the very place Timoleon was besieging. The Corinthian general suffered him to pass, and then followed in pursuit with his cavalry and his light infantry. Icetes crossed a river and drew up his forces on the other side, in a position which was difficult of attack because of the steep banks and the river between them. When the army of Timoleon came up on the other side a strange contest arose between the officers. Each wanted to be first in the attack, and there was therefore some danger of a confused and disorderly onset. To avoid this, Timoleon declared that the matter should be decided by lot, and for this purpose he took the rings of the officers and shook them up in his robe. The first that was drawn out happened to have upon it a trophy as a seal. The officers hailed the omen with joy. They declared that they would wait for no other lot, and the whole army marched hastily down to the river. So fierce was their onset that the enemy scarcely stood the first shock. Their men were soon in full flight, throwing away their arms as they ran, and leaving a thousand dead upon the field. A few days later Timoleon captured Icetes alive, and the tyrant's son was also brought to him bound by the soldiers. Both suffered death as tyrants and traitors to their country. After Timoleon had returned to Syracuse, the wife and daughters of Icetes were also tried publicly, condemned to death, and executed. This appears to be the event in Timoleon's life most worthy of blame, for, if he had interposed, the women would have been spared.

Timoleon next marched against Mamercus, defeated him, and slew above two thousand of his men. Of the slain a considerable number were Carthaginians. Their countrymen now sued for peace, which Timoleon granted upon certain conditions, one of which was that the Carthaginians should give up all friendship and alliance with the tyrants. This treaty reduced Mamercus to despair. He endeavoured to sail to Italy to obtain aid, but the crews of his galleys, instead of proceeding thither, returned to Sicily and delivered up his town of Catania to Timoleon. Meanwhile Mamercus escaped to Messina, and took refuge with the prince of that place. Thither Timoleon marched, and invested it by land while his fleet blockaded it by sea. The Prince of Messina, despairing of a successful defence, endeavoured to escape by sea, but was seized by his own subjects. He was exposed to the derision of the people in the theatre, scourged and then put to death. Thereupon Mamercus surrendered himself to Timoleon to take his trial at Syracuse. He was brought before the people in that city, and endeavored to make an oration to them which he had prepared for the occasion. But the people would not hear him, and received him with noise and clamour, so that the fallen tyrant perceived that they had made up their minds to show him no mercy. In despair, he cast off his upper garment, rushed through the theatre, and dashed his head against the stone steps with the object of killing himself. He was, however, taken up alive, and suffered the death that is decreed for thieves and robbers.

Thus did Timoleon root out tyranny from the island of Sicily and put an end to the wars. He found the whole island turned almost into a desert by its calamities, so that even its natives could hardly endure to live in it. Yet such order did he bring back to it, and so desirable did he make it, that strangers flocked to settle in it. The cities, which had been sacked and left desolate, were now peopled again under the protection of Timoleon, who so aided and supplied the settlers that he was beloved by them as though he had been the founder of their cities. Indeed, to such a degree did he enjoy the love of the Sicilians in general, that no war seemed finished, nor law enacted, nor lands divided aright, unless the matter were first revised by him. He was the master-craftsman whose hand was required to put the finishing touches to every work and to reduce all to perfect beauty.

Timoleon himself ascribed all his successes to fortune. When he wrote to his friends at Corinth, or when he addressed the people of Syracuse, he often said that he owed much to the Goddess of Fortune, since she had chosen to save Sicily under his name. In the house which the Syracusans had in gratitude given him in the city, he built a chapel and offered sacrifices to Chance, while he dedicated the house itself to Fortune. But most of his time he spent in his country house, which they had also given him, in the company of his wife and children, who had joined him from Corinth. He never returned to his native city nor took part in the troubles of Greece, avoiding the insatiable pursuit of glory and power which has wrecked so many great men. He was content to remain in Sicily, enjoying the blessings which he had established, and seeing around him so many cities and such great numbers of peoples happy through his means.

But, as one writer says, every republic must have its impudent slanderer as surely as every lark must have a crest on its head. Thus it was at Syracuse, where two demagogues arose and attacked Timoleon. When the people would have refused to hear the first of these, Timoleon stilled the tumult. 'I have,' said he, 'undergone many dangers and labours in order that the meanest Syracusan may, if he wishes, have recourse to the laws.' And when the second made many charges against him, his only answer was to say, 'I cannot thank the gods enough for permitting me to live to see all Syracusans enjoying the liberty of saying what they think fit.'

It was a happy fortune which kept Timoleon at a distance from the calamities which, during his lifetime, came upon Greece, and which kept his hands unstained with the blood of his countrymen. His victories, more remarkable than those of any other Greek of his age, were at the expense of foreigners and tyrants, and few of his trophies cost his countrymen a tear.

When he was well advanced in years, and had lived long in great prosperity, blindness came upon him. The affliction seems to have been the result of a family weakness together with the advance of years. It was borne by Timoleon with patient fortitude, and the honour and respect paid to him in his blindness by the Syracusans were truly admirable. They frequently visited him themselves, and also brought to him all strangers who spent some time in the town, in order that the visitors might have the pleasure of beholding the deliverer of Syracuse. In their assemblies they decided the less important affairs themselves, but consulted him in all great matters. On these occasions Timoleon was carried in a litter through the market-place to the place of assembly, where he was saluted by all the people. Having returned their salutations, and been informed of the subject under discussion, he delivered his opinion. Then, amidst the applause of the people, he was carried out again by his servants, and the rest of the public business was transacted without him.

Thus in his old age he was cherished as the father

of his people, until at last he died of a slight illness, full of years and honour. The people of Syracuse buried him with great magnificence. His bier, splendidly adorned, was carried by young men over the ground on which the citadel and palace of the tyrants had formerly stood, and was followed by many thousands of men and women clad in white robes and crowned with garlands. The lamentations of the people and their praise of the dead hero showed that the stately procession was no formal show, but the outward sign of deep sorrow and affection. When, at length, the bier was laid upon the funeral pile, a herald made proclamation, saying: 'The people of Syracuse inter Timoleon the Corinthian at the public charge, and decree that he shall be honoured through all time in annual games as the man who uprooted the tyrants, conquered the barbarians, repeopled great cities which aforetime lay desolate, and restored freedom to the Sicilians.'

ALEXANDER

THE life of Alexander forms a kind of sequel to the lives of Aristides and Themistocles. The great deeds of the earlier heroes were mainly concerned in stemming and turning back the flood of war, in the shape of the Persian armies, which threatened Europe. About a century and a half later the positions were reversed. The young Macedonian king and his army burst into Asia, not indeed like a flood, for the number under his command was small for so great an invasion, but rather like a mountain torrent sweeping all before it by its impetuous rush. In swift ruin the Persian empire was toppled over, and in the most wonderful series of victories in the history of the world Alexander carried his arms beyond the limits of the known world to the river Jhelum or Hydaspes.

The marvellous victories and conquests of Alexander were accomplished in a comparatively short time, for he was only in his thirty-third year when he died. He was not merely a soldier and conqueror. He was a statesman of wide views, with a settled policy of blending together the different peoples under his rule. It was for this purpose that he educated Persian youths in the Greek manner and encouraged intermarriages between his Asiatic subjects and his Macedonians. He also planted many Greek colonies in his conquests, and though most of them were probably founded merely for military reasons, they ultimately became centres from which the civilisation of Greece was spread. Nor did he neglect the material interests of his wide domains. His death indeed occurred at a time when he was engaged in devising great plans for the drainage of the fever-stricken marshes around Babylon and for the irrigation of the district. Some writers suggest that his death was the result, not so much of the drunken debauch of which Plutarch tells, as of a fever which he contracted while thus engaged.

The wonderful success of Alexander was not without an injurious effect upon his character. The hardy, simple and temperate Macedonian warrior-king gradually became more and more like the Eastern despots he had conquered. He made his manly Macedonians grovel on the ground in his presence, and gave way to fits of ungovernable fury, such as that in which he slew his old friend and comrade-in-arms, Clitus, who had saved his life in battle.

When Alexander died the burden of his vast empire proved too heavy for any other shoulders to bear, and it soon broke up into a number of kingdoms ruled by his generals and successors.

ALEXANDER was the son of Philip, King of Macedon, and of Olympias his wife. Among other strange and great events that occurred about the time of his birth, it happened that the temple of Diana at Ephesus was destroyed by fire on the very day upon which he was born. The wise men, who were then at Ephesus, looked upon the fire as a sign of still greater misfortune to come. They ran through the city, beating their faces and crying, 'On this day is born he who shall be the scourge and destroyer of Asia.' Thus they interpreted the omen.

The statues and paintings of Alexander preserve his features for our view. The characteristic turn of his head, which leaned a little to one side, and the quickness of his eye, which many of his successors and friends sought to imitate, are best shown by the statues. The paintings of Apelles were not very successful in depicting his complexion, for the painter made the skin too brown, whereas Alexander was fair with a ruddy tinge in his face.

As a youth Alexander showed an ambition which had something great and splendid in it, and which, in its character, was beyond his years. It was not every sort of honour that he coveted, nor did he seek it by any kind of path. In this he was unlike his father, who, although a great conqueror, was as vain of his eloquence as any professed speaker could be, and who recorded his victories in the Olympic chariot-races in the impressions upon his coins. On the other hand, Alexander, when he was asked by some why he did not run in the Olympic race—for he was fleet of foot—replied, 'I would indeed run if I had kings to contend with.'

Ambassadors from Persia happened at one time to come to the court in the absence of King Philip. The young Alexander therefore received them in his father's stead, and surprised them much by his courtesy and his sound sense. He asked them no trifling nor childish questions, but inquired concerning the distances between places, the roads through the upper provinces of Asia, the character and mode of government of their king, and the sources of the strength and power of the Persian kingdom. The ambassadors were astonished, and regarded the famous shrewdness of Philip as less wonderful than the genius of his son.

Whenever news came that Philip had taken some strong city or won some great battle, the young prince, instead of appearing delighted at the success, used to say, 'My father will make so many conquests that there will remain nothing for me to do.' His desires were not for pleasure or riches, but for valour and glory. Therefore he looked upon each new conquest made by his father as limiting his own field of distinction.

Upon one occasion a certain Thessalian brought a horse named Bucephalus to the court of Philip, and offered it for sale to the king. Philip with the prince and many nobles went out into a field to see the horse tried. The animal, however, showed himself to be extremely vicious and intractable. So far from allowing himself to be mounted, he would not even bear to hear the word of command, and turned fiercely upon all the grooms. Philip was angered that so wild and vicious a horse should have been brought to him, and commanded that he should be taken away. But Alexander, who had watched the animal very carefully, exclaimed, 'What a splendid horse is being lost for want of the skill and spirit to manage him!' This he said not once but several times, till at last the king replied, 'Young man, you find fault with your elders as if you could manage the horse better than they.'

'That I certainly could,' said the prince.

'And what will you forfeit,' asked his father, 'if you fail?'

'The price of the horse,' answered Alexander.

Thereupon the whole company laughed. The king and his son, however, agreed upon the conditions. Alexander at once ran to the horse, and laying his hand upon the bridle turned the animal so as to face the sun. It seems that the prince had observed that the horse had been terrified at his shadow which was previously cast before him; and which moved as he moved. Next, so long as the animal continued to be nervous and frightened, Alexander kept patting him and speaking soothingly to him. When he had become quieter, the prince gently let fall his mantle, leaped lightly upon the horse's back, and got a firm seat. Then with a light hand upon the reins, and without the use of whip or spur, Alexander set the horse going. He soon found him going freely, and that the creature now desired only to run. He then put the horse to a full gallop and urged him on with voice and spur. Philip and his courtiers were at first silent with fear as to what would happen. But when they saw that Alexander controlled the steed, and that he turned him round and brought him straight back with ease, all except Philip burst into shouts of applause. As for the king, he shed tears of joy, and said,

'Seek another kingdom, my son, for Macedonia is too small a field for your abilities.'

Philip perceived that his son was of a disposition which would not readily submit to commands, but was rather to be led to the path of duty by the gentler force of reason. He therefore used persuasion with him rather than commands. The king saw, too, that his son's education was of great importance. Therefore he entrusted it, not to ordinary teachers, but to Aristotle, the most learned and famous of the philosophers. By him Alexander was instructed not only in moral and political knowledge, but also in the more profound branches of science. The prince valued learning highly, as is shown by a letter which he wrote to the philosopher in which he said, 'For my part, I would rather excel in the higher parts of learning than in power and dominion.' The *Iliad* of Homer he called a portable treasury of military knowledge. So he certainly thought, for he had a copy, corrected by Aristotle, which he was accustomed to carry with him in a casket upon his expeditions. This casket, it is said, he used to place under his pillow with his sword.

When Alexander was but sixteen years of age, his father departed on a certain expedition, and the prince, though so young, was left as regent. During his regency the people of a subject town rebelled. The prince at once attacked and overthrew them, seized their town, and planted it with a colony of people. He also, while a youth, distinguished himself in a great battle with the Greeks, and is said to have been the first to break the Sacred Band of the Thebans.

The great talents which Alexander showed thus early in life caused the king to be very fond of him. But after Philip had cast off Olympias, the mother of Alexander, and had taken another wife, dissensions arose between the father and son which grew at last into open quarrel. Therefore Alexander, having first taken away his mother, withdrew himself from the court and kingdom of his father. While he was thus absent Philip was murdered. Many believed that Olympias was concerned in inciting the murderers, and Alexander did not escape without some suspicion. It is, however, certain that he caused diligent search to be made for the murderers, and that he had them punished.

Alexander was only twenty years of age when he was thus called to the throne. He found the kingdom torn in pieces by dangerous parties and fierce hatreds. There was also a danger of losing the conquests which his father had made, for the barbarian nations hated subjection, and longed for the rule of their native kings. Moreover, though Philip had subdued Greece by his victories, he had not had time to accustom the Greeks to his yoke. He had, indeed, rather thrown affairs into confusion than produced any firm settlement.

The young king's advisers, alarmed at the troubles which threatened, counselled him to give up Greece, and to endeavour to recall the wavering barbarian nations to his rule by persuasion and gentle treatment. Alexander, on the contrary, was of opinion that the only way to secure and establish his kingdom was to act with spirit and resolution. He therefore marched at once into the barbarian lands, and penetrated as far as the Danube, where he overthrew one of the kings of the barbarians in a great battle.

Some time after this Alexander received news that the Thebans had revolted, and that the Athenians were following the same course. He therefore advanced at once through the Pass of Thermopylæ, resolved to show his antagonists, who had taunted him with his youth, that in action at least he was a man. When he first appeared before Thebes he was willing to deal mildly with the people. He offered that, if the two leaders of the revolt were given up, he would pardon all others. The Thebans gave a proud answer and invited, by the sound of trumpet, all who loved freedom to join them in recovering the liberty of Greece. Alexander then let loose his Macedonians, and the fight began with great fury. The Thebans, who were greatly outnumbered, fought with the utmost courage and resolution. But when the Macedonian garrison which had been holding the citadel of the town sallied out and attacked them in the rear, the Thebans were surrounded on all sides, and most of them were cut to pieces. Their city was taken and plundered, and it was then levelled with the ground. More than six thousand of the Thebans were slain in the battle. Of the survivors, those who had opposed the revolt and some few others were spared, but the rest to the number of thirty thousand were sold as slaves.

The wretched town suffered various and terrible calamities. One party of Alexander's troops destroyed and despoiled the house of a Theban lady of rank and honour. When they had departed with their booty, their captain, who had shamefully ill-treated the lady, demanded whether she had not some hidden treasure of gold and silver. She replied that she had. Taking him alone into the garden, she showed him a well into which, she said, she had thrown all her treasures when the city was taken. The officer stooped down to examine the well narrowly, and as he did so, the woman pushed him in, and hurling stones upon him, killed him. At that moment his soldiers returned, seized and bound the lady, and carried her before Alexander. The king saw by her high and fearless bearing that she was a woman of rank and attainments. He asked her who she was. 'I,' said the Theban lady, 'am the sister of a Theban general, who fell fighting against your father for the liberty of Greece.' The king admired her answer and her courage in slaying the officer who had ill-used her. He gave orders that she and her children should be set at liberty.

Alexander expected that the rest of Greece, terrified by the dreadful punishment inflicted upon Thebes, would submit in silence. Whether his fury, like that of a lion, was now satiated with blood, or whether he wished to efface the memory of his cruel treatment of Thebes, he treated Athens with leniency. It is said, indeed, that the calamities he brought upon the Thebans long weighed upon his mind, and that he therefore afterwards treated others with less severity. It is certain that he attributed some misfortunes that befell him to the anger of the god Bacchus, the avenger of Thebes. And there was not a single Theban who survived the destruction of the city, who was ever refused a favour by Alexander.

As for the Athenians, he forgave them, although they sympathised with the Thebans, and received such as escaped from the general ruin of their town with all imaginable kindness.

A general assembly of the Greeks was afterwards held at the Isthmus of Corinth. It was there resolved that the different states should furnish men for a war against the Persians, and Alexander was elected captain-general. At this time many statesmen and philosophers came to congratulate the young king, who hoped that the famous Diogenes who was living at Corinth, would be of the number. Finding, however, that the philosopher took but little notice of the king, Alexander went to visit him. Diogenes was basking in the sunshine at the time, and on the approach of the king with a numerous company of followers raised himself slightly. Alexander, in an obliging tone, spoke to the philosopher, saying, 'Is there anything, Diogenes, in which I can be of service to you?' 'Nothing,' replied the latter, 'except to stand a little on one side so that you may not keep the sun off me.' Alexander, we are told, was astonished to find his power and majesty so little regarded. His courtiers ridiculed the philosopher, but the king, who saw something great in the contempt of Diogenes for rank and riches, exclaimed, 'If I were not Alexander, I would be Diogenes.'

The number of the troops which Alexander led upon his expedition into Asia was, according to some, thirty thousand foot and five thousand horse; according to others, thirty-four thousand foot and four thousand horse. He was but slenderly furnished with money for

ALEXANDER AND DIOGENES

the food and pay of his men. Nevertheless, though his resources were so small, he dealt generously with his friends before his army embarked. To one he gave a farm, to another a village, to another the revenue of a town, to another an office of profit, and so on. He thus disposed of nearly all the estates of the crown, and caused one of his courtiers to ask him what he had kept for himself. 'Hope,' said the king. 'In that case,' said the courtier, 'we who are to share in your labours will also share in your hopes.' He therefore refused to take the estates allotted to him, and some others followed his example. In this spirit Alexander and his army crossed the Hellespont.

Meanwhile the generals of King Darius had assembled a great army, which they had posted along the banks of the river Granicus. This army Alexander had to defeat if he was to enter the gates of Asia. Many of his officers were alarmed at the strength of the position they had to attack, for they had to cross a deep river, the banks of which were held by a great force. One of the Macedonian generals also objected that it was too late in the day to attempt to force the passage. Alexander, however, was not to be persuaded. Followed by thirteen troops of horse, he dashed into the stream. His men advanced under a shower of arrows, while the rushing river often bore them down or dashed its waves over them, so that the attempt to cross seemed almost mad. Alexander, nevertheless, held on, and at length by desperate efforts arrived at the opposite bank. There the slippery mud gave but a poor foothold for his horses, and, before the soldiers could form up in order, they were fiercely attacked by the Persians, who charged shouting loudly. Horse against horse, spear against spear, sword against sword, a desperate hand-to-hand combat was waged.

The fight pressed hard upon Alexander, for he was beset by numbers who marked his buckler and the great plume of white feathers upon his helmet. A javelin pierced one of the joints of his breastplate, but he escaped unhurt. Then two officers of great renown attacked him at once. Alexander avoided the blow of the first, and smote the other so shrewd a stroke upon the breastplate that the spear shivered in his hand. Then the king, drawing his sword, pressed upon this antagonist. Meanwhile, the officer whom he had at first avoided, wheeled his horse beside Alexander, and rising in his stirrups smote the king with a battle-axe. So dire was the blow that it sheared off crest and part of the plume, and cut through the helmet even to the hair. But, as the officer was about to repeat the blow, Clitus, the foster-brother of Alexander, ran him through with a spear, and at the same time the king despatched the other adversary.

While this furious combat was waged by the cavalry, the Macedonian phalanx crossed the river, and the infantry then joined in the fight. The resistance of the enemy was now but short. All broke and fled except a body of Greek hireling soldiers in the pay of Persia. These made a stand upon some high ground and sent a message asking for quarter. Alexander, influenced by anger rather than reason, refused, and at once advanced to attack them. He met with a desperate resistance, and his horse, which, however, was not the famed Bucephalus, was killed under him. In this part of the fight Alexander lost more in killed and wounded than in all the rest of the battle, for here he had to do with seasoned soldiers whose courage was heightened by despair. Nevertheless, in the whole battle Alexander lost, it is said, but thirty-four men killed, while the enemy lost twenty thousand foot and two thousand five hundred horse. The king sent the greater part of the spoil to his mother, but, in order that the Greeks might have their share in the glory of the day, he sent them presents of some portions of it.

This victory had a great and immediate effect upon Alexander's prospects. Sardis, the chief pride of the Persian empire upon the seaward side, submitted. All the other cities followed its example, with the exception of two which Alexander stormed.

The victor was now in some doubt as to what course he should pursue: whether by a rapid advance to stake all upon the fate of a single battle with King Darius, or whether to reduce the maritime provinces as a base for future operations. At this time, we are told, he received great encouragement from a strange occurrence. A stream suddenly changed its course and, overflowing its banks, threw up a plate of brass, upon which in ancient characters was inscribed a prophecy that the Persian empire should one day be destroyed by the Greeks. Alexander's hopes were fortified by this event, and he hastened to reduce the whole coast of Asia Minor. When he took the town of Gordium he found there the famous chariot which was fastened by cords made of the bark of the cornel-tree. This 'Gordian knot' was cunningly contrived, the cords being twisted many private ways, and the ends of the cords artfully concealed. Alexander was informed of tradition, firmly believed among the people, that the empire of the world awaited the man who could untie the knot. The king, so most historians say, solved the problem by cutting the knot with his sword, though one writer affirms that he did actually untie it.

By the time Alexander had completed the conquest of the maritime provinces of Asia, King Darius had taken his departure from his town of Susa. He was filled with confidence because of the vast number of soldiers in his army, which mustered six hundred thousand men. He was, moreover, encouraged by a dream which his wise men interpreted in a manner such as they thought would please the king. A still greater encouragement to Darius was given by the long stay which Alexander made in the seaward provinces. The Persian monarch attributed this delay to fear, but it was in truth due to the sickness of Alexander, caused, some say, by the great fatigues of the campaign, or, as others have it, by bathing in the very cold waters of a certain river. His condition was very serious, yet his physicians did not dare to give him any medicines, for they feared that if the king died, as was probable, they would be accused of poisoning him. One physician there was, however, Philip by name, who, though he saw fully the danger to himself, was nevertheless impelled by the desperate condition of the king, and by gratitude for past favours, to attempt the cure. He found Alexander quite ready to submit to his treatment, and indeed anxious to do so, for he burned with impatience to be able to carry on the war.

While the medicine was being prepared, there came a letter from an officer warning Alexander to beware of Philip, who, so the writer affirmed, had been prevailed upon by Darius by the promise of presents of vast value and the hand of the Persian king's daughter in marriage, to poison his master. Alexander, without showing the letter to any other person, put it under his pillow.

The time for the trial of the medicine having come, Philip, with the king's friends, entered the sick-chamber bearing the cup of medicine in his hands. The king took it from him without any sign of suspicion, and at the same time handed the letter to the physician, so that while the one drained off the draught, the other read the letter. It was indeed a striking situation. The king's countenance, by its open and untroubled expression, showed his confidence in the physician, while Philip's face reflected his indignation at the abominable charge. Protesting his fidelity, he threw himself down by the king's bedside, beseeching his master to be of good courage and to trust in his care. The medicine was indeed of so powerful a nature that the king lay a long time speechless and insensible from its effects. But, after he came to himself, he was soon cured by his faithful physician, and was able to show himself to his Macedonians, who were consumed with anxiety until he was able to come in person among them once more.

There was in the army of Darius a Macedonian fugitive who was well acquainted with the character of Alexander. This fugitive, seeing that Darius was preparing to leave the plains and to march through narrow mountain passes in quest of Alexander, implored the Persian monarch to remain where he was, so that in the open plains he might have the full advantage of his vast superiority in numbers. Darius objected that if he did so, the enemy would fly without coming to action, and that Alexander would thus escape him. 'If that is your only uneasiness,' replied the Macedonian, 'you may dismiss it from your mind. Be assured that Alexander will come to seek you, and that he is, indeed, already on the march.'

Darius, however, would not listen to these representations. He pressed on to meet Alexander, while the Macedonian king advanced by another way. Thus it happened that the armies passed one another in the night, and both therefore turned back. Darius now strove to recover his former camp, and to disengage his army from its difficult position. He was by this time conscious of his mistake in moving into a region hemmed in between the mountains and the sea, and so intersected by streams as to be impracticable for cavalry. Moreover, the broken nature of the ground prevented the vast host of Persian foot-soldiers from acting except in small divided parties. Alexander rejoiced at the good fortune which enabled him to meet the enemy in a position so favourable to his smaller forces, and hastened to attack Darius before the Persians could emerge into open country. But if fortune favoured

Alexander as to the scene of the battle, his own skilful arrangement of his forces contributed still more to the victory which he gained. As his army was very small compared with the Persian host, he took great care to prevent it from being surrounded. He threw out his right wing beyond the enemy's left. There he fought in person in the foremost ranks, and put the Persians to flight. He was, however, wounded in the thigh. According to one writer, he sustained the wound in hand-to-hand fight with Darius. Alexander himself, however, in an account which he gave of the battle, does not mention by whom the injury was inflicted. He merely states that he received a sword-wound in the thigh, and that it had no serious consequences.

A hundred and ten thousand of the enemy were slain. The victory was a signal one, and only the capture of Darius was lacking to its completeness. The Persian king escaped narrowly, having a start of his pursuers of about half a mile. Alexander captured his chariot and his bow and returned with them to his Macedonians. He found the troops loading themselves with the plunder of the Persian camp. They had reserved for their master the tent of Darius, in which he found officers of the household in splendid attire, rich furniture and much gold and silver. As soon as he had taken off his armour, he proposed to refresh himself in the bath of Darius. 'Say rather,' said one of his friends, 'in the bath of Alexander, for the goods of the conquered belong to the conqueror.' Alexander looked round upon the golden basins, vases and vessels of various kinds, the splendid furniture of the apartments, and inhaled the air heavy with fragrant odours. As yet the young king scorned such luxury, and in contempt said, '*This* it seems it is to be a Persian king.'

As Alexander was sitting down to table, word was brought to him that the mother, the wife and the two daughters of Darius were among the prisoners. The royal captives had seen the chariot and bow of the Persian king, and, concluding that he was dead, had broken out into loud lamentations. Alexander sent to inform them that Darius was living. Further, he assured them of his protection. His actions were even more humane than this message. The ladies were provided with rich robes and with many servants, and in all ways treated with the utmost honour and respect.

The young king was, at this time, a man of very temperate life. His indifference to the pleasures of the table was well exemplified by one of his sayings. A certain queen, who was greatly indebted to him, was accustomed to send him every day choice foods, and at last she sent some of her best cooks and bakers to him. Alexander, however, said, 'I have no need of these, for I was supplied with better cooks by my tutor. They are a march before day to prepare for my dinner, and a light dinner to prepare for my supper.' He also added that the same tutor had been accustomed to examine his clothes and the furniture of his chamber to prevent needless or luxurious articles being given to him by his mother.

Nor was Alexander so much addicted to wine as has been supposed. True, he was accustomed, in times of leisure, to sit a long time at table. The time, however, was spent more in talking than in drinking. Moreover, when business called, he was not to be detained by wine or sleep or by any kind of pleasure. This fact is sufficiently shown by the innumerable great actions which crowd his short span of life.

On days of leisure Alexander was accustomed, as soon as he had risen, to sacrifice to the gods. He then took his dinner, and the rest of the day he spent in hunting, or in settling disputes among his troops, or in reading and writing. When he was upon a march which did not require haste, he used to exercise himself upon the way in shooting and in throwing the javelin, or in dismounting from his chariot and mounting again when it was going at full speed. His conversation was more agreeable than that of most princes, for he was by no means lacking in the graces of society. His chief fault in this respect arose from his vanity. He was accustomed not only to boast himself concerning his doings, but also allowed others to flatter him most fulsomely.

After the battle of Issus, Alexander sent to Damascus to seize the stores of Darius which had been left there when the Persians advanced to the battle. He employed the Thessalian cavalry for this purpose, as a reward for their distinguished conduct in the battle. These troops enriched themselves with the booty, nor did the rest of the army go without ample spoil. The Macedonians, having thus once tasted of the treasure and the luxuries of the Persians, hunted for the wealth of their antagonists with the eagerness of hounds following a scent.

Alexander considered it a matter of great importance to subdue the maritime districts before he went further. All places made submission to him except the city of Tyre, which he besieged for seven months. During that time he built great mounds of earth from which his engines cast missiles against the town, and on the seaward side he invested the place with two hundred galleys.

About the middle of the siege he made an expedition against the Arabians who dwelt in the mountains of Anti-Lebanon. There he ran great risk of his life through his anxiety for his teacher Lysimachus, who, in spite of his age and infirmity, insisted upon accompanying him. When they came among the hills and dismounted from their horses in order to proceed upon foot, the infirmity of Lysimachus caused him, and Alexander with him, to lag behind the rest of the party. Night came on, and the enemy was known to be at no great distance, but Alexander would not leave his companion, who by this time was worn out with fatigue and the weight of his years. Thus it happened that while the king was encouraging his old tutor and helping him on, the two became more and more widely separated from the troops. The night was dark and very cold, and Alexander was in some doubt how to proceed. In his perplexity he saw at a distance a number of scattered watch-fires which the enemy had lighted. He resolved to depend upon his swiftness and activity, and upon the boldness by which he was accustomed to extricate his Macedonians from every danger. He ran to the nearest watch-fire, slew two of the soldiers who guarded it, seized a lighted brand,

and ran to rejoin his own party. His men soon kindled a huge fire. Many of the enemy, supposing from its size that the fire had been made by a large body of men, fled in alarm, while the few who attacked were driven off with considerable loss. By these means the night was passed in safety.

As for the siege of Tyre, it came to an end in this way. Alexander, on account of the long and severe fatigues which his troops had undergone, permitted most of his soldiers to rest, while only a few were left to keep the Tyrians occupied. At this time one of the soothsayers of the Greeks, having offered sacrifice and inspected the entrails of the victim, boldly declared that they showed that the city would be taken that very month. Those who were standing by laughed his prophecy to scorn, for that very day was the last of the month. The king perceived that the soothsayer was disconcerted by this ridicule. He therefore called out his forces by sound of trumpet, and ordered a much more vigorous assault upon the town than he had intended. At the same time those who had been left behind in camp ran to help their comrades, and so furious was the attack that the Tyrians were forced to yield, and the city was taken that day as the soothsayer had foretold.

One day a casket was brought to Alexander, which appeared to be one of the most curious and valuable things which had been found among the treasures of Darius. The king asked his friends what was most worthy of being kept in such a case. Some said one thing, some another, but Alexander decided the question by saying, 'Of all things the *Iliad* of

Homer is the most worthy.' And indeed, if what the people of Alexandria say be true, Homer was no bad counsellor to him. They tell us that after Alexander had conquered Egypt, he determined to build there a great city to be peopled by Greeks and to be named after himself. Further, it is said that on the advice of his architects he caused the site to be marked out in a certain place, and was preparing to lay the foundations when a wonderful dream caused him to choose another position. He dreamed that a grey-haired man of a very venerable appearance came to him and quoted the lines wherein Homer refers to the Pharian island fronting the mouths of the Nile. Thereupon Alexander left his bed and repaired to Pharos, which at that time was an island lying a little above one of the mouths of the Nile, though later it was connected with the mainland by a causeway. Alexander no sooner saw the place than he perceived how well fitted it was for his purpose. It is a tongue of land, a great lake being on one side, and on the other the sea, which here forms a capacious harbour. These advantages caused Alexander to declare that Homer, in addition to his other admirable qualities, was an excellent architect. He therefore ordered a city to be planned suitable to the conveniences of the ground. For want of chalk, his architects marked out the plan of the city with flour, which answered well enough upon the black soil.

While the king was looking with pleasure upon the design for the city, there suddenly arose from the river and the lake a vast multitude of birds of various kinds. The cloud of birds settled down upon the place, and ate up all the flour which had been used in marking out the lines. Alexander was disturbed by this event, which seemed to him to be an unfavourable omen. His diviners, however, reassured him and encouraged him to proceed with the work. They told him that the occurrence was a sign that the city he was about to build would be blessed with such plenty that it would be able to supply all who came to it from other places.

Alexander left the carrying out of the plan for his city of Alexandria to his architects. Meanwhile he went to visit the temple of Jupiter Ammon. The journey thither was long and laborious, and was, moreover, attended with two great dangers. One of these was the possibility that the supply of water might fail in the midst of the desert which had to be crossed. The other lay in the great sand-storms which sometimes arise in the desert, when the wind raises waves of sand so great that on one occasion, at least, they engulfed an army of full fifty thousand men. When these difficulties were represented to Alexander, he refused to consider them. Fortune had aided him so much that his resolution could not be shaken, and his courage inspired a love of adventure so great that he sought to overcome difficulties of every kind. During his march through the desert, Alexander received such assistance from the divine powers as gave some colour to the idea which was spread abroad that the conqueror was himself of divine descent, being, it was said, the son of Jupiter. In the first place, copious and constant rain fell. Thus the travellers were not only freed from all fear of thirst, but the moistened sand was made firm to the foot, so that they travelled easily and at the same time the air was cleared and cooled.

It is said by some that when Alexander had passed the desert and arrived at the temple, he was received by the oracle as being indeed the son of Jupiter. Certainly, among the barbarians, he assumed a lofty bearing as if convinced of his divine origin. But among the Greeks such claims were but little advanced by him. Indeed, long after this time, when he was wounded by an arrow, he said, 'My friends, this which flows from my wound is mortal blood, and not the ichor which flows in the veins of the immortals.' It appears, then, that Alexander did not believe that he was divine, and that he only made use of the idea in order to increase his power over others.

After his return from Egypt into the country round about Tyre, Alexander did honour to the gods with sacrifices and stately processions. He also entertained the people with music and dancing and with the representation of tragedies, played by the greatest actors and mounted with the most splendid scenery. It was about this time that he received a letter from Darius offering to make peace. The Persian king was willing to cede all the territories lying west of the river Euphrates, to give his daughter to Alexander in marriage, and to pay a ransom of ten thousand talents for the prisoners. When Alexander informed his friends of these proposals, one of them, Parmenio by name, said, 'If I were Alexander, I would accept them.' Thereupon the king replied, 'So would I if I were Parmenio.' The answer which he returned to the proposals was to the effect that if Darius would come and submit, he should have the best of treatment, but if he did not do so, Alexander must set out in quest of him.

Having made this declaration, the king began his march. He was recalled, however, by the news that the wife of Darius was dead, and he returned in order to bury her with the greatest magnificence. He then sent one of her servants to the Persian king to acquaint him with the loss of his consort. Darius loudly lamented the death of his consort in captivity. But when he heard of the honours which Alexander had rendered to her, he admired the noble spirit of the conqueror. Lifting his hands to heaven, he prayed to his gods that he might restore the fortunes of Persia, and in victory display a like spirit to Alexander, but that, if it were decreed that the glory of Persia should now fail, none but Alexander might sit upon his throne.

Alexander subdued all the land on the western side of the Euphrates, and then began his march against Darius, who had taken the field again with an army of a million men. The great battle between the Persian and Macedonian forces is known as the battle of Arbela, though in truth it was fought not at that town, but at a neighbouring village.

The two armies having come in sight of one another, Darius kept his men under arms during the night, and held a general review of the troops by torchlight. Alexander, on the other hand, allowed his troops to rest, while he himself offered sacrifices in front of his tent. The oldest of his friends, Parmenio in particular, were astonished at the vast number of torches which glowed in the enemy's camp, and by the tumult of noise, like the roar of the sea, which arose from it. The sights and sounds plainly showed the vast numbers of men which the Persians had brought into the field, and the Macedonian officers doubted whether their army could withstand the onset of such an army if the battle were fought in daylight. They therefore waited upon Alexander, when he had finished the sacrifice, and advised him to make a night attack upon the enemy, in order that the darkness might hide from his troops the fearful odds against them. Thereupon the king made the famous reply, 'I will not steal a victory.' Some have thought that the answer was inspired by the vanity of a young man. Others, however, regard it as a wise reply, since the speech itself was likely to inspire his troops with confidence, and it was also necessary for Alexander to defeat his enemy in open battle. A victory snatched by night would leave Darius the pretext that he had been defeated through the darkness, just as he had before ascribed his defeat to his being hemmed in between the mountains and the sea, and in his great empire he could easily raise another army. But the defeat of his vast army in open daylight would be the ruin of his hopes, and would utterly break down his spirit.

When his friends had gone, Alexander retired to rest within his tent. He is said to have slept that night much more soundly than usual, so that, when his officers came to attend him, they were surprised to find him still fast asleep. They therefore themselves gave orders for the troops to take their morning repast. Then, the occasion being urgent, Parmenio entered the king's apartment and called him loudly two or three times by name. When Alexander awoke, his officer asked him how he could thus sleep as soundly as though he had already won the victory, whereas he had, indeed, still to fight the greatest battle ever fought in the world. The king smiled and answered, 'Surely we may regard ourselves already as conquerors. Darius now stands to face us, and we should rejoice that we no longer have to pursue him across desolate wastes.' As soon as he had thus replied to Parmenio, Alexander put on his helmet, for in other respects he was already fully armed. He wore a short coat closely girt about him, and over that a breastplate of strongly quilted linen. His helmet was of iron, but polished so that it shone like burnished silver. To this a gorget of the same metal, set with precious stones, was fitted. His sword, the weapon he was accustomed to use in battle, could not be excelled for lightness and fineness of temper. But the belt which he wore in all his fights was more splendid than the rest of his armour, and upon its decoration the utmost skill had been lavished. When drawing up his forces in order of battle or when reviewing them, he spared Bucephalus on account of his age, and used another horse. But he constantly used the famous horse as his charger in battle, and on this occasion he had no sooner mounted him than the signal for battle was given. Before the battle began, Alexander made a speech of some length to the Thessalians and other Greeks in his army. He found that they in their turn strove to add to his confidence, and called loudly to him to lead them against the barbarians.

Then shifting his javelin into his left hand, Alexander stretched his right hand to heaven, and called upon the gods to defend and strengthen the Greeks if he indeed were the son of Jupiter.

At that moment the chief soothsayer who, clad in a white robe and wearing a crown of gold, rode by Alexander's side, pointed to the heavens. There the soldiers saw an eagle flying over the king and, as it appeared, directing his course against the enemy. Animated by this sight, they burst into shouts of encouragement; the cavalry charged at full speed, and the infantry rushed like a torrent upon the foe.

In the battle Alexander showed the same calm courage and excellent judgment that he had shown in his answer to Parmenio before the conflict. For the left wing, which was commanded by Parmenio, was almost broken by a charge of the enemy's horse, and at the same time the Macedonian baggage in the rear was attacked. Thereupon Parmenio sent a message to Alexander telling him that his camp and baggage would be taken if he did not at once send troops from the front to the rear to defend them. The message was brought to the king at the moment when he was about to give the right wing, where he commanded in person, the signal to charge. 'Parmenio must be mad,' said he, 'not to remember that the spoils belong to the conquerors, and that the conquered need not concern themselves about their baggage and treasures, since their best hope is an honourable death.'

The fury of the charge of Alexander's right wing

broke the barbarian host before the first ranks were well engaged. Alexander pressed hard upon the fugitives, striving to break into the midst of the host where Darius fought in person. For the Persian king could be plainly seen among his royal guards from a distance. He was mounted upon a lofty chariot, and was moreover, readily recognised by his great stature and by the beauty of his features. A numerous body of chosen cavalry stood in close order around the chariot, and appeared ready to receive the attack firmly. But the approach of Alexander was so terrible, as the fugitives were driven back upon those who still stood their ground, that most of the cavalry broke and fled. A few of the best and bravest, however, stood firm and met their deaths in front of the king's chariot. There they fell in heaps, and falling, strove to hinder the pursuit, for even in the pangs of death they grappled with the Macedonians and, lying on the ground, clung to the legs of the horses as they charged over them.

King Darius was now in the most pressing danger. His own troops, placed in front to defend him, were driven back upon him. The wheels of his chariot were half buried among the dead bodies, so that it was almost impossible to turn the chariot round. Moreover, the horses which drew it were mad with fear. They plunged wildly up and down among the heaps of the slain, and were no longer under the control of the charioteer. The king was therefore obliged to leave his chariot and his arms and to escape upon horseback. Probably he would not have escaped at all, had not Parmenio just at this time again sent messengers to Alexander begging him to come to his assistance, as a good part of the enemy's forces opposed to him still held their ground. Some have thought that in this battle the old general Parmenio showed some lack of spirit, whether because age had dulled his courage, or because he felt some jealousy of Alexander's power and arrogance. The king, though vexed at being thus checked in the pursuit, sounded a retreat under pretext of the gathering darkness and his weariness of the carnage. Riding to that part of the field where the issue of the battle had been represented as doubtful, he found that the enemy had by this time been totally defeated and put to flight.

The battle having ended in this manner, the Persian empire appeared to be destroyed, and Alexander was acknowledged King of Asia. The first thing he did was to render thanks to the gods by magnificent sacrifices. Next he made splendid presents of houses, lands and governments to his friends. He then traversed all the provinces of Babylon, which at once submitted to him. In one of these districts the king was particularly struck by the sight of a great gulf of fire from which the flames streamed continuously, as if from an inexhaustible source. Not far from this a flood of naphtha flowed from the ground in such volume that it formed a lake. This liquid is very inflammable. It takes light from a fire at a distance, and all the air between is filled with a sheet of flame. The natives, to show the king the inflammability of this liquid, sprinkled drops of it along the street which led to his lodgings. Then, standing at one end, they applied their torches to the first drops. The flame sped along swifter than thought, and instantly the street was all ablaze.

It happened that an attendant, who waited upon Alexander when he bathed and who anointed him with oil, was often successful in amusing the king. One day he proposed, as a jest, to anoint a boy with the naphtha, saying that if it took fire upon the lad it must indeed be allowed to be an extraordinary substance. The boy readily consented to the test, but as soon as his body was anointed with it, the oil immediately burst into flame. He must have been burnt to death, had it not been that there were many attendants present with vessels of water for the service of the bath. As it was, the flames were put out with great difficulty, and the poor boy felt their effects as long as he lived.

When Alexander took possession of the town of Susa, he found in the king's palace there fifty thousand talents in coined money, besides the royal furniture and other treasures of incalculable value. Among other things there was purple fabric of the value of five thousand talents which, though it had been laid away for a hundred and ninety years, still retained its first freshness and beauty of colour. We are told that amongst their treasures the Persian kings used to put jars filled with water brought from the Nile and the Danube, as a symbol of the extent of their dominions and of their mastery of the world.

The entry into Persia itself was difficult because of the rugged nature of the country. Moreover, the passes were guarded by the bravest of the Persians, in order to protect Darius who had taken refuge there. But a man, half Greek and half Persian by birth, offered his services to Alexander, and showed the king how he might enter the country by taking a roundabout way. The first bodies of the enemy that fell into his hands were slaughtered in vast numbers. Alexander himself tells us that he ordered no quarter to be given, because he thought that such an example of severity would at this time be of service to his affairs. It is said that in Persia he found as much gold and silver coin as he had done at Susa. There were besides such vast stores of other treasures that they loaded ten thousand pairs of mules and five thousand camels.

Alexander wintered at the city of Persepolis and remained there four months, in order to give his troops time to rest and refresh themselves. There he took his seat under a golden canopy upon the throne of the Persian kings. One of his followers, a Corinthian who had been a close friend of Alexander and of his father Philip, wept with joy at the sight. 'How unfortunate are those Greeks,' he exclaimed, 'who have died without beholding Alexander seated on the throne of Darius.'

When the conqueror was on the point of marching again in pursuit of Darius, he gave a great entertainment to his friends. After the company had drunk freely, one of the women who was present, Thais by name, exclaimed, 'I have borne great hardships in wandering about Asia, but this day brings its reward. But how much greater would be my joy if I could set fire to the palaces of Xerxes, the king who laid Athens in ashes. Then should it be said in days to come that even the very women who followed in the train of Alexander were more powerful to avenge Greece upon the Persians than all the Greek generals who lived before him.' The company hailed the speech with applause and shouts of approval, and pressed the king to agree to the proposals. At length he yielded, leapt from his seat, and, with a garland upon his head and a torch in his hand, led the way. The rest followed, shouting joyously and dancing as they went, and spread themselves around the palace. The Macedonian soldiers, when they heard of the frolic, also seized lighted torches and gladly ran to join the revellers. They thought that the burning of the palace showed that Alexander intended to return home, and not to fix his seat finally among the barbarians. Such is the account generally given of the burning of the palace. Some, however, say that it was not done out of a drunken frolic, but after cool consideration. In any case, Alexander soon regretted the act, and gave orders that the fire should be extinguished.

The conqueror was naturally extremely generous, and the vast treasures he had acquired increased his inclinations in this direction. Moreover, he was gracious in his manner of giving, so that his bounty had an irresistible charm. Thus one of his foreign soldiers laid the head of the enemy whom he had slain at the king's feet and said, 'Among our people, sir, a gold cup is the reward for such a present.' 'An empty one, I suppose,' answered the king with a smile, 'but I will give you one filled with good wine, and, moreover, I will drink your health.' One day a Macedonian, who was a poor man, was driving a mule laden with the king's money. The beast fell tired, and the man then took the burden upon his own shoulders. He carried it some distance until he tottered under the weight, and was ready to drop from exhaustion. At that moment Alexander happened to see him, and was informed of the circumstances. 'Bear up a little longer, friend,' cried he, 'and carry it to your own tent, for it is yours.'

He was indeed generally more displeased with those persons who refused his presents than with those who asked for favours. Hence he wrote to one of his friends, saying that he should no longer regard him as a friend if he rejected the marks of his esteem.

He had given nothing to a certain youth who was accustomed to play at ball with him, because the young man had not asked for anything. One day Alexander, the youth and others were playing at ball. The king noticed that when the ball came to the young fellow, he always threw it to others of the party, never to Alexander. 'Why do you not throw the ball to me?' asked the king. 'Because you do not ask for it,' was the answer. The king laughed at the reply, and immediately gave the youth presents of great value.

A certain jester chanced to offend Alexander. Friends interceded for him, and the man himself with tears in his eyes besought forgiveness. At length Alexander consented to pardon him. Thereupon the jester at once said, 'If your majesty really does pardon me, I trust you will give me some substantial proof of it.' And the king did so to the extent of five talents in money.

He found that, on account of the wealth they had gained, his chief officers set no bounds to their luxury. They fed on the most extravagant delicacies, and were profuse in spending in other ways. Thus, one wore silver nails in his shoes, another had many camel loads of a special kind of earth brought from Egypt with which he was rubbed before going into the wrestling-ring, another had hunting-nets many miles in length. Many used rare essences instead of oil after bathing, and had special servants to attend to their baths and others to make their beds. Alexander reproved their falling away from the stern temper of the soldier in the manner of a philosopher. 'It is strange,' said he, 'that you, who have fought so many glorious battles, do not know that labour and exercise woo sleep better than dainty beds. How can you, comparing the Persian mode of life with our Macedonian manners, fail to see that luxury makes men the slaves of pleasure, while toil and labour ennoble them? How can the man whose hands are too delicate to wait upon his own dainty body hope to manage his horse and make his armour glorious? Surely the conquerors should scorn to do as the conquered did; far greater and nobler should their actions be.' Thenceforth, as an example, he exercised himself in war and hunting with less care for his safety than before, and constantly exposed himself to danger and fatigue.

When he marched again against Darius he expected to have to fight another battle. He received intelligence, however, that the king had been treacherously seized by Bessus, one of his own officers, and was held prisoner by him. Alexander then dismissed his Thessalian troops, and sent them home with the present of a large sum of money over and above their pay. With his cavalry he hastened in pursuit of Bessus, who aspired to the sovereignty, in order if possible to rescue Darius from him. The pursuit was long and difficult, and three thousand three hundred furlongs were covered in eleven days. The chief hardship was the scarcity of water, from which the troops suffered more than from fatigue. On one occasion while they were on the march, some Macedonians, who had filled their bottles at a river, came up, bearing the water upon mules. These men saw that the king was greatly distressed by thirst. They at once filled a helmet with water and offered it to him. Alexander asked them for whom they had brought the water. 'For our sons,' they replied, 'but the life of our prince is of more importance to us than the lives of our children.' The king took the proffered helmet, but as he was about to drink, he looked round and saw his horsemen with heads bent forward looking eagerly at the water. He thereupon returned the helmet without drinking. He thanked the people who offered the water, but said, 'If I alone drink, my men will be dispirited.' His cavalry, admiring his self-restraint and unselfishness, broke into loud cries of applause. 'Let us march!' they cried, spurring their horses, 'we are neither tired nor thirsty, and under such a king we feel ourselves more than mortal men.'

All the troops who followed him in his pursuit of Bessus were equally devoted to his cause, but only sixty of them managed to keep up with him until he reached the enemy's camp. There the horsemen rode over treasures of gold and silver that lay scattered about. Then they came to a number of carriages, filled with women and children. Though the charioteers had abandoned them, the horses continued to draw the vehicles along. Alexander's troops pressed on, expecting to find Darius in the leading part of the throng. At length, after eager search, they found him lying in his chariot, pierced with many darts. He was near his end, but had strength enough to ask for water to quench his thirst, and a Macedonian brought the dying king some cold water. He drank and afterwards said 'Friend, the measure of my misfortunes is complete in that I am unable to reward thee for this act of kindness. But Alexander will reward thee, and the gods will reward him for his humanity to my mother, my wife and my children. Tell him that I grasp his hand, for in sign thereof I take thine.' So saying, he took the hand of the Macedonian and immediately expired. When Alexander came up he was deeply concerned at the death of the Persian king, and covered the dead body with his own robe.

Bessus, the murderer of Darius, afterwards fell into the hands of Alexander, and the death of the king was avenged in this manner. Two straight trees were bent towards each other, and a leg of the prisoner fastened to each. Then the trees were released, and as they sprang back violently to their natural positions, the body of Bessus was torn asunder.

The corpse of Darius was embalmed and sent to

his mother, and Alexander ordered that it should be given all the honours of a royal funeral.

The king next moved into the region about the Caspian, which appeared to him not less than the Euxine in size, but with waters sweeter to the taste. Here some of the barbarians fell suddenly upon a party of Alexander's men who were leading Bucephalus, and captured him. This provoked the king so much that he sent a herald to threaten them, their women and children with utter extermination if the horse were not returned. But when the barbarians brought back Bucephalus and surrendered to the king, he treated them mercifully, and even paid a ransom for the horse to those who had captured him.

Thence Alexander marched into Parthia. Here he first assumed the dress of the Persian kings whose dominions he had conquered. This he did, either to please his new subjects by conforming in some degree with their customs, or in order to impress his Macedonians with a deeper respect for his dignity. At first he used the dress only before the people of Asia, or among his personal friends within doors. In time, however, he came to wear it in public and during the despatch of business. The sight of their king dressed after the manner of the Asiatics was very distasteful to his Macedonians. However, in view of his other virtues, they thought that he might well be suffered to indulge his vanity without question. Indeed, some indulgence was due to a prince who had endured such hardships, and who, moreover, had but lately been wounded in the leg by an arrow, so that the bone was shattered and splinters of it were taken from the wound, and who had for a time lost his sight through a blow on the back of the neck, and who nevertheless continued to expose himself to every danger. So little did he indulge himself that on one occasion, when he had attacked and routed a body of the enemy, he pursued them for over twelve miles, though he was suffering severely from illness at the time.

He gradually came more and more to adopt the manners of the Asiatics, while at the same time he persuaded them to adopt some of the Macedonian fashions. In this way he hoped to weld the two peoples together. With the same object he chose out thirty thousand boys from among his new subjects, and engaged masters to teach them Greek and to train them to arms after the Macedonian manner. Further, he himself married Roxana, the daughter of one of the enemy's captains. This marriage was entirely a love-match on the king's part, but it nevertheless helped to gain the confidence of his new subjects.

Among the Macedonians Philotas, the son of the old general Parmenio, had great authority. Not only was he valiant and tireless in battle, but no man, except Alexander himself, was more generous or more faithful in friendship. But he was proud and arrogant, and affected a magnificence beyond the condition of a subject. Hence he was exposed to dislike and to suspicion. His father Parmenio warned him, saying, 'My son, be less.' But Philotas would not take warning, and among his friends spoke of all the great actions of the war as having been accomplished by himself and his father.

ALEXANDER

As for Alexander, he was, said Philotas, a mere boy who enjoyed the title of conqueror through the labours of others. These things and other indiscreet sayings were carried from mouth to mouth till they reached the ear of the king. Moreover, about the same time, a certain Macedonian formed a plot against Alexander's life. Some of those who were privy to the plot sought access to the king in order to give information, but they were prevented from seeing him by Philotas. This circumstance confirmed the king's suspicions. Philotas was seized, put to the torture and executed. Immediately after his death Alexander sent orders for the execution of his innocent father, Parmenio. This cruel act struck terror into the hearts of the king's friends. For the old general had shared in nearly all the conquests of King Philip and was the principal, if not the only one, of the old counsellors who had encouraged Alexander in the invasion of Asia. Moreover, upon that expedition he had been followed by three sons. Of these two had been slain in battle, and he himself now unjustly shared the fate of the third.

Not long afterwards the murder of Clitus, the king's foster-brother, happened. He was one of a company who had been feasting with Alexander, and like the king and most of the others, was inflamed with wine. It happened that somebody began to sing some verses ridiculing certain of the Macedonian officers who had lately been beaten by the barbarians. The older friends of the king were greatly offended by the song, but Alexander bade the singer go on. Thereupon Clitus, who was naturally hasty in temper and who had drunk

THE QUARREL BETWEEN ALEXANDER AND CLITUS

too much wine, burst out, 'It is not right to make a jest among barbarians and enemies of Macedonians, who are better men than the laughers, though they have met with misfortune.' The king answered, 'Clitus pleads his own cause when he calls cowardice misfortune.' Clitus started to his feet and cried, 'Yet it was my cowardice that saved your life from the Persian's sword. And it is by the blood and wounds of the Macedonians that you are grown so great that you disdain your father, Philip, and claim to be the son of Jupiter.'

Alexander was greatly angered by this reply. 'Thus,' he said, 'dost thou talk and stir up the Macedonians to mutiny. Dost thou expect to enjoy long the power to do so?'

'What indeed,' retorted Clitus, 'do we enjoy, and what reward have we for our toils? Do we not envy those who died without seeing Macedonians shut out from access to their king by Medes and Persians?'

Clitus went on in this rash manner, and the king retorted with equal bitterness. Thus the quarrel grew until Alexander, angered beyond endurance, hurled a missile at his friend and looked about for his sword. One of his guards had, however, removed it in time, and the company gathered round the king endeavouring to assuage his fury. It was in vain, however. Alexander broke from them, called upon his guards, ordered his trumpeter to sound the alarm, which would have assembled the whole army, and struck him in the face when he found him unwilling to obey.

Meanwhile Clitus, who refused to make any

submission, was with difficulty forced out of the room by his friends. Very soon, however, he was mad enough to return by another door, and to shout out the words of the poet:

'Is it thus that Greece repays her warriors? Shall one man claim the conquests won by thousands?'

As he said these words and was putting aside the curtain over the doorway, the king snatched a spear from one of his guards, ran at his foster-brother and thrust him through the body. Clitus fell to the ground, and expired with a groan.

Alexander's rage disappeared immediately. He came to himself and poked round upon his friends, who stood speechless with horror at the deed. Hastily he withdrew the spear from the dead body, and placed it to his own throat. His guards, however, seized his hands, and by force carried him into his own chamber. There for a long time he lay in tears and lamentations and in speechless grief. At length, however, the words of his soothsayer and the exhortations of his philosophers prevailed upon him to return to the affairs of his dominions.

When Alexander was on the point of setting out upon his expedition to India, he found that his troops were so laden with spoils that they were quite unfit to march. Early in the morning, when they were about to start, he therefore first set fire to his own baggage and that of his friends, and then gave orders that all the rest should be consumed in the same way. Inspired by the king's example, few of his soldiers were displeased at the order, and many received it with applause. All that was not needed was burnt; the rest was shared with those who were in want. This greatly encouraged Alexander in his design. By this time, too, the king had become very severe in punishing disobedience or other offences. He put one of his friends to death for refusing to stay in a fortress of which he had been placed in charge, and with his own hand shot a rebellious Asiatic officer dead with an arrow.

About this time there happened an event that was looked upon as a good omen of the success of Alexander's expedition. A servant who had charge of the king's equipage opened the ground near the river Oxus in order to pitch the king's tent. There at once welled forth a spring of a liquid, which at first was oily and dirty, but afterwards ran perfectly clear, and neither in smell, nor in taste, nor in clearness differed from the real oil of olives, though no olives grow in that country. It seems that Alexander was greatly pleased by this incident. The soothsayers said that it betokened that the enterprise would be hard and difficult, but that its result would be glorious, since the gods give oil to refresh men after their labours. In truth, during this expedition Alexander met with great dangers and received grave wounds, while his army suffered very severely from the lack of food and water and from the climate. The prince indeed was ambitious to prove that courage can triumph over fortune, and that nothing is impossible to the bold and brave. In this spirit his remark was framed on an occasion when he besieged a certain fort situated upon a rock so extremely steep that the summit appeared inaccessible. He inquired of one of his Asiatic officers what the character of the defender was. Being told that he was of a timorous nature, the king remarked, 'Then we can take the fort, for there is no strength in its defence.' In the event, he managed to terrify the defender and to make himself master of the fort.

When he was besieging another fort situated on an equally steep height, he saw among the company marching to the assault a young Macedonian who bore his name, Alexander. 'You must bear yourself gallantly, my friend,' cried the king, 'in order to do justice to your name.' He was told afterwards, and was much concerned at the news, that the young man fell whilst fighting with the most glorious courage.

When Alexander had entered India, the king who ruled the territory between the Indus and the Jhelum came to him and proffered friendship, and his offer was accepted. But when the invader came to the banks of the river Jhelum he found his progress barred by the army of a king named Porus which lined the opposite bank. Alexander himself left an account of his contest with Porus in his letters.

The river Jhelum ran between the two armies and, on the bank opposite Alexander's troops, Porus drew up his elephants to dispute the passage of the stream. In these positions the armies lay for some little time, and every day Alexander caused a great bustle and noise to be made in his camp, so that the enemy might become accustomed to the tumult and less ready to take the alarm. Then, under cover of the darkness of a wild and stormy night, he managed, with a part of his infantry and a chosen body of horse, to reach an island in the stream at some distance from the Indians. While they were upon the island, a most violent storm of wind and rain with terrible lightning and thunder burst upon them. In spite of this awful storm, and in spite of the fact that several of his men were killed before his eyes by the lightning, Alexander pushed on into the stream to gain the opposite bank. But the river, swollen by the rains, had burst its banks on that side and formed a kind of bay. Hence Alexander's troops found the landing very difficult, and the ground broken and undermined by the stream. On this occasion he is said to have uttered the famous saying, 'Will my Athenian friends believe the dangers I have undergone in order that they may be the heralds of my fame?' Thus one writer records, but Alexander himself only tells us that he and his followers quitted their boats, and in full armour waded through water breast-high to the shore.

When his troops were landed, Alexander marched with his horse-soldiers two and a half miles in advance of his infantry. He judged that he could easily beat off an attack if made by the enemy's cavalry only, while if infantry were brought against him his own foot-soldiers would have plenty of time to march up and join in the battle. His judgment proved to be sound. The enemy sent against him a body of a thousand horse and sixty armed chariots. These he easily defeated, capturing the chariots and slaying four hundred of the cavalry. Porus now understood that Alexander himself had passed, and therefore brought up against him the whole Indian army, except such a force as seemed necessary to prevent the crossing of the rest of the Macedonians. Alexander, seeing that the enemy was superior in numbers, and that his centre was strengthened by the elephants, did not choose to make an attack upon that part. He himself fell upon the left wing, while by his orders one of his officers attacked the right. Both wings were broken and rolled back upon the elephants in the centre. There they rallied, and the combat became of a more confused and desperate character. So obstinately was the battle contested that it was not until the eighth hour of the day that the victory was won by the Macedonians.

Most historians say that Porus was a good deal over six feet in height, and that, though he rode on one of the largest elephants, yet such was his height and bulk that he appeared of proportionate size to the animal on which he was seated. His elephant throughout the battle gave extraordinary proofs of sagacity and of care for his master. So long as King Porus was able to fight, the animal defended him with the greatest courage and kept all his assailants at a distance. When, at length, the elephant perceived that the king was ready to sink from the multitude of wounds from darts which he had received, the animal knelt slowly down to prevent his master from falling, and with his trunk drew out every dart from the king's body.

When Porus was taken prisoner, Alexander asked him how he wished to be treated. 'Like a king,' said the Indian prince. 'Is there nothing else you wish to request?' replied Alexander. 'No,' said Porus, 'for everything is included in the word "king."' Alexander not only restored his dominions to him, but also added some very extensive territories which he had conquered.

In this battle with Porus, Bucephalus received several wounds from which he died some time afterwards. One writer, however, gives another account, and says that the famous horse died of age and fatigue, being by this time thirty years old. Alexander lamented him as much as though he had lost one of his faithful friends. So indeed he regarded him. In the place where Bucephalus was buried, near the river Jhelum, he built a city, which he called Bucephalia in honour of the wonderful steed.

The fierce battle with Porus lessened the ardour of the Macedonians, and caused them to resolve not to advance farther into India. In that fight they had defeated, but with difficulty, an enemy who brought only twenty thousand infantry and two thousand cavalry into the field. They therefore resolutely opposed Alexander when he wished to cross the Ganges, for they were told that the river was four miles broad and a hundred fathoms deep, and that the opposite bank swarmed with a vast army of two hundred thousand foot, eighty thousand horse, eight thousand chariots and six thousand war-elephants.

Alexander was deeply vexed and indignant at the refusal of his men to follow him farther. For a time he shut himself up in his tent and refused to come forth. At length, however, the prayers and remonstrances of his friends and the entreaties of his soldiers prevailed upon him to show himself again amongst his army. He now, since he was unable to advance farther into India, formed the design of sailing down the river until he reached the ocean. He caused a number of rafts and boats to be made, and upon these his army was carried down the river. On the way he attacked the cities which lay near the stream, and forced them to submit to him. He was, however, very near being killed by a certain people called the Malli, who are said to be the most warlike of the peoples of India. Some of the defenders had been driven from the walls of their city, which he was attacking, by the missiles cast by his soldiers. He was himself the first man to climb the wall, but, immediately he was on the top, the scaling-ladder by which he had climbed broke. The king was now, with but two or three companions, exposed to the darts which the enemy hurled at them from below. In this emergency Alexander poised himself and then suddenly leapt down from the wall into the very midst of the enemy. Fortunately he alighted on his feet and, fortunately too, the enemy were astounded and took the flashing of his arms in the sun as he leapt down for lightning or for some supernatural splendour. They soon recovered themselves, however, and, seeing the king attended only by two of his guards who had leapt down with him, they attacked him hand-to-hand. Alexander fought against overwhelming odds with desperate courage, but he was wounded through his armour by their swords and spears. Then one of the enemy, who stood a little farther off, drew his bow with such strength that the arrow pierced the king's breastplate and entered his ribs. He reeled under the shock, and fell upon his knees.

Thereupon the Indian ran in with his scimitar drawn to despatch the king. The two guards sprang in front of him, but one was at once killed and the other wounded. The latter, however, kept up the fight as well as he could, and meanwhile Alexander struggled to his feet, and struck down his assailant. He was, however, wounded again more than once, and at length he received such a blow upon his neck from a club that he reeled against the wall for support, and stood thus facing the foe. In this strait he was rescued by the Macedonians, who by this time had got into the town. They surrounded their king, and having beaten off his assailants, carried his senseless body to his tent.

Alexander was quite insensible; indeed, it was currently reported in the army that he was dead. With great difficulty his attendants sawed off the shaft of the arrow which stuck in his breast. With equal trouble they took off the breastplate, and they then found that the arrow head, which was of the breadth of three fingers, was firmly embedded in the bone. The king fainted under the operation of withdrawing it, and was on the point of expiring. He recovered after a while, however, but was extremely weak, so that he was for a long time confined to his tent. When he had sufficiently recovered, he was carried on his way in a litter along the waterside. Even in this condition he subdued a large tract of land and many considerable towns.

Alexander took seven months in descending the

river to the ocean. There he took ship and sailed to an island, where he landed and sacrificed to the gods. He then prepared to set out on his return. He ordered his admiral Nearchus with the ships and some of the troops to sail along the coast, keeping it upon the right hand, and so return to the Persian Gulf. With the rest of his army Alexander set out to return by land. For sixty days his way led him through an inhospitable country, where his army suffered severely. So many men did he lose that he did not bring back from India more than a fourth part of the army with which he entered it, an army which numbered no less than one hundred and twenty thousand foot and fifteen thousand horse. Disease, bad food and torrid heat destroyed multitudes, while famine played still greater havoc with their numbers. The country was sterile and untilled, and even the natives lived upon wretched fare, for they had no flocks save a few miserable sheep.

Having with great difficulty struggled through this country, the army of Alexander entered Gedrosia (Baluchistan). There the soldiers found provisions in abundance, for not only is the land more fertile in itself, but the princes and great men of the neighbourhood hospitably supplied food. Here Alexander gave his men time to rest and refresh themselves, while he entertained them with feasts and public displays. Afterwards, for seven days, the army continued its march in a riotous procession, as revellers rather than soldiers, through the province bordering the Persian Gulf. The king himself had a platform built upon a magnificent chariot drawn by eight horses, and upon this platform the king and his chief friends revelled night and day. Behind came many other carriages covered with tapestry or hangings of purple or shaded by freshly gathered branches of trees. In these rode the rest of the king's generals and favourites, crowned with flowers and flushed with wine. Throughout the whole army there was scarcely to be seen a shield, a helmet, or a spear. In place of these weapons of war the soldiers bore flagons and goblets and cups, which they filled from huge vessels of wine. Thus the army advanced to the music of flute and trumpet, with song and dance and drunken frolic.

In Gedrosia Alexander was joined by his admiral Nearchus, and received an account of the voyage from the mouth of the Indus. So delighted was the king with the description he received that he formed the great design of sailing himself from the mouth of the Euphrates with a great fleet to circle the coasts of Arabia and Africa, and to return to his dominions by passing into the Mediterranean by way of the Pillars of Hercules. But meanwhile the report of the great difficulties which Alexander had met with in his Indian expedition, and the great losses his army had sustained, had been spread abroad. These reports, together with the expectation that Alexander would never return alive from the sea-voyage which he now contemplated, incited many of his subjects to revolt. Some of his generals and governors, too, for the same reasons, fancied themselves released from the king's authority, and began to display their insolence and greed and to rule unjustly. Indeed, the whole empire was disturbed and ripe for revolt.

In consequence of this unsettled state of affairs,

Alexander gave up his project. Having determined to carry war into the maritime provinces, he sent his admiral to sea again, and himself marched to punish his lieutenants. One of these he slew with his own hand. Another he found had laid in no provisions for the army, but had collected three thousand talents in money. The king bade him offer it to the horses, and when they refused it exclaimed, 'Of what use is such a provision to me at this time?' and at once ordered the officer to be taken into custody for his negligence.

When Alexander entered Persia he gave this money to the matrons of the country, after the custom of the Persian kings. Here he found the tomb of the great King Cyrus broken open, and gave orders that the man who had wrought the destruction, though a person of some importance, should be put to death. Alexander was much affected by the inscription upon the tomb, which set forth vividly the uncertainty and transitory nature of earthly greatness. He ordered the epitaph, which was in the Persian language, to be inscribed also in the Greek tongue upon the tomb. It was as follows: 'I am Cyrus, the founder of the Persian empire. O man! whosoever thou art, envy me not the little space of earth that covers my body.'

Here, too, at a great feast which he gave to his friends and officers, Alexander promised that the one who should drink the most wine should be crowned as a victor. The man who carried off the prize by drinking a prodigious quantity survived the debauch but three days. Others, we are told, drank to such excess that forty-one of them died in consequence.

ALEXANDER

When Alexander arrived at the town of Susa, he married his chief officers to Persian ladies of high rank, with the purpose of uniting the Macedonian and Persian peoples, and himself set the example by taking the daughter of Darius as a second wife. Moreover, he also gave a great entertainment to those Macedonians who had already married Persian women. It is said that no less than nine thousand guests sat down to the banquet, yet such was the king's magnificence, that to each one he presented a golden cup. Indeed, he even paid the debts of his guests, so that the whole cost of the entertainment reached a stupendous sum. Among those who claimed the king's bounty was a veteran officer, who falsely declared that he was in debt for such and such a sum. The king paid the amount, but afterwards discovering the fraud, dismissed the offender from the court, and deprived him of his rank in the army. There was no fault to be found with this man as a soldier, and he had indeed lost an eye in circumstances in which he displayed great courage and fortitude; for, when as a youth he was serving at a siege under King Philip, the father of Alexander, he was wounded in the eye by a dart shot from one of the engines of war. In spite of his wound, he would not quit the field, nor even suffer the dart to be withdrawn, until he had helped to repulse the enemy, and driven them back into the town. The old soldier was now so overwhelmed with shame and despair at the disgrace which he had brought upon himself that it was feared that he would take his own life. To prevent this the king not only forgave him but also ordered him to keep the money.

Alexander was greatly delighted with the progress of the thirty thousand Persian boys whom he had left under proper masters for their training, and whom he now found grown handsome in looks, and active and skilful in their military exercises. The favour which he showed to them and to other Persians excited, however, the jealousy of his Macedonians. They complained that the king neglected them after their great services. The anger of Alexander at this mutinous spirit, however, brought them back to their obedience, and they besought forgiveness. The king after a time relented; those who were too old for service were indeed sent home, but they were loaded with presents. Alexander ordered further that, when they arrived in their native land, honour should be paid to them in the theatres and public places. He commanded, moreover, that the pay of those who had died in his service should be continued to their children.

When Alexander came into Media and had despatched urgent affairs of business, he gave himself up to the celebration of games and festivities. But in the midst of these rejoicings and carousings his chief friend and favourite, Hephæstion, fell sick of a fever. In his illness the young officer could ill brook the low diet that suited his condition. Taking advantage of the absence of his physician at the theatre, he ate a hearty meal and drank a flagon of ice-cold wine. As a consequence of this excess he grew rapidly worse, and in a few days died.

The grief of Alexander at this event passed all reason. He caused the wretched physician to be crucified.

The horses and mules he ordered to be shorn, and the battlements of neighbouring cities to be pulled down in sign of mourning. For a long time he forbade the sound of the flute and of all manner of music in his camp. This extravagant mourning continued until he received an oracle which enjoined him to revere his dead friend and to sacrifice to him as a demi-god. In order to do this, Alexander made an expedition against a neighbouring people. Having conquered them, he put all the males above the age of boyhood to the sword. This terrible slaughter he called a sacrifice to the soul of his dead favourite.

When the king was advancing towards Babylon he was met by his admiral Nearchus, who had sailed up the river Euphrates after completing his expedition upon the ocean. The admiral informed his sovereign that certain wise men had come to him, and strongly urged that Alexander should not enter the city of Babylon. The king, however, neglected the warning, and continued his march. Soon, however, he was disturbed by signs which he took to be unfavourable omens. As he drew near the walls of the city, he saw a number of crows fighting, some of which fell dead at his feet. He learnt also that the governor of Babylon had consulted the gods concerning him, and that the omens foretold something terrible. Moreover, one of the largest and finest of the lions that were kept in the town was kicked to death by an ass. On another occasion a man, dressed in the royal robes and wearing the regal diadem, was found sitting in profound silence upon the throne of Alexander. The man was put to death, but the strange event, added to the other signs and portents, greatly disturbed the mind of the king. He became the prey of despair and of suspicion, and gave way to the most violent outbursts.

Now that he had once given himself up to superstition, his mind was so disturbed by vain fears and imaginings that he turned the slightest event, if at all unusual, into a sign and a portent, and his court was crowded with sacrificers and soothsayers. However, having received some favourable oracles, he to some extent recovered his spirits and gave himself up once more to feasts and entertainments.

One day he made a great feast to his admiral Nearchus. Afterwards, according to his wont, he went to refresh himself in the bath before retiring to rest. In the meantime, however, there came one of his friends to invite him to a carousal. Alexander would not refuse him. At his friend's table the king drank all that night and the next day. The debauch brought on a fever from which, after lying ill some ten days, the mighty conqueror died.

PHILOPŒMEN

PHILOPŒMEN, who was born about the middle of the third century before Christ, was the greatest hero and patriot of the declining years of Greek liberty.

After the death of Alexander the Great, a number of the Greek states rose in rebellion against Macedonia, but were defeated. A time of great confusion, which lasted about half a century, followed, but in the period immediately preceding the times of Philopœmen, Macedonia was again master of the whole of Greece, with the exception of Sparta.

Freedom was, however, again brought to Greece by the growth of two leagues of allied states, of which at this time the more important was the Achæan League. In former days this had been merely a league of a number of cities on the north coast of the Peloponnesus, but it was now extended, and in the boyhood of Philopœmen it included most of the Greek cities except Sparta and a few other places of less importance.

The exploits of Philopœmen as general of the Achæan League were thus performed largely against Sparta, the greatest of the Greek states outside the league. Philopœmen was fully conscious of the danger to Greek independence from the presence of the Romans in his *country. He did all that he could to prevent any pretext being given them for making Greece a Roman province.*

When Philopœmen died, a victim of that disunion among the Greek states which was the ruin of ancient Greece, his country was still, in name at least, independent of Rome. But its independence was rapidly dying, and within forty years of the death of the last of the ancient Greek heroes, his land had become a province of the widespreading dominions of Rome.

THE father of Philopœmen was a native of the city of Megalopolis, and was in all respects a remarkable man. He died while his son was very young, and the lad's upbringing was therefore undertaken by a friend who had been sheltered in times of adversity by his father. He repaid the debt by his care of the orphan lad, and by training him from infancy in noble sentiments and lofty virtues.

When Philopœmen was past the age of childhood, two citizens of Megalopolis had the principal charge of him. They were men distinguished alike by learning and by their deeds, but of all their actions this, that they had had the training of Philopœmen, came to be their greatest distinction. For in after-years their pupil proved to be the last of the many excellent generals that Greece produced, and was therefore beloved exceedingly, being, as it were, the child of his country's old age.

Philopœmen was not plain in face, as some have supposed, for his statue shows otherwise. Nor is the idea of his homeliness of feature borne out by the story

PHILOPŒMEN

of his hostess at Megara, for her mistake arose from the unaffected easiness of his manner and the plainness of his dress. That lady, having received word that the general of the Achæans was about to pay her a visit, fell into a great flurry and bustle to provide suitably for so distinguished a guest, and was particularly disturbed because her husband did not happen to be at home to assist her. In the midst of her preparations Philopœmen arrived and, as he was dressed very plainly, his hostess took him to be one of the general's servants. Glad of the unexpected help, she therefore asked him to assist her in the work of the kitchen. He immediately threw off his cloak and began to chop some wood. While he was thus engaged the master of the house returned and, astonished at seeing the general thus employed, exclaimed, 'Whatever does this mean, Philopœmen?' The general replied to his question with a broad country accent and said, 'I am paying the penalty of my plainness.'

As to the manners of Philopœmen, it appears that his pursuit of honour was attended by too much roughness and passion. He succeeded in imitating Epaminondas, whom he took as his model, in energy, shrewdness and scorn of wealth, but, on account of his hasty temper, he never equalled the temperate and frank conduct of that hero in political disputes. Hence he seemed fitted rather for war than for politics. Indeed, from childhood he delighted in everything connected with the military art, and occupied himself eagerly in all exercises connected with it, such as riding and the use of arms. As his body seemed to be well built for wrestling, his friends advised him to practise that art. Thereupon he inquired whether skill in wrestling would interfere with his efficiency as a soldier. They told him the truth, that the manner of life and condition of body necessary to make a good wrestler were quite different from the training suitable for a soldier. The wrestler must live a regular life as regards food and exercise, and be governed entirely by the rules of training. The soldier, on the other hand, must be inured to the most extreme changes in his manner of living, and be trained to go without food or sleep for long intervals. Philopœmen on learning this not only abstained from wrestling himself, but afterwards, when he became general, did all in his power to bring the sport into disrepute, because it spoilt men as soldiers who were otherwise most fitted for war.

When he had passed out of the hands of his instructors, he frequently engaged in private forays with some of his fellow-citizens into the territories of Sparta. In these incursions he was always the first to march out and the last to return. His leisure he spent in hunting, or in the tillage of his estate outside the town. Thither he went every evening and slept upon a hard bed like one of his own labourers. In the early morning he worked in the fields with his vine-dressers or his ploughmen before returning to the town to take part in public affairs.

Philopœmen was thirty years old when Cleomenes, King of Sparta, surprised Megalopolis by night and, having forced his way through the city guard, seized the market-place. Philopœmen rushed to aid his fellow-citizens but, though he fought with the most desperate valour, was not able to drive out the attackers. He succeeded, however, in giving the citizens time to escape out of the town, and himself retired the last of all. Indeed, he escaped with great difficulty, for his horse was killed under him, and he himself was wounded. When the fugitives had reached the town of Messene, the Spartan king offered, if they would return, to restore their city with their lands and goods to them. The people were disposed to accept this proposal gladly, for they were in haste to return to their homes. Philopœmen, however, strongly advised them not to do so. In a speech to his fellow-citizens he pointed out that the Spartan king offered them their goods, because he wanted to be lord of a populated city and not of a deserted one. Further, Philopœmen reminded them that the king could not long remain in the town to gaze on empty walls and houses, but must soon be driven away by the very desolation of the place. His arguments dissuaded the citizens from returning, but nevertheless furnished the Spartans with a pretext for plundering the town.

Soon after these events Antigonus, King of Macedonia, came to the assistance of the Achæans against the King of Sparta. The latter had taken up a strong position on high ground which Antigonus resolved to force. Philopœmen and his fellow-citizens were stationed with the cavalry and, together with the Illyrian foot-soldiers, formed one wing of the army. They were ordered to wait quietly until they received the signal from the other wing, where Antigonus was stationed in person. This signal was to be given by the hoisting of a red robe upon the point of a spear.

The Achæans kept their ground as they were ordered, but the Illyrians disregarded the general's commands and charged the Spartans. They were separated from the horsemen on their wing by this movement, and the brother of the Spartan king, seeing the gap thus made in the line, ordered a body of his light-armed infantry to charge through and attack the rear of the Illyrians. They did so, and soon threw them into confusion. Philopœmen now saw that the condition of affairs was critical, and that immediate action by the horsemen was necessary to drive off the light-armed infantry. He made a suggestion to that effect to the officers of King Antigonus. But, in view of the king's orders and the fact that Philopœmen had, up to this time, no special reputation as a soldier, they refused to do as he proposed. Philopœmen then took matters into his own hands, and with his fellow-citizens himself attacked the light infantry. At the very first shock the enemy was routed and driven off with great slaughter.

When he had thus retrieved the position of affairs on that wing, Philopœmen dismounted from his horse in order to assist in a further attack on the enemy. In his horseman's coat of mail and other heavy armour, he was making his way across a space of marshy, boggy ground when he received a terrible, though not mortal, wound from a javelin. The missile passed completely through both thighs, the point coming out on the farther side. For a little while Philopœmen stood unable to move, his legs being, as it were, riveted together by the weapon. He knew not what to do, for the leather thong in the middle of the javelin made it so difficult to draw the missile out of the wound that none of those who were near would venture upon the attempt. At the same time the battle was at its fiercest; honour and the lust of combat impelled Philopœmen to take his part in it. Therefore, with astonishing resolution, he moved his legs this way and that, until at length he broke the staff of the javelin, and then had the pieces pulled out of the wounds in his thighs. Being thus set free, he rushed through the foremost ranks and charged the enemy sword in hand, at the same time animating the troops by his voice and the splendid courage of his example.

When the victory was thus won for Antigonus, that general, in order to test his officers who had been in command on the wing, asked who had given orders for the cavalry to charge before the signal was made. In order to excuse themselves, they told him that they had been obliged against their will to come into action, because a certain young man of Megalopolis had begun the attack too soon. Antigonus smiled. 'That young man,' said he, 'acted like an experienced general.'

The conduct of Philopœmen in this battle naturally brought him great reputation. Antigonus was anxious to have his services, and offered him a command of considerable importance in his army. The young soldier declined, however, because he knew that he could not well bear to be under the orders of another. He was anxious, however, not to be idle, and wished above all things to exercise and improve his military skill. He therefore sailed for Crete in order to take part in the wars in that island. There he served for a long while, and gained so much renown that when he returned he was at once made general of the horse by the Achæans.

He found the cavalry in a very bad state. Many men, who should have served themselves, shunned the duty, and sent substitutes in their stead. Moreover, the horsemen were badly mounted, for their horses were picked up anywhere when the men were called out on service. The soldiers were badly disciplined and lacking in military skill, and as a consequence they made very timid soldiers. Former generals had connived at these abuses in order to curry favour with the cavalry, who had special power in the state and great influence in the distribution of rewards and punishments.

Such personal considerations had no influence with Philopœmen. He sought to bring his men to a proper sense of honour by all possible means, and he did not shrink from using punishment where necessary. He also practised them continually in drills, reviews and sham fights. By these means he soon wrought an extraordinary improvement in their skill and spirit, and so disciplined them that their evolutions were executed as though the whole body was controlled by a single will.

In a battle which they fought with other Greeks, the general of the enemy's horse advanced beyond his own lines and charged at full speed upon Philopœmen. The Achæan general avoided his blow, and with a spear-thrust laid him dead upon the ground, whereupon the enemy at once broke and fled. Philopœmen was now everywhere celebrated as uniting the personal courage of youth with the wise prudence of age, and as being equally great in actual combat and in skill to command.

He used his reputation and influence to persuade the Achæans to improve their arms and method of warfare. They had been accustomed to use small shields and lances which were much shorter than the Macedonian spears. Such arms put them at a disadvantage in close combat. Philopœmen persuaded them to adopt a close formation, to use large shields which could be locked together to form a continuous front, to wear heavy armour and to carry long spears. He turned their love of display to account by inducing them to expend their money not, as they had been wont to do, upon fine clothes and household goods, but on the splendour of their arms and armour. Through his influence the shops were soon filled with plate, sent to be broken up in order that breastplates might be made to gleam with gold, and shields and bridles made bright with silver studs. Whilst the artificers were thus employed, the young men practised horsemanship or the use of arms, and the women adorned helmets with coloured plumes and military cloaks with embroidery. By these means Philopœmen greatly increased the military spirit of his men and their efficiency in war.

At this time the Achæans were involved in war with Machanidas, King of Sparta, who with a powerful army was aiming at the conquest of the whole of southern Greece. In pursuit of this object, he attacked the town of Mantinea, and Philopœmen at once took the field and marched against him. The two armies took up positions not far from the town, each force including a good number of hired soldiers in addition to its own native troops. Early in the battle Machanidas attacked and put to flight a body of spearmen who were placed in front of his opponent's position. Elated with his success, he continued the pursuit instead of carrying his attack against the main body of the Achæans.

Philopœmen, though to some the day seemed to be lost, made light of this early reverse. He let Machanidas sweep on in full pursuit and, when the king was at some distance from the field of battle, commenced an attack upon the main body of the Spartan army. By reason of the absence of the pursuers, he was able to extend his line beyond the enemy, and to attack them both in front and flank. They were unable to withstand the onslaught, and were routed with such slaughter that four thousand Spartans, it is said, were left dead upon the field.

Philopœmen now turned to meet Machanidas, who was returning from the pursuit. As the victorious Achæans came up, Machanidas sought to cross a broad and deep ditch, which lay in his way, in order that he might escape. Philopœmen hastened to prevent him if possible. A struggle ensued between them which was not so much like a combat between two generals, as a fight between two wild animals, or rather, between a hunter and a wild beast. The tyrant's horse, which was a powerful and spirited animal, forced by violent spurring leapt down into the ditch at the very moment when Philopœmen, and two comrades who always fought by his side, rode up. The general's friends levelled their spears at the king, but Philopœmen, being determined himself to settle affairs with the enemy, prevented their attack. He saw that the tyrant's horse, rearing high in his endeavours to gain the opposite bank, covered the tyrant's body. Philopœmen therefore turned his own horse aside, and thrusting with his spear bore Machanidas to earth in the ditch. The statue of Philopœmen, in the attitude in which he thus killed the tyrant, was afterwards set up by the Achæans as a memorial both of the personal exploit and of the victory.

The warlike skill of Philopœmen was a great obstacle to the designs of Philip of Macedon, who thought that if the general were once removed the Achæans might be brought under the power of the Macedonians, as they had formerly been. The king therefore secretly sent assassins to murder him, but the treacherous plot was fortunately discovered in time. The attempt brought upon Philip the hatred and scorn of all Greeks, who saw in the great deeds of Philopœmen a revival of the ancient glories of their race.

The very name of Philopœmen was, indeed, a terror to the enemies of the Achæans. Thus it happened that when a false report came to the Bœotians, who were besieging a certain town, that Philopœmen was advancing to the relief, they immediately fled, although their scaling-ladders were actually planted against the walls of the town. On another occasion Nabis, who had succeeded Machanidas as tyrant of Sparta, surprised and took the city of Messene. Philopœmen, who at the time was out of office, endeavoured to persuade his successor in the generalship to go to the aid of the people of the town. The general refused to do so, however, because, as he pointed out, the enemy was actually within the city, and the place therefore lost beyond remedy. Thereupon Philopœmen himself set out, taking with him his own fellow-citizens, who were ready to follow him anywhere. When Nabis was informed that he was near at hand, the king did not dare to await attack, though his men were actually quartered in the town. As Philopœmen came up, Nabis stole away through another gate of the city, and thus Messene was rescued.

Thus far every action of Philopœmen shows the greatness of his character. But he has been much censured because at this juncture he went a second time to take part in the wars in Crete. This action has been represented as a desertion of his own country at a time when Megalopolis was so hard pressed by the attacks of Nabis, that the citizens were closely shut up within the walls of the town, and were obliged to sow corn in the very streets because the enemy was encamped almost at their gates. On the other hand, it is to be said that, as the Achæans had chosen other generals, Philopœmen was out of employment, and that he took service in Crete on account of his natural hatred of idleness, and his desire to keep his military skill in constant practice.

In Crete he again greatly distinguished himself, and performed many remarkable exploits, so that he returned home with much honour. On his arrival he found that the Romans were in Greece, that their consul

Flaminius had beaten Philip of Macedon, and that Nabis of Sparta was engaged in war with both Romans and Achæans.

Philopœmen was at once chosen general by the Achæans. Venturing upon a sea-fight, however, he found that experience is as necessary in naval combats as in warfare by land. He was worsted on account of his lack of skill. Moreover, the old ship which he had fitted out and manned with his fellow-townsmen, proved so leaky that it was in great danger of foundering. His failure made the enemy despise his abilities as a leader at sea. They therefore ventured to lay siege to a town on the sea-board, and felt so secure from attack that they neglected to keep proper watch. They were punished for their over-confidence, for Philopœmen landed in the night, burnt their camp and killed a great number of them.

A few days later, as he was marching through a difficult mountain pass, he came suddenly upon the army of Nabis. The Achæans were terrified by their position, for it seemed impossible to escape from the narrow pass, so strongly was it held by the enemy. Philopœmen now showed his skill in that most important part of the art of war, the drawing up of an army in proper order. He called a halt, surveyed the nature of the ground, and in a little while, without hurry or confusion, altered the disposition of his forces to suit the occasion, and to remove the disadvantage in which his army was placed. Then falling upon the enemy he put them to flight. He noticed that the fugitives did not fly to take refuge in the neighbouring town, but that they dispersed themselves in small bodies over the surrounding country. The region was rugged, with clumps of woodland here and there, and was broken up by deep ditches and watercourses, so that cavalry could not act in it. Philopœmen therefore did not pursue the enemy, but proceeded to encamp. He judged, however, that the scattered bodies of fugitives would, after nightfall, endeavour to draw together in the town. He therefore set many bodies of Achæans, who lay hidden sword in hand, in ambush in places around the town. Great numbers of the enemy as they stole back to the town were slain by these bodies, so that the greater part of the army of Nabis was destroyed.

Some time after this Flaminius made peace with Nabis, and Nabis himself was assassinated. The affairs of Sparta now fell into the utmost confusion. Philopœmen seized the opportunity, came upon the town with his army, and partly by force, partly by persuasion, induced the city to join the Achæan League. The gaining over of so great a town was of high importance to the Achæans, and raised the reputation of Philopœmen among them to the highest pitch. The chief inhabitants of Sparta were also grateful to him, for they hoped now to enjoy the advantages of liberty. They therefore, having sold the house and goods of Nabis, made a public decree that the money derived from the sale should be given to Philopœmen.

So well known, however, was the independence of Philopœmen that not one of them was willing to undertake the task of offering the money to him. One and all excused themselves. As last, however, they induced one of their number, who was bound to the general by ties of friendship, to broach the matter to their liberator. The messenger arrived at Megalopolis, and was welcomed by his friend. But when he saw the simplicity of the general's mode of life, the plainness of his food, and his indifference to wealth, the envoy of the Spartans did not venture to set forth the true object of his visit, but gave some other reason, and so departed. He was sent a second time with the same result, but during a third visit he, with some difficulty, brought himself to mention the matter. Philopœmen heard him with pleasure, but went at once to Sparta, and refused the gift. He advised them not to tempt good men, who were already their friends, with money, but to use it to stop the mouths of the corrupt, who might otherwise do the state an injury. Such was his noble contempt for wealth.

Some time afterwards, when another officer was general of the Achæans, the Spartans fell under the suspicion of intending to withdraw from the league. The general determined, therefore, to march against them, and punish them. Philopœmen endeavoured to dissuade him, recognising that the quarrels of the Greeks would furnish the Romans with a pretext for taking away their independence. The general persisted in his intention, however, and with the Roman consul Flaminius entered the Spartan territories. Philopœmen then took a course which, though not strictly within the law, shows the noble daring of his character. Though he held no office at the time, he threw himself into the town, and shut the gates in the faces of the Achæan general and the Roman consul. Moreover, he succeeded in healing the dissensions among the Spartans, and in bringing back the city into allegiance to the Achæan League.

Nevertheless he afterwards, at a time when he was again general himself, took a fierce revenge upon Sparta for the murder of some of his friends. He put a number of the citizens to death, threw down the walls of the town, and deprived it of a great part of its territories. Pursuing his vengeance further, he unjustly deprived the Spartans of their liberties and their form of government, and abolished the Spartan discipline in which they had trained their youths. In place of their ancient customs he imposed Achæan institutions. Thus the sinews of Sparta were cut and the haughty city made tame and submissive, though, some time after, the Romans allowed the citizens to cast off the Achæan customs, and to re-establish, as far as might be, their ancient institutions.

As time went on, the power of the Romans in Greece increased, and pressed hard upon the Achæan League. Nor were there wanting Greeks who favoured the Romans. The orators especially inclined to their interest. In these times of difficulty Philopœmen struggled as a patriot for his country, like a good pilot struggling against a storm. One of his fellow-citizens, a man of great weight with the Achæans, but strongly inclined to court the favour of the Romans, declared in council that, in his opinion, the Romans should not be opposed or thwarted in any way. Philopœmen heard him for a time in speechless indignation, but at last he could restrain himself no longer. He burst out with the question, 'You wretched fellow, why are you in such haste to see the end of Greece?' And in this spirit he opposed the growth of Roman power which, he saw clearly, was sapping the liberties of Greece.

When Philopœmen was seventy years of age, he was elected general of the Achæans for the eighth time. He hoped, however, not only to pass his time of office without war, but to spend the remainder of his life in peace, for the spirit of hostility among the Greek states was weakening with their failing power, like the symptoms of violent illness abating with the loss of bodily strength. But the gods willed otherwise; the aged general was to fall like one who, having run a race with matchless speed, stumbles at the very goal.

There was a certain citizen of Messene, Dinocrates by name, a man of evil life, who hated Philopœmen. He found means to draw Messene away from the Achæan League, and the report ran that he intended to seize another town as well. At the time Philopœmen lay sick of a fever at Argos, but directly the news came, he set out for Megalopolis, and reached it in one day, though it was fifty miles distant. Thence he soon led forth a body of horsemen, all young men of noble birth, who followed him as volunteers out of personal affection and for the love of glory. With these he marched towards Messene and, coming upon the forces of Dinocrates upon a certain hill, attacked them and put them to flight. Suddenly, however, a further body of five hundred of the enemy came up, and the fugitives seeing them rallied among the hills. Philopœmen now saw that he was in danger of being surrounded, and retreated over rough and broken ground. He himself fought in the rear, in order to cover the retreat of his young soldiers, and often turned to face the enemy so that he might give his men time to escape. Old as he was, none of the enemy dared to engage him in hand-to-hand fight, but only shouted and rode about him.

As he often faced around in this manner, he gradually became separated from the main body of his retreating troops, and at last found himself alone amidst a number of the enemy's horsemen. Even then they did not venture to attack him hand-to-hand, but hurled their javelins at him from a distance. Thus they drove him into a steep and rocky place where he could scarce, by continual spurring, force his horse to go.

The aged warrior was still active through constant exercise, so that his years were no obstacle to his escape. But he was weakened by sickness and wearied with his journey, so that he could no longer sit his horse so firmly as he was wont, while the animal stumbled and struggled over the broken ground. At last the rider was thrown from the saddle upon the rocks; his head was injured by the fall, and he lay on the ground insensible, so that his enemies believed him to be dead. But when they turned him over to strip him of his arms, Philopœmen raised his head and opened his eyes. Thereupon his enemies gathered around him, bound his arms behind his back, and bore him off with vile indignities and abuse.

The people of Messene, elated by the news,

flocked to the city gates to see the entry of the captive. But when they saw the hero of Greece dragged along with humiliations so unworthy of the glory of his deeds, not a few were touched with pity, even to tears, at the sight. Some indeed began to recall the benefits they had aforetime received at his hands, and how their city had been delivered by him from the tyranny of Nabis. Nevertheless a few, to please Dinocrates, talked of putting the captive to torture and to death as a dangerous and relentless enemy, the more to be dreaded on account of the treatment he had received, if they were foolish enough to allow him to escape. After much discussion he was thrown into a dungeon called the Treasury, the entrance to which was closed by a huge stone, and into which neither air nor light was admitted. There, having swung the stone into place and set a guard about it, they left him.

Meanwhile his fugitive cavalry, recovering from their panic, discovered that their leader was not with them. They halted and with loud shouts called him by name. No reply came, so that they feared Philopœmen was dead. They then began to blame themselves for basely escaping at the expense of the life of the leader who had exposed himself so freely on their behalf. After much search and inquiry about the country, however, they learnt the truth and carried the heavy tidings home.

The Achæans deemed the loss of Philopœmen the worst possible calamity. They resolved at once to send an embassy to Messene to demand that he should be given up, and in the meantime, in case of refusal, they began to prepare for war.

But Dinocrates feared above all things that delay might save the life of Philopœmen. He resolved, therefore, to compass his death before the Achæans could take action to save him. So, when darkness had fallen and the people had gone away from about the dungeon, he caused it to be opened. Then he sent in one of his servants bearing a cup of poison, and ordered him not to leave the place until Philopœmen had taken the fatal draught. The servant found the captive lying down wrapped in his cloak. He was not asleep, however, for sadness and vexation kept him awake. When he saw the light and a man standing by him with the draught of poison, he raised himself up as well as his weakness would allow and, taking the proffered cup, asked for news of his cavalry. He was told that they had almost all escaped, whereupon, nodding his head in sign of gladness, he said, 'Thou bringest good tidings, and we are not unfortunate in all respects.' Then, without another word and without a sigh, he drank the poison and again lay down. So low had he been brought by weakness that he died almost without a struggle.

All Achaia was filled with grief at the news of his death. The youth and the delegates of the different towns at once went to Megalopolis, and determined to take vengeance against the town of Messene. Having chosen a general, they entered its territories, and so ravaged the country that the Messenians were driven to open the gates of the city. Before the avengers entered, Dinocrates and those citizens who had voted for putting

PHILOPŒMEN IN PRISON

Philopœmen to death, forestalled their vengeance by killing themselves. Those who had voted for putting him to the torture suffered a worse fate, for they were carried off to be put to a more painful and shameful death.

The remains of Philopœmen were burnt by his countrymen, and the ashes enclosed in an urn. Then, in ordered march and with funeral solemnities, the army returned to Megalopolis. First came the infantry, wearing crowns of victory and dragging along the fettered captives. Next came the general's son, surrounded by the chief Achæans and bearing aloft the urn, which could scarcely be seen for the garlands and wreaths which covered it. The march was closed by the cavalry, fully armed and superbly mounted.

As the procession passed along the countryside, the people of the towns and villages flocked out as if to meet a general returning from a glorious campaign, and so, with all honour and respect, joined in the solemn march and attended the remains of Philopœmen to his town of Megalopolis.

His burial was worthy of his great deeds; many statues were set up, and many honours paid to his memory by the Grecian cities, and the Messenian prisoners were stoned to death at his tomb.

CORIOLANUS

THE *life of Coriolanus falls within the early history of the Roman Republic, when the mastery of Rome over other neighbouring cities and peoples was, as yet, uncertain and unstable. The chief events narrated by Plutarch in the life of Coriolanus fall within the first few years of the fifth century before Christ. The story exhibits the ruin of a noble nature by pride. The ardent young soldier, taught to consider valour in battle the greatest of all virtues, performs in early manhood deeds of courage worthy of the demi-gods of early tradition. To the pride derived from such success is added the pride of rank felt by an arrogant and overbearing nature. His scornful contempt of the commons leads to his fall, and at once resentment overpowers the finer qualities of his nature, and the patriot becomes the leader of his country's enemies. One strain of tenderness, however, remains, and he forgoes the full exaction of his revenge in response to the prayers of his mother Veturia and his wife Volumnia, whom Plutarch calls respectively Volumnia and Virgilia.*

The life of Coriolanus illustrates the earlier stages of that struggle between patrician and plebeian, of rich and poor in Rome, which we shall find growing still more bitter, and breaking out into the bloodshed of civil brawls, in the lives of the Gracchi.

The life of Coriolanus as told by Plutarch is closely followed by Shakespeare in the stately drama of **Coriolanus**, *though the order of events is in some places altered by him.*

CAIUS Marcius was of a patrician family which gave many illustrious citizens to Rome. He was brought up by his mother in her widowhood, and his life shows that the loss of a father, though attended by many disadvantages, is no hindrance to the attainment of manly virtue. On the other hand, his life bears witness to the fact that a noble nature, if not moulded by discipline, will bring forth bad qualities with the good, just as the richest soil, if not carefully tilled, produces the most luxuriant weeds. His dauntless courage and resolution incited him to many great deeds, and enabled him to accomplish them with honour. But, at the same time, he was a man of violent passions and of great obstinacy, so that it was difficult for others to act in concert with him. Hence, the very persons who could not but admire his temperance, justice and courage, were unable to endure his imperious temper, and found his manner too haughty and overbearing for a citizen of a republic.

The young Marcius had an extraordinary natural inclination towards war, and from childhood was accustomed to the use of arms. And, since he thought that weapons of war were of little avail unless the bodily strength and activity were preserved and improved, he trained himself by exercise for every kind of combat. Hence, while his limbs were so active and lissome that he was fleet in pursuit, his muscular strength and weight were such that none could easily break away from his grip in wrestling. Indeed, those who were beaten by him in any contests in these sports consoled themselves by ascribing their defeats, not to their own lack of skill, but to the invincible strength of Marcius, which nothing could resist or tire.

While still very young he made his first acquaintance with war in the campaign against Tarquin, who had reigned in Rome and had been driven from the throne. The deposed king had fought many battles with ill success, and was now staking all upon a last desperate effort to regain his throne. He was aided by many of the states of Italy who took up his cause, not for any love for him, but because of their fear and envy of the growing greatness of Rome. In the battle which followed, Marcius distinguished himself in the sight of the dictator. For, seeing a fellow-Roman overthrown at no great distance from him, Marcius rushed to the assistance of his comrade, engaged the enemy and slew him. When victory had finally declared for the Romans, the general presented Marcius with a crown of oak leaves, which was the reward given, by the custom of Rome, to one who saved the life of a citizen.

The honours which Marcius gained early in life by no means satisfied his desire for glory. He was ever endeavouring to excel his previous exploits, and to add achievement to achievement. So conspicuous was his courage, that he received greater and greater honours from the generals under whom he served. The Romans at this time were engaged in several wars, and many battles were fought, from not one of which did Marcius return without a crown of honour, or some other distinction in witness of his valour. He valued these rewards of his courage mainly on account of the delight which they gave to his mother Volumnia, and he considered himself at the height of happiness when, with tears of joy, she embraced him, crowned with the prize of valour, amid the plaudits of the people. Indeed, he held himself bound to pay her the respect and duty which would have been due to his father had he been alive, over and above the honour due to her as his mother. He even married in compliance with her wishes, and after children had been born to him he still continued to dwell in his mother's house.

At the time when the reputation and influence which the courage of Marcius had gained for him were at the highest point, Rome was disturbed with internal troubles. The senate sided with the richer citizens against the commons of the city, who were treated by their creditors with intolerable cruelty. The goods of such as had property were seized, and either kept as security for debt or sold. Those who had nothing were dragged off to prison and there loaded with fetters, though their bodies were often covered with the wounds they had received while fighting for their country. The last expedition in which the Romans had been engaged had been against the Sabines, and, in order to induce the poorer citizens to serve, they had been promised that in future they should be treated more leniently, and by a decree of the senate the consul was appointed a guarantee of the promise. But when the commons had cheerfully undergone the dangers and toils of war, and had returned with victory, they found their lot in no way improved. Moreover, the senate disregarded their agreement, and without concern saw the commons dragged off to prison, or their goods seized and sold as before. The people were deeply angered at this breach of faith, and the city was filled with tumult and sedition.

These internal troubles encouraged the enemies of Rome. They invaded the territories of the city, and laid them waste with fire and sword. The consuls called upon all who were able to bear arms to send in their names, in order to form a force to repel the invaders, but so general was the discontent that not a man among the commons responded to the summons. It was now urgent that something should be done. A number of the senators were of opinion that some indulgence should be shown to the poor. Others, however, were absolutely opposed to any concession. Marcius in particular strongly held this view. He regarded the demands of the commons as an insolent attempt to decrease the powers of the patricians and believed that any yielding would only lead to further and greater demands. The senate debated the matter several times within a few days, but could come to no decision.

On a sudden, however, the commons took action. They arose one and all, marched out of the city, and, without committing any act of violence, withdrew to the height now known as the Sacred Hill. For they said: 'The rich have for a great while been accustomed to drag us from our dwellings in the city. Any place in Italy will furnish us with air and water and room for burial, and Rome offers us no other privilege than these, unless indeed it be a privilege to bleed and die for those who oppress us.'

The action of the commons thoroughly alarmed the senate, and some of those members who were most moderate in opinion and most popular with the plebeians, were chosen to go and treat with the people. The leader of this deputation was Menenius Agrippa, who, after much entreaty to the commons and many arguments in defence of the senate, concluded his speech with this celebrated fable:

'Once upon a time the members of the human body rebelled against the belly, which, they said, lay idle and useless, while they were all toiling without cease to satisfy its appetites. But the belly only laughed at the foolishness which they showed in not realising that though it did indeed receive all the nourishment into itself, it did so only that the food might be prepared for the use of all the other parts of the body.

'Such, my fellow-citizens,' said Menenius, 'is the case with regard to the senate and yourselves. For, in return for your labours, the consuls and government of the senate provide for the well-being of all the people.'

After this speech the commons were reconciled to the senate, but not before they had secured the appointment of five men, known as Tribunes of the People, to defend their rights upon all occasions. The commons now readily obeyed the orders of the consuls with regard to the war, and came forward to be enrolled as soldiers.

The privilege which the commons had gained by the appointment of tribunes was far from pleasing to Marcius, who looked upon it as lessening the authority of the patricians, and a considerable body of the nobles shared his opinion. Nevertheless Marcius exhorted those who thought with him not to be backward in serving their country, and to prove themselves the superiors of the commons in courage and patriotism.

The capital of the country of the Volscians, with whom the Romans were at war, was Corioli. This town was besieged by the Romans under their consul. The rest of the Volscian nation, alarmed lest their capital should be taken, assembled with the intention of falling upon the rear of the besieging army. The Roman consul therefore divided his force and, leaving part to continue the siege of Corioli, marched with the other troops to meet the Volscian army which was advancing to the relief of the town.

When the people of Corioli got wind of this division of the Roman forces, and saw the smallness of the body left to maintain the siege, they despised the strength of their besiegers, and sallied out of the town to attack them. At first their attack was successful: the Romans gave ground and were driven to their entrenchments. Their success, however, was checked by Marcius, who with a small party flew to the assistance of his fellow-citizens. He slew the foremost of the enemy and checked the career of the rest, while with a loud voice he called the Romans back, for he was no less dreadful in battle from the might of his arm than from the thunder of his voice, and from an aspect that struck terror to his enemies. Many of the Romans rallied to his call, and pressing hard upon their enemies drove them back in confusion.

It did not satisfy Marcius merely to repel the attack; he followed close upon the rear of the flying enemy, and continued the pursuit up to the very gates of the besieged town. There the Romans who had followed him halted, for showers of arrows were rained upon them from the walls, and there was none except Marcius so bold as to dream of entering, with the press of fugitives, within the walls of a city filled with warlike enemies. Such, however, was the hero's daring plan. 'See,' he cried, 'the gates are open, and assuredly rather for the victors than for the vanquished.' But few were willing to follow him as he broke through the enemy and forced his way into the town, while for a time no one ventured to oppose or even to face him. Once within the walls, he cast his eyes around and saw that but very few Romans had entered with him, and that these were dispersed and mingled with the foes. All now depended upon him, and, summoning up all his strength, he performed almost incredible feats, in which he displayed alike his mighty vigour, his marvellous agility and his extraordinary daring. His efforts overpowered the enemy, some of his antagonists fled to distant parts of the town, and others threw down their arms, so that the Roman commander was able to bring up the main body of his troops, and to enter the town without hindrance.

Thus the city was taken, and at once most of the soldiers fell to plundering the place. Marcius sternly rebuked this action. 'Shame it is,' said he, 'that we should run about for plunder, and thus keep out of the way of danger, while, perhaps at this very moment, the consul and the Romans under his command are engaged with the army marching to the relief of the town.' Though few would listen to him, he nevertheless put himself at the head of such as offered to follow him, and took the road which he knew would lead to the consul's army. He kept urging his small body of followers to hasten their march, and besought the gods to grant that he might arrive before the battle was over, in order that he might share in the glorious toils and dangers of his countrymen.

The consul's army was drawn up in order of battle, and the enemy was in sight when Marcius and his followers arrived. Many of the soldiers were startled at his appearance, for he was covered with the blood of battle and the sweat of his hurried march. But when he ran joyfully up to the consul, took him by the hand and told him that Corioli was taken, the consul clasped him to his heart, while those who heard the great news and those who did but guess at it were greatly animated and cried out with loud shouts to be led against the enemy. Marcius then inquired of the consul in what part of the enemy's array the bravest troops were stationed. He was told that those who had that reputation were placed in the centre. 'I beg of you, then,' said Marcius, 'that I may be favoured by being placed directly opposite to them.' The consul admired his spirit, and readily granted the request.

When the battle began with the throwing of spears, Marcius advanced beyond the rest of the Romans, and charged the centre of the enemy so furiously that it was soon broken. The wings, however, endeavoured to surround him, whereupon the consul in alarm sent a chosen body of troops to his succour. The fight then raged furiously around Marcius, and great carnage was made, but the vigorous attack of the Romans at last prevailed, and the enemy was put to flight. By this time Marcius was almost weighed down by wounds and weariness, but when others begged him on that account not to join in the pursuit, he replied, 'It is not for the conquerors to feel weary.' So he joined in completing the victory, in which the whole Volscian army was defeated, great numbers being slain and many made prisoners.

On the day after the battle, the consul caused his army to be assembled and then mounted the rostrum. First he returned thanks to the gods for the extraordinary success that had attended the Roman arms; next, he spoke of the great deeds of Marcius. In detail he recounted his gallant actions, of some of which he had been himself an eye-witness, while he had heard of others from the general in command of the troops left before Corioli. Finally, he ordered that, out of the great store of treasure and the number of horses and prisoners that had been taken, a tenth part should be given to Marcius. Moreover, the consul presented him with a splendid horse magnificently caparisoned, as a reward of valour.

The army received the speech of the consul with loud shouts of applause, and thereupon Marcius stood forward to reply. He was, he told them, happy in the approval of the consul, and gladly accepted the present of the horse. But as for the tenth part of the booty, Marcius continued, that seemed to him rather a reward in money than an honourable distinction, and he therefore begged to be excused from accepting it, and to be allotted only his single share with the others. He asked, however, to be allowed one favour. 'I have,' said he, 'a friend among the Volscian prisoners, a man of virtue and honour, bound to me by the sacred ties of hospitality. From wealth he is now reduced to servitude, and I should be glad to free him from one of the many woes which have befallen him, by preventing his being sold as a slave.'

These words of Marcius were hailed with louder applause than the consul's speech, for his conquest of the temptation of wealth was esteemed even nobler than his valour in battle. Even those who had before felt some envy and jealousy at the honours offered him, now realised that he was indeed worthy of great things, since he had so greatly declined them.

When at length the applause had died down and the multitude was silent, the consul spoke again. 'You cannot, my fellow-soldiers,' said he, 'force these gifts upon a man so firmly resolved to refuse them. Let us therefore give him something which it is not in his power to decline, and, in memory of his brave conduct at Corioli, let us decree that he be henceforth called Coriolanus.' Hence from that time Caius Marcius became Caius Marcius Coriolanus.

When this war was over, further trouble between the patricians and the plebeians arose in Rome. No new injury was done to the commons, but the city suffered from the consequences of former troubles, and the miseries which the people endured were used by demagogues to stir them up against the patricians. The previous quarrels had prevented corn from being sown in the territories of Rome itself, while the war had prevented supplies from being brought from other places. Thus there was a great scarcity of food, and factious orators made use of the want and misery of the people to assert falsely that the rich had planned the famine out of a spirit of revenge.

Just at this time, too, there arrived ambassadors from the people of the town of Velitræ, which had been so terribly scourged by plague that scarcely a tenth part of its inhabitants survived. They offered to surrender their town to Rome and begged that a colony might be sent to repeople the city. The wiser part of the Romans thought this a highly advantageous proposal for their city, since it would relieve the scarcity of provisions. They hoped also thus to rid the city of some of those who disturbed the peace. The consuls therefore chose some to form the colony, and further to heal the dissensions, selected others to serve in war against the Volscians, believing that when rich and poor, patrician and plebeian, came again to serve in arms against the common enemy, they would treat one another in a greater spirit of comradeship.

But the restless tribunes cried out against these proposals. They declared that the consuls and the patricians, not content with bringing famine upon the city, now designed to expose the people to the horrors of plague and to the slaughter of war. They persuaded the people that the rich, by thus bringing upon them the three greatest calamities to which mankind is subject, famine, plague and war, intended to compass their utter ruin. Stirred by their speeches, the commons refused both to form the colony and to go on service in the war.

The senate was now in some doubt as to the course to be pursued. Marcius, however, by this time not a little elated by the honours he had received and by the consciousness of his own abilities, took a foremost part in opposition to the tribunes of the commons. Through his influence, therefore, the colony was sent out, heavy fines being inflicted upon those who refused to go. But as the commons still held out against serving in the war, Marcius mustered a body of his own dependents and of such volunteers as he could raise. With these he made a foray into the territories of the enemy. There he took great store of corn and many cattle and slaves. He kept no part of the plunder for himself, but led his troops back to Rome laden with the booty. Those of the citizens who had held back from the war now repented of their obstinacy, and looked with envy upon the men who returned with such great store of provisions. Upon Marcius, too, they looked with an evil eye, regarding his power and honour as rising upon the ruin of the people.

Soon afterwards Marcius stood as a candidate for the consulship. At first the commons seemed disposed to think more kindly of him, and to be sensible of the shame of rejecting a man so distinguished in family, in courage, and in services to the state. When, as it was the custom for candidates for the consulship to do, Marcius stood in the Forum clad in a loose gown without a tunic, and showed the wounds and scars he had received in many glorious battles fought during seventeen successive years, the people, struck with admiration for his valour, decided to make him consul.

But when the day of election came, the suspicions of the people were aroused. Marcius was conducted with great pomp to the Campus Martius by the senate in a body, and the patricians bestirred themselves on his behalf with more vigour and energy than had ever before been known. The people now began to reflect that a man so much in the interests of the senate and so strongly favoured by the nobles might, if he became consul, utterly deprive the commons of their liberties. Influenced by these reflections, the people rejected Marcius, and elected others to the office.

The senators were very much incensed at this action of the commons, which they regarded as directed against them rather than against Marcius. But he for his part bitterly resented his rejection, and gave free vent to his anger. Unfortunately, he appeared to think that there was something great and noble in freely expressing his angry feelings, and his character was wanting in that calmness and moderation which are the chief political virtues. He went away from the meeting-place greatly disturbed by his defeat, and full of bitterness against the people. Some of the proudest and most high-spirited of the nobility, who were devoted to him as their instructor in war and their leader in every expedition, further inflamed his anger by their words.

In the meantime great stores of corn were brought to Rome, some bought from other parts of Italy, and some sent as a present from the King of Syracuse. Affairs appeared, therefore, to be in a more encouraging state, and it was hoped that the troubles which disturbed the city would disappear with the scarcity of food which had given rise to them. The senate was immediately called together, and the people stood about in crowds awaiting the decision as to the disposal of the food. They expected that the corn which had been bought would be sold at a moderate rate, and that the supplies which had been sent as a gift would be distributed free. Some of the senators proposed that this should be done. Marcius, however, stood up, strongly censured those who spoke in favour of the commons, and called them traitors to their order. He told the senate that by yielding to some extent to the demands of the people, they had encouraged their insolence and disorder. Instead, therefore, of yielding further to their demands with regard to the distribution of the corn, they should seek rather to take from them the privileges which had already been granted. Especially, Marcius declared, should they abolish the office of the tribunes of the people, by whose appointment the authority of the consuls had been lessened.

This speech was hailed with delight by the young senators and most of the rich men. Some of the older men, however, foresaw the consequences, and opposed his proposals. They were indeed justified, for the result was disastrous. The tribunes who were present, seeing that there would be a majority in the senate in favour of the proposals, ran out to the people assembled without, and called upon them to rally to the support of their own magistrates. A tumultuous mob soon gathered together, and when the speech of Marcius was recited, the people were on the point of breaking into the senate. The tribunes, however, dissuaded them, and succeeded in directing the fury of the mob especially upon Marcius. They impeached him in due form, and sent for him to come and make his defence.

The messengers who were sent on this errand, however, were spurned away. The tribunes then went themselves with their attendant officers to lay hands upon Coriolanus and bring him by force. Upon this the patricians rallied to his defence. They drove off the tribunes and beat their officers until, at length, nightfall put an end for a time to the struggle.

Early next morning crowds of the enraged commons began to flock to the Forum from all quarters. The consuls were now greatly alarmed at the outlook. They hastily convened the senate, and proposed that in the present dangerous position of affairs they should use their best efforts to allay the anger of the commons.

The majority of the senate agreed in the wisdom of this course. The consuls, therefore, went out to the people and did all they could to pacify them. Though they complained of the tumultuous behaviour of the commons, they spoke favourably to them, and declared that, as to the price of the corn and other provisions, there should be no cause of difference between the senate and the populace.

A great part of the people were moved by the speech of the consuls, and it was evident that they were ready to compose their difference with the senate. The tribunes, however, interposed. They declared, that since the senate spoke thus moderately, the commons for their part were willing to meet them in the same spirit. They insisted, however, that Marcius should come before them, and answer to the charges of inciting the senate to destroy the privileges of the people; of refusing to obey the summons of the tribunes, and of beating their officers and thus stirring up civil war. The object of the tribunes was, either to humble the proud spirit of Marcius if he should submit, or, in the event of his refusing, which they deemed the more probable event, for they knew the man, to make the quarrel between him and the commons incurable.

Marcius stood before the people as if he intended to make his defence, and the populace stood in silence awaiting what he had to say. But when he began to speak, instead of the submissive language they had expected, the commons heard a bold accusation of themselves. Moreover, not only his words, but also his haughty tone and fierce looks, expressed his scorn and contempt for them. Then his hearers lost all patience, and the boldest of the tribunes, after consulting with his colleagues, proclaimed that the tribunes condemned Marcius to death, and called upon their officers to seize him, carry him to the Tarpeian rock, and there hurl him over the precipice. However, when the officers came to lay hands upon him, many, even of the plebeians, were shocked at the idea, while the patricians at once ran with loud shouts to his assistance. Some of them surrounded him to prevent his arrest, while others besought the people to think better of their decision. But in the tumult little regard was paid to words and entreaties for a time. It was soon evident, however, that Marcius could not be taken without much bloodshed, and the friends of the tribunes therefore besought them to alter the unlawful sentence they had pronounced, and to promise that a fair trial should be given to their antagonist. Somewhat moved by these appeals, the tribune who had called for the execution of Coriolanus asked the patricians by what right they took Marcius out of the hands of the people. The nobles answered by another question: 'By what right,' said they, 'do you dare to attempt to drag one of the worthiest citizens of Rome to a dreadful and unlawful death?'

'If that be all your complaint,' said the tribune, 'you shall have no further pretext for your opposition to the people, for the man shall have his trial. You, Marcius, we cite to appear on the third market-day, then to satisfy the people of your innocence if you can. By their votes your fate shall be decided.' The nobles had to be satisfied with this compromise, and withdrew, thinking themselves fortunate in being able to carry Marcius off upon any terms.

The third market-day was yet some while off, and as war broke out against the people of Antium, the senate had some hopes of evading bringing the matter to the judgment of the commons. Peace, however, was soon made, and the senate met frequently in order to find means, if possible, of refusing to give up Marcius to judgment without causing further trouble with the plebeians. The boldest of the senators declared that their order would be ruined if they once allowed the right of the commons to sit in judgment upon one of their number. Others, however, were of opinion that it was wiser to give way to the demand.

When Marcius saw that the senators, perplexed between regard for him and fear of the violence of the people, were undecided how to act, he spoke himself to the tribunes. 'What accusation,' said he, 'do you bring against me, and upon what charge am I to be tried before the people?' They answered that he would be tried for treason against the commonwealth, and for designing to set himself up as a tyrant. 'If that is the charge,' said Marcius, 'I refuse no form of trial, and am ready to make my defence to the people, provided that no other charge is made against me.' The tribunes agreed to this condition, and promised that the trial should turn upon the point of treason to the commonwealth alone.

When the people were assembled, however, the first thing the tribunes did was to alter the method by which it had long been the custom for the votes to be taken. They contrived thus to give the balance of power to the meanest and most turbulent of the people, who were by their device enabled to outvote those who were of some standing and character, and who had borne arms in the service of the state. In the next place, notwithstanding their promise, they passed over the charge against Marcius of treason in seeking to make himself master of the commonwealth. Instead, they brought up his speech against lowering the price of corn, and for abolishing the office of the tribunes. Moreover, they advanced quite a new charge, namely that he had divided the spoils of his expedition against Antium amongst the volunteers who had followed him, instead of bringing them into the public treasury.

The last charge, being quite unexpected, confused Marcius the most, and the praise which, in his reply, he gave to his followers in the expedition only served to incense those who had refused to serve in that war. Thus it came about that he was condemned, the sentence being perpetual banishment from Rome.

The commons looked upon the sentence as a great victory for their order, and showed more elation at their triumph than ever they did at a victory on the battlefield. In the streets of Rome it was not necessary to look at the dress or any marks of distinction to tell which man was a patrician and which a plebeian. He whose face showed exultation was a plebeian, and he whose looks revealed dejection was a patrician.

But, amidst the triumph of enemies and the dejection of friends, Marcius himself stood unmoved and unhumbled. His carriage was still haughty, and his countenance composed, but his calm concealed hot anger and fiery indignation. First he repaired to his own house, and there embraced his weeping wife and mother, and besought them to bear his banishment with fortitude. Then he hastened to one of the city gates, whither he was conducted by the whole body of patricians. Thus, asking nothing and receiving nothing at any man's hand, he left Rome.

Coriolanus spent the next few days at some of his farms near the city. His mind was agitated by a thousand different thoughts which anger and resentment prompted, and by plans from which he sought not advantage for himself, but revenge against the people of Rome. At last he determined to stir up a bitter war between Rome and some neighbouring people. For this purpose he determined first of all to approach the Volscians, for he knew that they were still strong in men and in wealth, and he judged that they were rather embittered against Rome than absolutely subdued by their former defeats.

There was, dwelling at the town of Antium, a certain man named Tullus Aufidius, who was highly distinguished among the Volscians for his courage, wealth, and noble birth. Marcius was well aware that of all the Romans he himself was the most hated by Tullus, for the two warriors had in several engagements exchanged threats and defiances, and had thus added personal enmity to the hatred which existed between their nations. Nevertheless, Marcius determined to approach Tullus with regard to the design which he had formed. He knew that, more than any of the other Volscians, his former enemy longed to be revenged upon the Romans for the evils which his country had suffered at their hands. Marcius therefore disguised himself and in the evening stole into the town of which he had been so bitter an enemy. Though he met many people in the streets, no one recognised him, and he passed without hindrance through the place until he came to the house of Tullus. He at once entered, made his way to the fireplace without saying a word, and, covering his face, calmly sat down. The people of the house were much astonished at the curious proceedings of the stranger, but there was so much dignity in his appearance that they did not disturb him, but went and told Tullus, who was at supper, of the unknown visitor. Their master at once rose from the table, and coming to the place where Coriolanus sat by the fireplace, asked him who he was, and upon what business he had come.

Coriolanus uncovered his face, paused awhile, and then spoke thus. 'If thou dost not know me, Tullus, I must be my own accuser. I am Caius Marcius, who have brought many evils upon the Volscians, whereof my other name, Coriolanus, is sufficient proof. That name is now the only reward left to me for all my labours and exploits; of everything else I have been stripped through the malice of the commons and the cowardice of those of my own order. Therefore have I come to you to offer my services to the Volscians that I may avenge them and myself upon Rome. Be assured that I shall fight better for you than ever I did against you.'

Tullus was delighted to hear Marcius speak thus.

Taking him by the hand, he said, 'Rise, Marcius, and be of good courage. The offer which you make of yourself is beyond all value. The Volscians, I assure you, will not be ungrateful.' He then led him to his table, and entertained him honourably. For the next few days the two consulted earnestly about the proposed war against Rome. Meanwhile that city was still greatly disturbed by the enmity between the nobles and the commons, which indeed had been increased by the recent expulsion of Coriolanus.

Tullus and Marcius, therefore, in secret conference with the principal Volscians, begged them to avail themselves of these dissensions, and to fall upon the Romans while they were thus weakened. There was, however, a truce for two years with Rome, and the more honourable of the Volscians shrank from the disgrace of breaking the pact. A pretext for doing so was, however, furnished by the Romans, for, acting upon some suspicion or false report, they proclaimed, on the occasion of certain public games, that all the Volscians who were in the city should leave it before sunset. Some say that this was done in consequence of a stratagem of Marcius, who, it is said, caused false intelligence to be taken to the consuls to the effect that the Volscians intended to attack the Romans during the games and to set fire to the city.

The proclamation greatly exasperated the Volscians, and Tullus was careful to feed their resentment and to magnify the insult. By so doing he at last persuaded them to send ambassadors to Rome, to demand that all the lands and cities which had been taken from the Volscians in the late war should be restored. The senate of Rome heard these demands with indignation, and replied that the Volscians might indeed be the first, if they pleased, to take up arms in spite of the truce, but that, if they did, the Romans would be the last to lay them down.

Tullus now called a general assembly of his countrymen and advised them to send for Marcius. He urged them to forget the injuries their former enemy had inflicted upon them, and assured his hearers that those evils would be far outweighed by the benefits which Marcius could confer upon them as their ally. The Roman was accordingly sent for, and made a speech to the assembly. His hearers now found that he could speak as well as fight, and perceived that he possessed ability as well as courage. They therefore willingly appointed him as general in conjunction with Tullus.

Marcius, thus made general, feared that much time would be lost in preparations for the war, and that the favourable opportunity for attacking the Romans would thus be lost. Therefore, leaving the magistrates of Antium to collect troops and necessary stores for the war, he set out with a body of volunteers, but without any regular levy of troops, and raided the Roman territories. There he made so much booty that the Volscians found it difficult either to consume it in camp or to carry it off. But the injury he inflicted upon the Romans by the loss of all this spoil was of less consequence than the harm he contrived that the raid should cause them by increasing the suspicion and dislike between the nobles and the commons. For, while Marcius ravaged the whole countryside, he was very careful to spare the lands of the patricians, and to prevent their goods from being carried off. Hence, while the nobles blamed the commons for causing the present troubles by the unjust expulsion of Marcius, the people, for their part, accused the patricians of inciting him to attack their lands out of a spirit of revenge. Thus Marcius attained his object of increasing the division between the two parties, while at the same time his success increased the warlike confidence of the Volscians. When he was satisfied that he had accomplished these objects, he drew off his troops without hindrance.

Meanwhile the Volscian forces had been assembled with great rapidity. So numerous were they, that it was decided to divide them into two parts, of which one was to be left to garrison the Volscian towns, while the other marched to attack Rome. Coriolanus then left it to Tullus to decide which of the two bodies he would command. The Volscian replied that his colleague was not at all his inferior in valour, and hitherto had been more successful. Therefore Tullus considered that the Roman general should lead the attacking army, while he himself saw to the defence of the towns and to the supply of stores to the invaders.

Marcius, thus given sole command of the attacking force, first marched against a Roman colony which, as it surrendered without resistance, he would not suffer to be plundered. Next he laid waste the lands of the Latins, expecting that the Romans would be forced to risk a battle in defence of this people, since they were their allies. The Latins sent urgent messages to Rome praying for assistance. But the commons showed no eagerness in the cause, and the consuls, whose term of office was nearly expired, would not run any risk. The Latins were therefore left to their own resources. Town after town which resisted the Volscian army was carried by assault, the inhabitants sold as slaves and the houses plundered, though Marcius was careful to spare such as surrendered voluntarily to him. At last he arrived at a town but little more than twelve miles from the walls of Rome. There he put to the sword almost all who were of an age to bear arms, and took much plunder.

These successes so excited the Volscians that those who had been left to garrison the towns came hurrying to join his army, declaring that they would have no other general but him. Indeed, his fame spread throughout Italy, for all were astonished that one man could make so vast a change in the position of affairs.

But in spite of the pressing danger, disorder and confusion continued in Rome. The commons still refused to fight, and spent their time in plotting, in making seditious speeches, and in complaints against the nobles. But a most wonderful change occurred when news came that Coriolanus had laid siege to Lavinium, where the sacred symbols of the gods were kept, and whence the Romans derived their origin, since it was the first city built by their ancestor Æneas. For, strangely enough, the commons now proposed to recall Coriolanus and reverse the sentence against him, while, still more strangely, the senate rejected the proposal. Either the senate was moved by a perverse spirit of opposition to everything which the commons proposed, or they were now filled with resentment against Coriolanus because he sought the total ruin of Rome, though he had only been injured by a part, and that the least notable part, of the citizens.

The news of the attitude of the nobles still further enraged Coriolanus. Quitting the siege of Lavinium, he marched in a fury against Rome, and encamped some five miles from its walls. The appearance of his army struck terror to the citizens; the women ran through the streets uttering cries of despair, the aged with tears prayed for succour at the altars of the gods, all courage and all counsel were quelled by fear.

But the terror which damped the valour of the Romans also stifled their quarrels. The senate saw their folly in refusing the wish of the commons for the recall of Coriolanus, and in indulging their anger against him at a time when they were powerless to protect themselves. All were now ready to agree to the sending of ambassadors to offer Coriolanus liberty to return to the city, and to beseech him to put an end to the war. For this purpose a number of senators were chosen, and, as they were all either friends or relations of Coriolanus, they doubted nothing of a favourable reception. But when they came to the Volscian camp they found a greeting other than they had expected. Being led through the host of their enemies, they came at last to the place where Coriolanus was seated in council with a number of the great officers of his army. He received them as strangers, and, with an air of great haughtiness and severity, bade them declare the business which had brought them. With a humility that befitted the present position of their affairs, the ambassadors delivered the petition of the Roman senate.

When they had spoken, Coriolanus answered in words which showed much bitterness and the deep resentment he felt against Rome. Further, as general of the Volscians, he demanded that the Romans should restore all the lands and cities they had taken in former wars, and that they should admit the Volscians to the freedom of their city. He gave them thirty days to consider his demands, and, having dismissed them, at once withdrew his army from the Roman territories.

There were not lacking among the Volscians men to misrepresent the action of Coriolanus in this matter. Among these was Tullus, who was moved not by any injury which he had received, but by envy and jealousy at finding himself displaced by Marcius from the first place in the esteem of the Volscians, who now looked upon Coriolanus as their chief leader. Private hints were first thrown out by the dissatisfied, and then the murmurings grew that Coriolanus had acted treasonably to their cause. True, he had not betrayed either their cities or their armies, but, said they, his treason was shown by his allowing the Romans a respite of thirty days in which they might compose their differences and re-establish their strength.

The delay, however, was not spent idly by Coriolanus. He wasted the lands of the allies of Rome, and, in the space of the thirty days, took seven large and populous towns to which the Romans did not venture to send any help. Indeed, that people seemed suddenly to become as lacking in warlike spirit as if their bodies had been smitten with palsy.

When the term was expired, Coriolanus again appeared before Rome with all his forces. The citizens then sent another embassy to him, imploring him to lay aside his resentment and to draw off the Volscian army. He replied that, as general of the Volscians, he would give them no answer, but, as one who was still a Roman citizen, he advised them to humble themselves, and to come to him within three days to express their full submission to the demands he had made. He warned them also that, if they decided otherwise than as he advised, it would not be safe for them to come again to his camp with nothing but empty words.

When the ambassadors reported the ill-success of their mission, the senate was almost in despair. As a last resource, it was decided to send all the priests of the gods, the ministers of the sacred mysteries and the diviners to endeavour to bend Coriolanus from his purpose. They went forth, therefore, wearing their robes and carrying the symbols of their sacred offices, and came to the Volscian camp. Coriolanus did indeed suffer them to be admitted to his presence, but he showed them no other favour, and treated them as sternly as he had the other ambassadors. He bade them, in short, either accept his former proposals, or prepare for war.

When the priests returned, the Romans felt that they had exhausted all their resources. They resolved to keep close within the city, and to defend the walls, but they had little hope except that perchance some accident might occur to save them. Everywhere there reigned terror and confusion and forebodings of coming disaster.

In this time of peril and dismay, an inspiration came to a certain noble lady named Valeria, who with many others of the most illustrious matrons of Rome was making her supplications for the preservation of the city in one of the temples. Acting upon a divine impulse which suggested a means by which Rome might yet be saved, she rose and called upon the other noble matrons in the temple to proceed with her to the house of Volumnia, the mother of Coriolanus. When they entered they found Volumnia seated, with her son's children upon her lap and his wife by her side. The Roman matrons approached, and, speaking for her companions, Valeria said: 'We come to you, Volumnia and Virgilia, not by any orders of senate or consuls, but in the name of our common womanhood. For we believe that our gods, hearing our prayers, put it into our minds to come to you to beseech you to accompany us to the camp of Coriolanus. For if you can by your prayers save the city, greater will be your glory than that of the Sabine women who charged the mortal enmity between their fathers and their husbands to peace and friendship.'

After Valeria had spoken thus, and the other matrons had joined in the appeal, Volumnia replied. 'We share,' said she, 'in the general misfortune of our country. But we are, my friends, especially unhappy since Marcius is lost to us, his glory dimmed and his virtue gone, and we see him surrounded by the enemies of his country, not as a prisoner, but as their commander. And to us it appears a calamity that Rome has become so weak that she must needs repose her hopes upon us women. For ourselves, we know not whether Marcius will have any regard for us, since he has none for his country, which he was wont to place before mother and wife and children. Take us, however, and do with us as you please. If we can do nothing more, we can at least die at his feet in beseeching safety for Rome.'

So, taking the children of Virgilia with her, Volumnia went with the other matrons of Rome to the Volscian camp. When they approached, Coriolanus, who was seated upon the tribunal with the chief officers of his army, was greatly surprised and agitated. He endeavoured, however, to retain his wonted sternness of appearance, though he perceived his wife and mother at the head of the party. But feelings of affection mastered him; he descended from the tribunal, and hurried to meet them. First he embraced his mother, then his wife, and afterwards his children, nor could he refrain from tears and other signs of natural affection.

At length, seeing that his mother desired to speak, he called his Volscian counsellors around him, and Volumnia thus set forth the purpose of her mission: 'You see, my son, by the sadness of our looks and our attire, the sorrow which your banishment has brought upon us. And think within yourself whether we are not the most unhappy among women, since the sight of you, which should have been the most pleasing to our hearts, is now the most dreadful. For Volumnia beholds her son and Virgilia her husband encamped as an enemy before the walls of his native city. Nor is the last consolation, prayer to the gods, left to us, for we cannot at the same time beseech them for our country and for you. Your wife and children must either see Rome perish or yourself. As for myself, I will not live to see this quarrel decided by the fortune of war. If I cannot persuade you to bring friendship between your countrymen and your present allies, then you must advance against Rome by trampling on the body of the mother who bore you. For it is not meet that Volumnia should live to see the day when her son shall either triumph over his native city, or be led a captive through its streets.'

Coriolanus listened to his mother while she spoke thus. But he made no reply, and, after waiting a long time whilst he still stood silent, Volumnia spoke again. 'Why are you silent, my son?' said she. 'Do you consider it a point of honour to guide yourself only by anger and revenge, and a disgrace to grant your mother's petition? Is it becoming for a great man to remember only the injuries that have been done him, and to forget the benefits he has received from his parents? Surely you, of all men, who have suffered so severely from ingratitude, should be most sensible to the claims of gratitude. The most sacred feelings of nature and of religion call upon you to grant my prayer, but if words will not prevail, this course only is left.' So saying, she, with Virgilia and her children, threw themselves at the feet of Coriolanus.

'O mother!' cried he, as he raised her from the

ground and tenderly pressed her hand, 'what is this that you have done? You have won a victory glorious for your country, but ruinous for me. I go, conquered by you, not by the arms of Rome.'

Next morning he drew off the army of the Volscians, amongst whom there were diverse opinions upon what had happened. Some blamed Coriolanus; others, who were inclined for peace, had no fault to find; while yet others, though they disagreed with the withdrawal from Rome, nevertheless could not find it in their hearts to blame the general for yielding to his mother's prayers.

In Rome it seemed as though the citizens had never been so sensible of the terrible danger which threatened the city as they were now that it was over. For immediately that they perceived from the walls that the Volscian army was being drawn off, all the temples were thrown open and were at once crowded with people, crowned with garlands, who offered sacrifices as for some great victory. In nothing did their joy appear more plainly than in the honour and gratitude which they paid to the women of Rome, to whom both senate and people ascribed the preservation of the city. In memory thereof the senate ordered that a temple should be built to the *Fortune of Women* at the public charge.

When Coriolanus returned to Antium, Tullus, who now both hated and feared him, resolved to compass his death. He therefore got together a number of persons to join him in the plot, and then called upon Coriolanus to lay down his authority as general and

CORIOLANUS AND THE MATRONS OF ROME

to render an account of his conduct to the Volscians. To this demand Coriolanus replied that, since he had received the office from the Volscian people, he was ready to surrender it if they so desired, but not otherwise. He further declared that he was prepared at once to give an account of his behaviour to the people of Antium if they wished him to do so.

The people of the town being therefore assembled, certain orators endeavoured, in accordance with the plan which had been formed, to stir them up against Coriolanus. But when the general stood up to speak the violence of the tumult abated, and it appeared that the best part of the people were ready to hear him fairly, and to judge him with justice. Tullus was therefore afraid that he would escape, the more so as he was an eloquent man, and had, in spite of the withdrawal from Rome, rendered great services to the state. Therefore he and his fellow-plotters determined to act at once. Crying out that such a traitor ought not to be heard, nor suffered to play the tyrant over the Volscians, they rushed upon him in a body, and slew him upon the spot, no man present lifting a hand in his defence. Nevertheless it soon appeared that the deed had not the general approval of the Volscians, for they gave his body an honourable burial and adorned his monument with spoils and arms as became a mighty warrior and general. As for the Romans, they received the news of his death without any sign either of favour or of hatred. But they permitted the women of the city at their request to go into mourning for him for ten months, that being the term of mourning assigned by the laws for the loss of a father, a son, or a brother.

Events soon proved how necessary the abilities of Coriolanus were to the Volscians. First they became involved in a quarrel with their allies in which they lost many men, and afterwards they were defeated in battle by the Romans. There Tullus and the flower of their army were slain, and the Volscians were obliged to submit to humiliating terms of peace which made them subject to Rome.

THE GRACCHI

THE two Gracchi, brothers in blood, were both inspired with the sense of the evils produced by the decrease in the number of freemen and the increase in the number of slaves in the Roman state, and by the tendency of wealth to pass more and more into the hands of the few at the expense of the many.

Both Tiberius and Caius set themselves to remedy these evils, and, just as they were alike in the objects to which they devoted their lives, so they were also alike in suffering cruel and unjust deaths at the hands of their opponents.

Both brothers were inspired by noble and worthy motives, but of the two Tiberius, the elder, was the nobler and purer character. It must, however, be allowed that even Tiberius, in the heat of party strife, broke the laws in order to attain his ends. The handle which he gave to his enemies by so doing furnishes, however, little or no excuse for his brutal murder.

Caius, moved by a more fiery and vehement temper, and also perhaps by resentment at his brother's fate, was more violent and headstrong in his measures, and less free from personal ambition than Tiberius. Indeed, it is generally admitted that, though most of his measures *effected useful reforms, yet some were injurious to the state in the long-run. Nothing, however, can excuse the means by which the senate succeeded in compassing his death.*

The murders of the Gracchi and of their adherents mark the beginning of the series of bloody reigns of terror by which triumphant political parties avenged themselves upon their opponents during the latter years of the Roman Republic. The death of the two brothers left the nobles triumphant, until there arose to power the terrible, low-born Caius Marius, who took savage vengeance upon their party. Indeed, this violent and bloodthirsty party spirit in Rome furnishes the key to much that you will read in those lives which follow in this book; the lives of the Gracchi, of Caius Marius, of Julius Cæsar, and of Brutus.

Tiberius Gracchus perished in 133 B.C., Caius twelve years later.

TIBERIUS GRACCHUS

THE two Gracchi, Tiberius and Caius, were the sons of Tiberius Gracchus, who, though he was once censor, twice consul, and celebrated two triumphs, was even more distinguished for his virtues than his dignities. Hence, after the death of Scipio, the conqueror of Hannibal, he was deemed worthy to marry Cornelia, the daughter of that great man, although he had been rather at variance with Scipio than on terms of friendship with him.

The story is told that Tiberius once caught a pair of serpents, male and female, upon his bed. He consulted the seers as to what this strange event might mean, and was advised by them that he should neither kill both the serpents nor suffer both to live. Further, they told him that if he killed the male serpent his own death would follow, while if he killed the female his wife Cornelia would die. Now Tiberius loved his wife dearly, and, as he was much older than she, deemed it fitter that he should die rather than Cornelia. He therefore killed the male serpent and allowed the female to escape. Not long after he died, leaving no fewer than twelve children to the care of his wife. The sole charge of the house and children now fell upon Cornelia, and so nobly did she discharge her trust, and with such affection and wisdom, that it seemed Tiberius had not judged ill in choosing to die for such a woman. A monarch, Ptolemy, King of Egypt, paid his court to her and offered her a seat upon his throne, but she refused him.

All her children died during the time of her widowhood except three; a daughter, who married the younger Scipio, and two sons, Tiberius and Caius. These children were brought up with such care by Cornelia that they were considered to owe more to their training than to the gifts of nature, though they belonged to the noblest family in Rome, and were gifted beyond all others in mind and character.

While the two brothers strongly resembled each other in courage, in temperance of life, in generosity and in eloquence, yet there appeared no small difference between them in their actions and in their conduct of political affairs.

In the first place, Tiberius was gentle in manner and calm in behaviour, while Caius was fiery and energetic. This difference was shown in their different styles of speaking in public. Tiberius stood still and used gestures but little. But Caius strode from one end of the platform to the other and often threw his gown from his shoulder. His oratory was full of passion and of a kind to excite terror and fear, while the speech of Tiberius was of a gentler nature, and awakened the softer emotion of pity. Tiberius used well-chosen words and polished language, while Caius was more splendid and forcible in diction.

Similarly, Tiberius lived in a very plain and simple manner, while Caius, though moderate in comparison with other young Romans of his position, seemed luxurious when compared with his brother.

The differences between the brothers in speech and mode of living reflected the difference in their characters. Caius was aware that his ardent nature often caused him to lose control of himself when speaking, and led him to raise his voice too high, to indulge in words of abuse, and to lose the thread of his speech. He was, therefore, accustomed to station one of his servants, a sensible fellow, behind him when he was speaking, with orders to sound a note of warning upon a pitch-pipe whenever his master was beginning to show signs of anger and to raise his voice too high.

Such was the difference between the brothers. But, in the courage which they displayed against the enemies of the state, in their justice towards their fellow-citizens, in the sense of duty which guided their public actions, they were perfectly alike.

Tiberius was the elder of the two by nine years, and hence it came about that their work in political matters took place at different times. This was a great misfortune, for, could they have acted together, their strength would have been greater, and might well have been irresistible.

As the young Tiberius grew into manhood, he gained a great reputation for one of his years. This is shown by the following story. Appius Claudius, who had been both consul and censor, and whose merit had raised him to the rank of President of the Senate, took occasion at a public entertainment to address Tiberius, and to offer him the hand of his daughter in marriage. Tiberius was sensible of the honour, and gladly accepted the proposal. When Appius returned home, he called out to his wife directly he entered the house and told her that he had arranged for the marriage of Claudia their daughter. 'Why so suddenly as all this?' answered his wife. 'What is the need for such haste, unless, indeed, Tiberius Gracchus is the man you have chosen?'

Tiberius served in Africa under the younger Scipio, who had married his sister, and he was, therefore, on intimate terms with his general. He lived in Scipio's tent, so that he learned much from the general's genius and mental powers, which daily gave him subjects for admiration and imitation. Tiberius, indeed, excelled all others of his age in the army in discipline and courage. At the siege of a certain town he was the first to scale the walls.

After this expedition he was appointed quæstor, and it became his duty to accompany the consul Mancinus in the Numantian war. The consul was not lacking in courage, but nevertheless showed himself one of the most unfortunate generals the Romans ever had. But amidst a series of reverses and disasters Tiberius distinguished himself, not only by his courage and ability, but by the respect which he showed to his general in his misfortunes.

After having lost several important battles, Mancinus endeavoured to draw off his army by night.

The enemy, however, detected the movement, seized the Roman camp and, attacking the retreating army, cut up the rear. Indeed, they surrounded the whole force and drove the Romans into rough and broken ground, whence there seemed no chance of escape. Mancinus despaired of cutting his way through with the sword, and sent a herald to his foes to beg for a truce and to ask for conditions of peace.

The Numantians, however, refused to treat with the herald, and declared that Tiberius must be sent, for they would have dealings with no other. Their reason for this was partly respect for Tiberius himself, and partly respect for the memory of his father, whose honour and faith their people had experienced beforetime.

Accordingly Tiberius was sent as envoy to the enemy. By giving way on some points he gained others, and was thus the means of making a peace which saved the lives of twenty thousand citizens of Rome, in addition to the slaves and other followers of the army.

However, the Numantians carried off as plunder everything that was left in the Roman camp, and, amongst other things, the books which contained the accounts which Tiberius had kept as quæstor. These accounts were of great importance to him, and therefore, when he discovered their loss, he returned with a few friends to Numantia, although the army was upon the march. When he arrived, he called out the magistrates from the place, and asked them to restore the books. He pointed out that enemies might take the opportunity to accuse him of misuse of the public money if they learnt that he had lost the volumes, which alone contained the evidence to rebut such false charges.

The Numantians were pleased to have the opportunity of obliging him, and invited him to enter their city. As he stood debating in his mind the wisdom of doing so, they came up to him, took him by the hand, and begged him no longer to look upon them as enemies, but to have confidence in them as friends. Tiberius decided to trust them, and entered the town. There they first invited him to take food with them, and afterwards not only restored his books but also asked him to accept whatever else he chose from the plunder. Tiberius, however, would accept nothing except some frankincense, to be used in public sacrifices to the gods. He then embraced his former foes, and took his departure.

When he returned to Rome, he found the people very angry about the peace, which they considered a dishonour to the Roman arms. Tiberius was therefore in considerable danger, but the relatives and friends of the soldiers whose lives had been saved by the treaty made up a considerable part of the people, and they united to save him. They laid all the blame of the disgrace upon the consul, and said that as for Tiberius he had rendered the state great service by saving the lives of so many citizens. The general body of the people, however, would by no means allow the peace to stand. They demanded that the example of their ancestors should be followed, who, when their generals made a similar peace, sent the chief officers of the army back naked to

TIBERIUS GRACCHUS

the enemy, as being the ones responsible for the breach of the treaty through agreeing to such terms.

The people, however, showed on this occasion a great affection for Tiberius. For instead of sending back the quæstors and tribunes as well as the consul, as their ancestors had done, they decreed that Mancinus alone, naked and in chains, should be delivered up to the Numantians, but that the rest should be spared for the sake of Tiberius. Scipio, who at the time had great power and influence at Rome, appears to have helped to procure this decree.

It is probable that Tiberius would never have fallen into the misfortunes which ruined him, if Scipio had been at home to aid him in political matters. He was, however, engaged in war with Numantia when Tiberius was bold enough to propose his new laws.

These land laws of Tiberius arose from the following facts. It had formerly been the custom when Rome won new territory from neighbouring states to dispose of it in this manner. A part was sold, another part was added to the public lands, and the rest was divided among the needy citizens on condition of a small rent being paid to the public treasury. But when the rich began to oppress the poor and to shut them out from the land entirely unless they paid extravagant rents, a law was passed that no man should hold more than five hundred acres of land. This law checked the greed of the rich for a time, and the poor possessed their lands at the old rents. But after a while their rich neighbours began to seize upon their lands and to hold them, at first in the names of other persons, and then, as they grew bolder, in their own. After the poor Romans were thus driven out, the lands were cultivated for the rich by slaves and foreigners, and thus there was a lack of freemen all over Italy.

Lælius, a friend of Scipio, made some attempt to remedy these abuses, but, when he found that the opposition was very powerful, he gave up the idea, for he feared that his reforms could only be carried by the sword. But no sooner was Tiberius appointed Tribune of the People than he engaged in this very undertaking.

Some say that he was incited to do this by the complaint of his mother that she was known as the mother-in-law of Scipio and not as the mother of the Gracchi. But his brother Caius relates that when Tiberius was passing through Tuscany, he was filled with sorrow to see the countryside stripped of husbandmen and shepherds and almost uninhabited, save for the foreign slaves who tilled the lands of the rich, and that he then formed the plans which were to bring such great misfortunes upon himself and his brother. Certainly the people themselves incited him to become the champion of their cause, for on the porches, the walls, and the monuments of the city they put up writings beseeching him to restore their share of the public lands to the poor.

Tiberius did not frame the law without consulting some of the Romans most distinguished for virtue and position. And, indeed, a more moderate law was never made to remedy so much injustice and oppression, for those who deserved punishment for taking away the rights of the people and holding lands contrary to law were to be compensated for giving up their groundless claims. Moderate though the proposals were, they satisfied the commons, who were content to overlook the past, provided their rights were safeguarded for the future.

Nevertheless, the rich opposed the law out of greed, and assailed Tiberius with hatred and malice. They endeavoured to raise prejudice against the design, by asserting that he wanted to throw everything into disorder and to overturn the constitution. They failed, however, for, in a cause so just and glorious, the eloquence of Tiberius, which might well have carried less worthy proposals, was irresistible. Great was he when, from the public platform, he pleaded for the poor in such words as these:

'The wild beasts of our country have caves in which to shelter, but for the brave men, who have shed their blood in her cause, there is nothing but air and light. Houseless and homeless, they wander from place to place with their wives and children. What a mockery it is when the generals at the head of their armies exhort the soldiers to fight for the tombs of their ancestors and the gods of their hearths! For among all those numbers of men, there is perhaps not one Roman who has an altar that belonged to his forefathers or a sepulchre in which their ashes rest. The common soldiers fight and die to increase the luxury of those already rich and great, and those Romans, who are called the masters of the world, have not a foot of ground to call their own.'

Such speeches, delivered by a man whose heart glowed with interest in the cause, filled the people with enthusiasm, so that none of his opponents dared to answer him. They therefore gave up the attempt to debate the matter, and applied themselves to work upon another of the tribunes named Marcus Octavius. Now, the power of the tribunes lies chiefly in the negative vote, for if one of them stands out the rest can do nothing. At first Octavius was unwilling to oppose Tiberius, who was his friend, but when a number of the men of the highest rank applied to him, he gave way and prevented the passing of the law.

Tiberius was incensed by this. He now dropped his first moderate proposals, and brought in a more drastic measure by which the holders were commanded to give up immediately the lands which they held contrary to the laws. Daily disputes on the new bill arose in public between Tiberius and Octavius, but, even in the heat of debate, they used no abusive or insulting language concerning one another.

Tiberius saw that Octavius would suffer personal loss if the proposals were passed, because he held more land than the law allowed. He therefore offered, though his own fortune was not great, to make up out of his means whatever loss Octavius might sustain, if only he would withdraw his opposition and allow the law to pass. But Octavius refused to accept the offer.

Tiberius now endeavoured to force the passage of his Agrarian Law by bringing the machinery of the state to a standstill. He forbade the other magistrates to exercise the functions of their offices, and he set his own seal upon the Temple of Saturn, so that no moneys should be taken out, or paid into, the treasury. These measures aroused such resentment that a number of the wealthy Romans went the length of bribing assassins to murder Tiberius, who, to protect himself, was obliged to take to carrying a long narrow sword such as robbers use.

When the day of the voting came, some of the urns used for the ballot were carried off by partisans of the rich, and great confusion was thus caused. Those who were supporting Tiberius were in numbers sufficient to carry the point by force, and seemed about to do so. Then two men of consular rank approached Tiberius, fell at his feet, and with tears and prayers besought him not to carry this purpose into execution. He himself now recognised the dreadful consequences of such an attempt. He referred the matter again to the senate, but the influence of the rich was so great in that body, that nothing came of the debates on the measure.

Tiberius then adopted a plan which was neither moderate nor just. He resolved, since there appeared to be no other way of getting the law passed, to remove Octavius from the tribuneship. First, however, he again besought him to give way, but met with a refusal. Then he declared that since they differed on a point of such prime importance, it was impossible for both to continue in office. He proposed, therefore, that they should abide by the popular vote, as to which of them should resign office. This proposal also was rejected by Octavius.

Next day Tiberius convoked the assembly and, as Octavius still refused to agree to his proposals, put to the vote a decree depriving him of office. When, of the thirty-five tribes, seventeen had already given their vote in favour of this, and but one more was wanted to carry the decree, Tiberius stopped the proceedings, and once more besought his colleague to yield. Octavius listened, not without emotion, but with a firmness that cannot but be admired, refused and bade Tiberius do his worst. The bill therefore was passed, and Tiberius then ordered one of his freedmen to pull down Octavius from his tribunal. This shameful manner of expulsion should have awakened the compassion of the mob, but, so far from feeling pity, they attacked the expelled tribune. Indeed, it would have gone hard with him, had not a body of the landed party come to his rescue, and kept off the mob so that he escaped with his life. But such was the fury of the mob that one of his servants, who put himself in front of his master in order to shield him, had his eyes torn out by the raging crowd. This outbreak was quite against the wishes of Tiberius, and he hastened to do his utmost to appease the fury of the people.

The Agrarian Law was then confirmed, and three men were appointed to attend to the survey and distribution of the lands. They were Tiberius, his father-in-law Appius Claudius, and his brother Caius, who was then serving in the army under Scipio. Tiberius next filled up the vacant tribuneship by getting one of his own dependents put into the office.

The anger of the patricians grew more and more

bitter with these proceedings. In the senate they lost no opportunity of insulting Tiberius. Thus, for example, they refused him the use of a tent at the public expense, while he was engaged in dividing the lands, though such a grant was customary. Moreover, they allowed him only a very small sum for expenses.

Meanwhile, on their part, the people were becoming more and more exasperated. When it happened that a friend of Tiberius died suddenly, the people roundly declared that he had been poisoned. The fact that it was only with great difficulty that the body could be consumed on the funeral pyre confirmed their suspicions. The action of Tiberius on this occasion tended to stir up the anger of the people against the other party still more. Dressed in mourning, he led his children into the Forum, and commended them and his mother to the protection of the people, as though he considered his own life as good as lost.

Now, about this time a certain ruler died, who by his will left the Roman people his heirs. Tiberius at once proposed a law to the effect that the money thus bequeathed should be divided among the citizens to enable them to get tools for the working of the lands newly assigned to them.

These proposals again were very distasteful to the senate, and many accusations were levelled at Tiberius. One senator charged him with designing to make himself King of Rome, and stated that he had certain knowledge that a royal diadem and purple robe had been brought to the tribune to be worn when he assumed the title. Others accused him of consorting with mean and turbulent people; while yet another brought a charge of more weight and truth, affirming that he had been guilty of a great offence in deposing his fellow-tribune, whose person, according to the law, was sacred.

Tiberius himself felt that the step he had taken in deposing Octavius from office offended many of the commons, as well as the patricians. He defended himself by saying that the person of a tribune of the people drew its sanctity from the fact that it was devoted to the service of the people. But, he argued, if a tribune opposes the interests of the people, he loses that attribute, and can be deposed by the same power that set him up.

The supporters of Tiberius, being afraid of the threats and plots against him, now advised him that he should use all his influence to get his tribuneship continued for another year, for they considered that he would be in great danger if he were but a private citizen. Tiberius therefore, in order to secure reelection, brought forward other laws intended to please the people. He proposed to shorten the time of military service, and also that an appeal from the judges to the people should be allowed. It must be confessed that in some of his proposals, he seemed now to be inspired rather by an obstinate anger against the patricians than by regard for the public welfare.

When the time came for the vote to be taken, Tiberius and his friends saw that there was a poor

TIBERIUS GRACCHUS

attendance of the people, and that their opponents were likely to be the stronger party. They therefore spun out the proceedings by all means possible, and procured the adjournment of the meeting to the following day. Tiberius then, with every sign of mourning and distress, went into the market-place, and applied to the people for protection. He told them that he feared that he himself would be killed, and his house destroyed before morning. The people were deeply moved. Many of them set up tents outside his door, and kept guard over his house all night.

Next morning, omens of disaster were not lacking. Nevertheless, Tiberius set out for the Capitol as soon as he heard that the people were assembled there. As he went out of his house, he stumbled on the threshold, and struck it so violently with his foot that his toenail was broken and the blood flowed freely. He had gone but a little way farther when he saw, on his left hand, two ravens fighting upon a housetop, and, although as tribune he was surrounded by many people, one of the ravens let fall a stone which dropped close to his foot. Even the boldest of his supporters were disturbed by so evil an omen, except one who exclaimed: 'It would be a disgrace unbearable if Tiberius, son of Gracchus, grandson of Scipio Africanus, and protector of the people of Rome, should fail to go to the help of the people when they called upon him, for fear of a raven, forsooth!' He declared, too, that their enemies would not be content with laughing at them. They would point out to the commons, the speaker continued, that Tiberius was already acting with the insolent pride of a king in coming or not to the meeting-place as it pleased him.

At the same time there came several messengers from their friends in the Capitol, asking Tiberius to make haste, for everything was going as well as he could wish.

And indeed, when the assembly saw Tiberius approaching in the distance, they burst out into the loudest applause, and when he came up greeted him with delight, and formed a ring around him to keep all strangers at a distance. The colleague, whose appointment Tiberius had secured, then began to call over the tribes, but such was the excitement and the press of the crowd that nothing could be done regularly and in order. In the midst of the commotion a certain senator got upon a raised place, and, as he could not make his voice heard above the din, made a sign with his hand to Tiberius that he had something to say to him in private. The tribune therefore called upon the people to make way, and with much difficulty the senator got near to him. He told Tiberius that the senate was sitting, and that the landed party had applied to the consul to take action against the tribune, and further that, as they could not get the consul to consent, they had resolved to kill Tiberius themselves, and had armed a number of their friends and slaves for that purpose.

As soon as Tiberius communicated this news to those around him, they girt up their togas, seized the halberds with which the guards kept off the crowd, and broke them up to serve as weapons with which to beat off any attack. The people who were at a distance could not understand the cause of this disturbance, and Tiberius found it impossible, on account of the din, to let them know by calling out to them. He therefore touched his head with his hand as a sign to them that his life was in danger. At once some of his enemies, who were mingled with the crowd, ran to the senate and declared that Tiberius was claiming the kingly crown, for that was the interpretation they put upon the sign he made.

The report caused a great sensation in the senate. Nasica, one of the senators, rose and demanded that the consul should defend the commonwealth, and destroy this man who aimed at making himself tyrant. The consul answered that he would not begin the use of violence, nor put any citizen to death who had not been condemned by the laws, but that he would annul any decree contrary to the constitution that Tiberius should persuade the people to adopt.

Upon this Nasica started up and cried, 'Since the consul gives up the cause of his country, let all those who support the laws follow me.' Then, covering his head with the skirt of his toga, he hurried to the Capitol, followed by a number of others. The crowd did not resist them; indeed the people, out of regard for their rank, made way for the senators to pass, trampling upon one another and breaking the benches as they did so. The attendants of the senators had brought staves and clubs with them, while the patricians themselves seized the legs of the broken benches. Thus armed, they rushed upon Tiberius, killing or driving off such as stood in their way.

Tiberius himself, with many of his friends, sought to escape. One of his enemies laid hold of his toga, but he slipped it off, and continued his flight. He chanced, however, to stumble over the bodies of some of those who had already been killed in the onslaught, and fell. Before he could recover himself, one of the patricians struck him upon the head with the leg of a stool, and he was killed. Over three hundred others were slain in this fight, all by clubs and stones, and not one by the sword.

This is said to have been the first civil strife in Rome, since the expulsion of the kings, in which the blood of any citizen was shed. All other disputes had been settled by compromise, and so probably might this one have been if Tiberius had been moderately dealt with. But it seems that the conspiracy against him was caused rather on account of the personal hatred of the rich, than for the reasons which they publicly gave for the deed. This is shown by the cruel and disgraceful treatment of his dead body. Despite the entreaties of Tiberius's brother that he might be allowed to take it away, the nobles ordered that it, with the other bodies of the slain, should be cast into the river. Nor was this all, for, of his friends, some were banished and others put to death without trial. One, indeed, was shut up in a cask with vipers and other poisonous snakes and left thus to perish miserably.

The senate now sought to make peace with the

people. They no longer offered any opposition to the Agrarian Law, and they allowed the election of another commissioner, in place of Tiberius, to attend to the dividing of the lands. But the people deeply lamented the death of their tribune, and it was plain that they were awaiting an opportunity for revenge. Nasica was especially the object of their hatred, and they reviled him as an accursed wretch who had defiled the most sacred and most awful temple in Rome with the blood of a magistrate. Nasica was indeed constrained to leave Italy secretly, and to wander from place to place in foreign lands until he died.

CAIUS GRACCHUS

WHETHER it was that Caius Gracchus felt some fear of the enemies of his house, or whether he wanted to make them more hateful to the people, certain it is that at first, after the murder of his brother, he absented himself from the Forum, and kept himself close within his own dwelling. But he was, indeed, a very young man at the time, for Tiberius, who was nine years the elder, was not quite thirty years of age at the time of his death. However, it soon appeared that Caius was preparing to take part in public affairs.

He showed such powers of eloquence in the defence of one of his friends, that all the other orators seemed but children in comparison, and the people were transported with enthusiasm. The nobles, however, regarded the powers thus revealed with fear and apprehension, and at once began to take measures to prevent his advancement to the office of tribune.

His enemies were pleased to get rid of him when it fell to his lot to attend the consul as quæstor in an expedition to Sardinia. Caius, however, felt no uneasiness as to the result, for he had as good a talent for military matters as for oratory. Indeed, he thought himself fortunate in being sent abroad, for he had some natural apprehension, after his brother's fate, of taking any share in the politics of Rome.

It is a common opinion that Caius, of his own accord, became a violent political leader. This, however, is not true, and it seems to have been rather necessity than choice that brought him into politics. Cicero, the orator, tells us that Caius avoided all office, and had resolved to live in a private station, but that the shade of his brother Tiberius appeared to him. 'Why dost thou delay, Caius?' said the spirit. 'For us the Fates have decreed the same path and the same death for the people. There is no other way.'

Caius distinguished himself in Sardinia above all the other young Romans, not only in combat with the enemy, but also in justice to those who submitted, and in respect and assistance to his general. He excelled even the veterans in temperance, in simplicity of food, and in devotion to labour.

A severe and unhealthy winter came on while the army was in Sardinia, and the general demanded clothing for his men from the cities of the island. The towns, however, appealed to Rome against this burden, and the general was ordered to find some other means of supplying the needs of the army. Caius thereupon applied to the towns in person, and such was his influence that they voluntarily supplied the clothing.

The senate was alarmed at this instance of the popularity that attended Caius, and determined to keep him away from Rome. They therefore made a decree, that when the ordinary soldiers on service in Sardinia were relieved by others, the consul should remain, in order that Caius as quæstor should also be detained with him.

When this order came to Caius, his anger overcame him. In defiance of it he embarked and arrived in Rome when nobody was expecting him. Not only did his enemies now blame him, but the general body of the people thought it strange that the quæstor should return without his general. A charge was laid against him, but he defended himself so well that opinion was entirely changed, and it was seen that he had indeed been ill-used. 'I have served twelve campaigns, whereas I was obliged to serve but ten. I have attended my general as quæstor three years instead of the legal term of one year.' He added, moreover, 'I alone went out with a full purse and return with it empty, while others, having drunk the wine they carried out, return with the vessels filled with gold and silver.'

After this other charges were brought against him, but he cleared himself of all suspicion. Then, his innocence being fully established, he offered himself as a candidate for the office of tribune. The patricians exerted every effort in opposition to him, but such a great number came into the city from all parts to support him, that the meeting-place would not hold the multitude, and some of the people gave their voices from the housetops.

However, the patricians were so far successful that they prevented Caius from obtaining the first place in the election, and he was returned fourth on the list.

CAIUS GRACCHUS

But when he had entered upon the duties of the office, he soon obtained a leading place among the tribunes. This he owed partly to his gifts of eloquence, in which he greatly excelled the others, and partly to the memory of his brother's services and unhappy fate. Caius indeed constantly returned to this subject, and reproached the people for allowing the murder. 'Your ancestors,' he said, 'made war to avenge an insult offered to one of their tribunes. Indeed, they thought death itself not too heavy a punishment for a man who refused to make way for the tribune when he was crossing the Forum. But you suffered Tiberius to be bludgeoned to death before your eyes, and his body to be dragged shamefully through the city, and cast into the river.'

Such speeches were heard by great numbers, for his voice was so powerful that he could be heard by a multitude. Having thus prepared the way, he proposed two laws. The purport of the first was that any magistrate who had been deposed by the people should thenceforth be incapable of holding any office. This law was aimed at Octavius, the man who had been deprived of his tribuneship by the agency of Tiberius. The second proposed that any magistrate who banished a citizen without trial should answer to the people for his conduct. In this Caius struck at Popilius, who had banished the friends of Tiberius. Popilius, being afraid to stand the issue of a trial, fled from Italy. The other proposal Caius dropped because his mother Cornelia interceded for Octavius.

The people were quite content to have it so, for they honoured Cornelia greatly, not only on account of her sons, but also on account of her father. They afterwards erected a statue in her honour which bore this inscription

CORNELIA

THE MOTHER OF THE GRACCHI

Among the various laws which Caius passed to increase the power of the people, one related to the foundation of colonies and the division of the public lands. A second secured that the army should be clothed at the public expense. A third gave the vote to the Italian allies of Rome. A fourth was intended to lessen the cost of bread. A fifth related to the courts of law, and, more than any other of his proposals, lessened the power of the senate. Hitherto only senators had held the office of judges, but Caius proposed that three hundred men of the knightly order should be added to the three hundred senators as judges. In furthering this bill he exerted himself to the utmost in all respects. One thing was noted as especially remarkable. Before this time all orators when addressing the people stood facing the senate-house. Caius, however, now for the first time stood so as to face the Forum, and ever after this time adopted the new position. Thus, by a mere alteration of the posture of his body, he indicated a very great matter, no less indeed than the change of the government of the state from the rule of the nobles to the rule of the people, for his action intimated that the commons and not the senate should be addressed as the masters of the state. The people not only ratified this law, but also gave Caius the power to choose the three hundred judges from the knightly order, so that he found himself possessed of almost kingly power. Indeed, at this time, even the senate was ready to listen to his advice. He used his power to obtain decrees for the making of roads, for settling colonies, and for building public granaries. He had the supreme direction of all these matters, but he was far from thinking so much business a fatigue. Indeed, he threw such energy into his manifold duties, and despatched them with so much ease, that it appeared as though any matter he happened to have in hand at the moment was the sole thing to which he had to attend. Even those who both hated and feared him could not help marvelling at his tireless industry and the speed with which his undertakings were completed. As for the people, they were delighted to see their leader followed by such a press of architects, artificers, ambassadors, magistrates, soldiers and writers, all of whom he received with a kindly and dignified courtesy.

He took especial pains in the construction of the public roads, and in planning them had regard to beauty as well as to utility. They were drawn in straight lines across the country, and were either paved with hewn stones, or made of sand specially chosen because it readily bound together to make a hard surface. Ravines or deep hollows in the way were either filled up with rubbish or spanned by bridges, so that the road crossed them as a level way. He caused all the roads to be measured, and set up stone pillars to mark the distances, while here and there he built mounting-stones to assist travellers who rode without servants to get on their horses.

The people were loud in praise of the activities of Caius, and there was no mark of their affection which they were not ready to bestow upon him. In one of his speeches he told them that there was one favour which he should esteem above all others, though he should not complain if it were denied to him. The people imagined that by these words Caius meant that he desired the consulship, and that, indeed, he aspired to be both consul and tribune at the same time. They therefore waited with some anxiety for his declaration of this fervent desire when the day of election for the consulship came. They found, however, that instead of seeking the office himself, Caius wished to secure it for another, who by the tribune's influence was immediately elected. As for Caius, though he made no application for office, and did not even offer himself as a candidate, he was at once appointed tribune for a second time.

He soon found, however, that the senators began openly to show their hatred for him, and that the consul, who had been appointed through his influence, began to fall away from him. He therefore set himself to pass still other laws to secure the favour of the people. Such measures were the proposals to found various new colonies, and to grant to all the Latins the rights and privileges of the citizenship of Rome. The senate now resolved to undermine his influence in a new and unheard-of manner. Instead of opposing his proposals, however injurious they might believe them to be, they determined to agree to them, and even to outbid him in the contest for popular favour by adopting still more extreme measures to gratify and please the people. For this purpose they secured the help of one of the colleagues of Caius, Livius Drusus, who by birth and education, eloquence and wealth was one of the foremost Romans of his time.

Drusus entered willingly into the plan. He proposed laws without any regard to the interests of the state, but solely in order to flatter and please the people and thus outvie Caius. Thus, when Gracchus procured a decree for sending out two colonies, Drusus succeeded in sending out twelve, and selected three hundred of the meanest of the citizens for each. Again, Gracchus divided the public lands among the poor citizens on condition that they paid a small rent, but Drusus freed them from even that payment. And, when Caius procured the rights of citizenship for the Latins, Drusus went beyond him by securing a decree that the Latin soldiers should not be flogged for any fault even when they were upon active service. In all these measures Drusus was supported by the senate. Indeed, he sought to persuade the people that the patricians were the prime movers in these matters, and he thus succeeded in lessening the hostility of the commons to the senate.

When it had been decided to rebuild and colonise the city of Carthage, which had been destroyed by Scipio, it fell to the lot of Caius to superintend the work, and for that purpose he set sail for Africa. While he was employed there in re-establishing the town, his work was disturbed by several events of evil omen. The staff of the first standard was broken, what with the violence of the wind and the efforts of the ensign to hold it aloft. Another tempest swept away the sacrifices from the altars, and bore them beyond the bounds marked out for the city. Moreover, the marks of the boundaries were themselves seized by wolves, and carried away to a great distance. Nevertheless, Caius brought all into good order in the space of seventy days, and then returned to Rome.

He found his affairs in no very favourable condition. Drusus had taken advantage of his absence to charge one of the particular friends of Caius with stirring up the Italians to revolt. This man, Fulvius by name, was of a factious character, and though no proofs were given for the accusations against him, his violence and unwise conduct gave some colour to them. As his intimate friend, Caius to some extent shared in the odium which fell upon Fulvius. Moreover, it was remembered, that some time ago suspicion had fallen upon Fulvius, and to a less extent upon Caius, of being concerned in the death of the great Scipio Africanus, who died without any previous sickness, and upon whose body marks of violence were afterwards found. Caius therefore found that his influence was declining, and at the same time found that the power of one of his enemies, Lucius Opimius, was increasing, so that it was expected that Lucius would be made consul for the following year, and would use the influence of that position to attempt the ruin of the tribune.

Caius now removed his dwelling from the Palatine Mount and took up his abode among the meanest and poorest of the citizens near the Forum. He then proceeded to propose the rest of his laws. The senate, however, now felt strong enough to oppose him, and, as supporters of Caius came from all quarters, they persuaded the consul to order all persons who were not Romans by birth to depart from the city. It was indeed a strange and unusual proclamation that the friends and allies of the republic should not be allowed to remain in the city and should not be allowed to vote, although they held the rights of citizenship. Caius encouraged them to disobey the order, and declared that he would protect them if they remained in Rome. But he did not keep his word, and he even suffered one of his friends to be seized and taken away before his eyes by the consul's officers. Either he feared that resistance would only serve to show how much his influence had declined, or he was unwilling to give his enemies the pretext which they sought for having recourse to the sword.

It happened that at this time Caius quarrelled with his colleagues. There was to be a show of gladiators in the Forum, and most of the magistrates had caused stands to be built around the place, intending to make a profit by letting the seats for hire. Caius, however, insisted that the stands should be taken down, in order that the poor might be able to see the spectacle without payment. His orders being disregarded, he went with a body of his own workmen, and pulled down the scaffolds on the very night before the show. Next day the poor were, of course, pleased to find that they had an uninterrupted view of the combats, but the colleagues of Caius bitterly resented the manner in which he had taken affairs into his own hands. This seems to have been the reason why he did not obtain the tribuneship a third time. It appears that he really had a majority of the votes, but that his colleagues, incensed by his conduct, managed to procure a false and fraudulent return which made it appear that he had been rejected. Whatever may be the truth of this, for it is a matter of some doubt, it is certain that Caius did not bear his disappointment with patience. Moreover, his enemy Opimius was elected consul, and at once set himself to secure the repeal of many of Caius's laws, and to annul the establishment of the colony at Carthage, with the object of provoking him to some act of violence which would furnish an excuse for destroying him. For some time Caius bore this treatment patiently, but at length, instigated by some of his friends and especially by Fulvius, he began to stir up opposition against the consul.

The beginning of bloodshed was about no great matter. When the day came upon which the consul, Opimius, hoped to get the laws of Caius repealed, both parties took up positions in the Capitol early in the morning. First the consul offered sacrifice, and one of his officers, while bearing away the entrails of the victims, came up to the place where stood Fulvius and some others of the friends of Caius. 'Out of the way, ye rebel citizens,' said he, 'and make way for honest men,' and some say that at the same time he stretched out his hand with a gesture of contempt. At once Fulvius and the others fell upon him, and stabbed him to death with their long styles, the sharp pointed metal implements with which the Romans wrote on their tablets of wax.

The people were alarmed at this act of violence. As for the two antagonists, Caius and Opimius, the one was dismayed at the handle which had been given to his enemies, while the other rejoiced and sought to excite the people to avenge the death of his officer. But for the time, a torrent of rain which came on prevented any further outbreak of passion.

Early in the morning of the next day the consul caused the senate to be assembled. While he addressed the members within the senate-house, others exposed the naked body of the murdered officer on a bier outside, and then, as had been previously arranged, carried it through the Forum to the senate-house, with loud noise of mourning all the way. Opimius, who knew all about the whole farce, pretended to be very much surprised. The senators in a body went out to meet the body, and, placing themselves around the bier, gave vent to cries of grief and indignation, as if some terrible calamity had befallen the state. This pretended sorrow could not but excite disgust in the minds of those who remembered how Tiberius Gracchus, though holding the great office of tribune, had been murdered by the nobles, and his body cast into the river. They could not help contrasting that deed with the present action of the senators, who stood weeping around the bier of a mere hireling officer, a man who had perhaps been too severely punished, but who had brought his fate upon himself by his insolence. But, in truth, the pretended grief of the nobles had no other source than the intention to provide an excuse for procuring the death of the only remaining protector of the people.

Having returned to their meeting-place, the senators passed a formal decree by which they charged the consul to take every possible means to provide for the safety of the commonwealth and the destruction of the tyrants, for so they termed Caius and his chief supporters. Opimius, in order to carry out these orders, commanded the patricians to take up arms, and each knight to attend with two well-armed servants on the next morning. Fulvius, for his part, also prepared for the struggle, and got together a crowd of his supporters. Caius made no such preparations, but it was observed that, as he returned from the Forum, he stood for some time before his father's statue, and his sorrow was shown by his sighs and tears. He then retired without a word. Many of the commons who saw him were moved with compassion. They felt that they should indeed be dastards if they abandoned their leader to the fate that threatened him. They therefore, of their own accord, went to his house and mounted guard over it throughout the night. Silently, as men oppressed by a sense of the calamitous cloud that overhung the state, they kept watch and ward, taking intervals of rest by turns. In far otherwise did those who attended Fulvius pass the night. They spent the time with noise and riot, with carousing and boastful threats, and Fulvius himself was the first intoxicated of all the rabble rout.

So soundly did Fulvius sleep after his wine that it was with difficulty that his companions awoke him at daybreak. Then he and his followers armed themselves with the Gallic spoils which he had gained during his consulship, and thus equipped they sallied out with boastings and threatenings to seize the Aventine Hill. But Caius would not arm. He went forth in his toga, having only a small dagger beneath it, as though he were going upon ordinary business to the Forum.

As he left the house, his wife threw herself at his feet, holding him with one hand, while the other clasped her son. 'You do not now go forth, my dear Caius, as tribune or lawgiver,' said she, 'nor do I send you forth to a glorious war where death would be attended by honour. You expose yourself to the murderers of your brother. You go unarmed, as indeed a man should who would rather suffer than commit violence. But in so doing, you are throwing away your life without any advantage to the state. Party hatred reigns, justice is overborne by outrage and the sword. What confidence can we have either in the laws or in the protection of the gods after the murder of Tiberius? Must it indeed be my fate to go a suppliant to some river by the sea to pray that it will discover to me where its waves have cast up your dead body?'

Thus his wife poured forth her lamentations, but Caius, as gently as he could, disengaged himself from her arms, and walked forth with his friends in deep silence. In despair she caught at his gown, but in the act fell to the ground, and there lay a long time speechless. At length her servants took her up and carried her to her brother's house.

When all the party were assembled, Fulvius

listened to the advice of Caius, and sent his younger son into the Forum as a herald. He was a handsome lad, and approached the opposing party with modest air and tearful eyes to propose terms for an agreement with the consul and senate. Many of the senators were inclined to listen to these proposals. But the consul would have nothing to do with them. 'It is not the place of criminals,' said he, 'to treat with us by their heralds, but first to make submission, and surrender themselves to justice, before they sue for mercy.' He bade the young man not to return unless it were to say that the friends of Caius and Fulvius submitted to these conditions.

Caius was of opinion that all of them should now go and endeavour to come to an agreement with the senate. None of the others agreed with him, however, and Fulvius therefore again sent his son with much the same message as before. But the consul Opimius was bent upon proceeding to extremities, and in a hurry to begin hostilities. He immediately took the young herald prisoner, and marched against his opponents with a large body of foot-soldiers and a company of archers.

The arrows of the bowmen soon galled their adversaries so sorely that they were thrown into confusion, and sought refuge in flight. Fulvius hid himself in an old abandoned bath, but he was soon discovered and put to the sword. With him there perished his eldest son. As for Caius, he was overwhelmed with sorrow at the course events had taken. He was not seen to lift hand in the fray, and took shelter in the Temple of Diana. There he would have killed himself had not two of his most faithful friends prevented him, taken

THE PURSUIT OF CAIUS GRACCHUS

away his dagger, and persuaded him to seek safety in flight. Before he left the temple he is said to have knelt down and prayed to Diana that the Romans might be slaves for ever, in punishment for their base desertion of him. Indeed, upon proclamation of pardon, most of the commons had openly gone over to the other side.

The enemy pursued Caius with eagerness, and came up with him as he was crossing a wooden bridge. His two devoted friends bade him go forward, and then, taking their place side by side at the bridge head, defended the passage so that no man could pass till both the defenders had been overpowered and slain. Meanwhile Caius with but one servant fled onwards. He met many who encouraged him in his flight, as they might have cheered a runner on the racing-path. But, because they saw that his enemies were gaining upon him, none of them helped him, nor lent him a horse, though he besought them to do so. At length, a little in advance of his pursuers, he got to the Sacred Grove of the Furies, and there his life-scene closed. His faithful slave first killed his master, and then took his own life, though some indeed say that both fell alive into the hands of the enemy, and that the slave clung so close to his master to protect him that he was cut to pieces before Caius was despatched.

The bodies of Caius and of Fulvius and of all those who had been slain, to the number of no less than three thousand, were thrown into the river. Their goods were declared forfeit and were sold; their widows were forbidden to wear mourning; the dowry of the wife of Caius was taken from her. With still more savage cruelty, the younger son of Fulvius, who had not borne arms, and who had been taken prisoner when he came as a herald of peace, was put to death after the battle.

The consul Opimius lived, but lived to earn the execration of the people as one whose hands were stained with the blood of so many citizens. Moreover, he was afterwards infamous enough to take bribes from an enemy of the state. As for the commons, in a little time they lamented the Gracchi. They erected statues to their memory, and decreed that the places where they had been killed should be held sacred. Nay, some indeed offered sacrifices and paid their devotions to them as to the gods.

Cornelia bore herself in all these misfortunes with a noble greatness of soul. She said of the sacred places that they were memorials worthy of her sons. And of Tiberius and Caius she would speak without a sigh or a tear, and recount their triumphs and their sufferings as though she had been telling the story, not of her own sons, but of some ancient heroes. Thus she showed how a noble mind may learn to support itself against the pangs of sorrow, and that though Fortune may often get the better of Virtue, yet Virtue can always be the conqueror by rising superior to the blows of circumstance.

CAIUS MARIUS

THE long life of Caius Marius began about the middle of the second century before Christ. It falls naturally into two divisions; an earlier one in which the soldier of humble birth raised himself to the highest position in the state and rendered his country almost unequalled services, a later and shameful one in which his insane greed of power brought upon Rome and her provinces the horrors of a savage and merciless civil war.

It has often been said with truth that had Marius died after he had overthrown the Teutones and the Cimbri, he would have left behind him one of the most glorious names in Roman history. But he could not bear to surrender in time of peace the foremost position which he had won by his skill in war. He found himself outdistanced by others in the arts which win popularity in civil life, and he then stooped to the basest acts in order to maintain his power. His mad jealousy of his aristocratic rival Sulla led to the outbreak of the civil war. He fell, but after a series of hairbreadth escapes and terrible hardships he returned to Rome during the absence of Sulla for a spell of power, brief in duration, but long enough for a hideous slaughter of all whom he knew or imagined to be his enemies. Mad with the lust of

CAIUS MARIUS

blood, he abandoned Rome to his band of four thousand freed slaves, who for five days and nights murdered and pillaged at their will.

He died in time to escape the triumph of his rival Sulla, who in his turn took his vengeance in a second reign of terror in which some thousands of the party of Marius perished. Marius himself was beyond his vengeance, but his dead body was torn from its grave and cast into the waters of the river Anio. The poet Lucan tells how the ghost of the terrible old warrior was wont to appear and frighten the peasants from the plough when revolutions in the state were at hand.

CAIUS MARIUS was the son of humble parents, who earned their living by the labour of their hands.

As regards his personal appearance, a stone statue of him which I saw at Ravenna entirely bore out what is said of the hardness and severity of his character. He was always naturally inclined to deeds of courage and the exercises of war, and his character was formed rather by the discipline of the camp than by the training of civil life. Hence his temper was ungovernable when he was possessed of power.

It is said that he never studied Greek, and that he declared it to be absurd to study the language of a people who were the slaves of others. But had the character of Marius been softened by the influence of the Grecian muses and graces, he would never have brought a glorious military and civil career to so ill an end, nor have permitted his boundless love of power and selfish vainglory to lead him to close his career by an old age of ferocious cruelty.

It was not until somewhat late in life that Marius saw Rome, and learnt the habits of life in the city. Up to that time he had dwelt in a village among the Volscian mountains. There he lived in a fashion rude indeed as compared with the polished and artificial manners of a great city, but temperate and agreeable to the old Roman ideas of bodily discipline.

His first service in war was under Scipio Africanus, when that general was besieging Numantia. There he gained the special notice of his commander by his valour, in which he surpassed all the other young soldiers, and by the readiness with which he fell into the severer style of living which Scipio introduced among the soldiers, whose fibre had been weakened by luxury and extravagance. It is said, also, that he killed one of the enemy in single fight in the presence of Scipio.

Scipio rewarded the merit of the young soldier by several honourable distinctions. On one occasion it chanced that the conversation after supper turned upon the subject of generals. Thereupon one of the company, either because he wished to flatter Scipio, or because he really wished to resolve a doubt in his own mind, asked the general where the Roman people would find such another leader when he was dead. 'Perhaps here,' said Scipio, touching Marius, who was next to him, upon the shoulder. Such was the promise of Marius and such the discernment of Scipio.

It is said that the encouragement which Marius

derived from these words largely induced him to enter upon a political career. He obtained the tribuneship and established a reputation as a resolute and determined man, who would do nothing to please either senate or people if he judged it contrary to the interest of the state.

After Marius had served as prætor, he obtained by lot the government of the farther province of Spain. The country was still in a very savage state, for the natives were not yet sufficiently civilised to regard robbery as a dishonourable pursuit. Marius, however, is said to have broken up all the robber bands during his term of government.

Though he had by this time thoroughly entered upon political life, Marius possessed neither eloquence nor wealth, which were the two means by which politicians at that time were wont to prevail with the people. But he gained the popular favour by his determined character, his unwearied industry, and his temperate mode of life, and he increased so much in influence that he became connected by marriage with the illustrious house of the Cæsars. His wife was Julia, whose nephew Julius Cæsar, the greatest of the Romans, to some extent moulded his life upon the career of Marius.

There is a story which affords a striking evidence of the endurance of Marius. It is said that he suffered from varicose veins in both legs, and in order to rid himself of this trouble placed himself in the surgeon's hands. He would not allow himself to be bound for the operation, but held forth one of his legs to the surgeon, and, without flinching or groaning, bore the severe pain of the operation with a steady countenance and without uttering a sound. When, however, the surgeon was about to proceed to operate upon the second leg, Marius refused to hold it out, saying that the cure was not worth the pain.

When Metellus was made consul and given the command in the war against Jugurtha, he took Marius with him to Libya as his lieutenant. There Marius greatly distinguished himself. He took care, however, that his deeds should redound rather to his own credit than to that of his general. Indeed, he scorned to be a lieutenant of Metellus, and looked upon the war as a wide field of action in which he could display his courage to advantage and gather glory for himself. The service was full of hardships, but Marius shrank from no danger, however great. Nor did he think any detail too trivial for his attention, but in prudence and foresight surpassed all the other officers, while he lived on fare as hard, and endured hardships as great, as the common soldiers. Thus he gained the affections of the troops, to whom it was no small consolation to see him voluntarily taking part in their labours. Nothing indeed pleased the Roman soldier more than to behold his general eating the same dry bread as that upon which he himself subsisted, or sleeping upon a camp bed, or sharing in the actual labour of digging trenches and raising earthworks. The soldiers loved those officers who shared their labours and dangers more than those who distributed honours and money among them, and were more attached to a general who helped them in the work of the camp than to an officer who indulged them in idleness.

Thus Marius gained the devotion of the soldiers, and his fame and glory spread throughout Africa and extended even to Rome. The soldiers wrote to their friends at home extolling him, and saying that Marius should be made consul, since he was the only man capable of bringing the war to a fortunate end. These matters caused much anxiety to Metellus, who, however, was still more distressed by the affair of Turpulius. This man, and indeed the whole of his family, had long been faithful retainers of the family of Metellus, by whom Turpulius was made governor of an important town in the enemy's country. He treated the people of the town with great humanity and with an unsuspicious openness, which gave them an opportunity of delivering up the place to Jugurtha. Turpulius himself, however, was not injured when the place was taken, for the townsfolk prevailed upon Jugurtha to spare him. His escape uninjured caused a suspicion that he had betrayed the place, and Marius, who was one of the council of war, was most bitter in pressing the accusation against him. He prevailed upon most of the other judges, and thus it happened that Metellus, much against his own will and judgment, was forced to pronounce sentence of death against his friend. Shortly after his execution it became plain that the charge was false, and Metellus was overwhelmed with sorrow. The other officers could not but sympathise with him, but Marius openly gloried in his distress, and boasted of the part he had taken in the matter.

Metellus and Marius henceforth became open enemies. We are told that one day Metellus, by way of insult, said to his rival: 'You intend, then, to go home to seek the consulship. Will you not be content to wait and be consul with this little son of mine?' In spite of the gibe, Marius continued to apply for leave to go to Rome, and Metellus kept finding pretexts for detaining him in Africa. At last, however, when but twelve days remained before the election, he permitted his enemy to depart.

Marius had a long journey from the camp before he reached the coast. He covered the distance, however, in two days and a night. Then, before he embarked, he offered sacrifice, and the diviner, it is said, promised him success beyond his hopes. Cheered by the prophecy, he set sail, and with a fair wind crossed the sea in four days. The people received him with favour, and he proceeded to bring many charges against Metellus. In order to secure the consulship for himself, he further promised the citizens that if he were given the command he would either kill Jugurtha or take him alive.

He was elected with applause, and at once set about making his levies for the army. In doing this, he did not observe the custom of previous generals of admitting only persons of some property. He did not hesitate to enrol many needy persons and even slaves. He made many bold speeches, too, in ill-mannered and insulting style, which gave great umbrage to the patricians. Thus, for example, he declared that he had snatched the consulship as a prey from the feebleness of the rich and high-born. He told the people that for his part he boasted of his own wounds, and not of the glory of great ancestors. He frequently referred to generals of high birth, who had been unsuccessful in the war in Africa, as examples of high-born incapacity. 'Would not the ancestors of such men,' he asked, 'prefer for descendants such men as I am? They themselves achieved fame not by their birth, but by their courage and lofty deeds.' He used such language not merely out of vanity and arrogance, but because he perceived that the people took pleasure in these insults to the great, and that they regarded such arrogant talk as a mark of a man of parts.

Upon the arrival of Marius in Africa, Metellus was overcome with mortification. He had, in a measure, finished the war, since only the capture of Jugurtha was necessary to complete the victory, and now his enemy, a man who had risen to greatness by ingratitude to him, was come to snatch from him the glory of the victory. Unable to endure the mortification of meeting his successful rival, he withdrew and left to his lieutenant the task of handing over the army to Marius. But before the war was ended, the retribution of Heaven overtook Marius. For, just as he had robbed Metellus of the glory of his exploits, so he himself was robbed by Sulla, a matter which happened in this wise.

The King of Upper Numidia, Bocchus, was the father-in-law of Jugurtha, but gave him very little help in the war. He pretended that he hated his son-in-law's faithlessness, but really he feared the increase in his power. Now, however, that Jugurtha was a wandering fugitive, and had applied as a last resource to his father-in-law for shelter, Bocchus received him, though without any great show of affection, and at once proceeded to play a double game. Publicly he wrote to Marius on behalf of his son-in-law, and declared that he would defend him to the last, but privately he sent to Lucius Sulla, who had done him many services during the war, intending to betray Jugurtha into his hands. When Sulla arrived to take over the prisoner, however, the king was in some doubt whether he should not change the form of his treachery, and hold the Roman officer prisoner. But at length he resolved to adhere to his first plans, and accordingly delivered his son-in-law alive into the hands of Sulla.

In this event lay the seeds of the desperate and implacable enmity between Marius and Sulla which almost ruined Rome. For many, out of envy of Marius, gave Sulla the whole credit for the success. Sulla, too, seemed to claim it, for he caused a seal to be made representing the delivery of Jugurtha to him, and constantly used it to seal his letters. This bitterly incensed Marius, whose passionate ambition would not suffer him to brook the existence of a rival in glory. The enemies of Marius did not fail to claim that the foundations of success and the chief actions of the war were achieved by Metellus, and that the finishing stroke was due to Sulla. By such reasoning they sought to deprive Marius of the renown of being the greatest commander of his time.

CAIUS MARIUS

Soon, however, the danger which approached Italy from the west silenced the clamour which envy, hatred, and calumny had roused against Marius. For, casting about for an able pilot to take the helm of the ship of state in the terrible storm which threatened to overwhelm it, the people found that no rich or high-born Roman would stand for the consulship in this time of danger, and they therefore again elected Marius as consul, although he was absent from the city.

The danger was indeed great. No sooner had the Romans joyfully received the news of the taking of Jugurtha, than reports spread abroad of the coming of the Teutones and the Cimbri. And, though these reports appeared incredible as regards the numbers and strength of the enemy, it afterwards appeared that they fell far short of the truth. Three hundred thousand well-armed warriors marched in the barbarian hosts, and with them came their women and children, who were said to be much more numerous. These vast hordes sought lands where they might live and cities in which they might settle, just as beforetime the Celtæ had driven out the Tuscans and taken possession of the richest part of Italy.

It is not known whence came this cloud of people, which now hovered like a storm over Gaul and Italy, or who they were. Some, because the barbarians were a blue-eyed people of great stature, believe that they belonged to the German nations who dwell by the shores of the North Sea. Others suppose that they were a mixture of Celtic and Scythian peoples; others again, that they came from Cimmerian lands where day and night divide the year into two equal parts. But these are matters of doubt.

Most historians, however, agree that their numbers were greater rather than less than those we have mentioned. Their courage and their vigour was like a devouring flame. Nothing could withstand their onset, everything that came in their way was trampled upon or driven before them, like cattle before the herdsmen. Many strong armies under experienced generals, maintained by the Romans on guard beyond the Alps, were swept before them like chaff. Their successes drew the barbarians on towards Rome, for, having beaten all the Roman troops they had met and loaded themselves with plunder, they despised that people, and decided not to settle down anywhere until they had laid waste all Italy and destroyed Rome itself.

It was in the alarm which the news of these terrible foes caused that Marius was elected consul a second time, although it was against the law for any one to be elected in his absence. But it was felt that at such a time the law must give way to the public safety. Accordingly Marius returned with his army from Africa and, on the first day of his new consulship, led up his triumph for the war in Numidia. In this procession he showed the Romans a spectacle none of them had ever expected to see, Jugurtha a captive in chains. Nobody had ventured to hope that Rome would end the war while Jugurtha remained alive, so fertile was he in expedients, and of a nature at once so courageous and so cunning. It is said that his mind became unbalanced through his being led in the triumphal procession by his captors. After the triumph some tore the clothes from his body, and others, to secure his golden earrings, pulled them off and with them the lobe of the ear. He was then thrust naked into a deep pit in the prison, and in his madness cried out with horrid laughter, 'O Hercules, how cold is your bath!' Six days he struggled against famine, and then by his death paid the penalty of his monstrous crimes. It is said that three thousand and seven pounds of gold, five thousand seven hundred and seventy-five pounds of uncoined silver, and two hundred and eighty-seven thousand drachmæ in money were carried in this triumphal procession.

After the triumph Marius met the senate in the Capitol and, either through carelessness or vulgar ostentation, entered the place of assembly wearing his triumphal dress. Seeing, however, that the senate took offence at this, he went out and returned wearing the ordinary purple-bordered robe.

When Marius marched forth to meet the Cimbri, he constantly exercised his troops in various ways, such as in running and in making forced marches. More over, he made every man carry his own baggage and prepare his own food. Hence it came about that men who were fond of labour and obeyed orders promptly and without complaint came to be called *Marian mules*. Some, however, give a different account of the origin of this expression. They say that when Scipio was besieging Numantia, he determined to inspect not only the arms and the horses, but even the mules and the waggons. On this occasion Marius produced his horse, which he groomed himself and kept in excellent condition, and also a mule which in appearance, training, and strength far excelled all the others. The general was much pleased, and often spoke of these beasts of Marius, whence there arose the scoffing title of *Marian mule* for a persevering, plodding, and hard-working man.

A singular piece of good fortune favoured Marius in this expedition. The torrent of the barbarians turned aside for a time, and flowed towards Spain before it again shaped its course towards Italy. The respite gave Marius time to strengthen the discipline of his troops and to stiffen their courage. Moreover, it gave the soldiers an opportunity of learning what manner of man their general was. This was of great importance, for the first impression derived from his sternness and the severity of his punishments was unfavourable. But, when discipline was thoroughly established, the soldiers could not but admire the justice of Marius, and the success of the means which he had employed to train his troops. Even his harsh voice, his violent temper, and his ferocious expression of countenance came to be regarded by the soldiers not as things to be feared by them, but as things terrible to their enemies.

His strict but impartial justice contributed in some degree to his being elected consul a third time, a course which also appeared advisable to the Romans, because the barbarians were expected to make their invasion during the following spring, and the citizens wished to retain Marius as their commander for the struggle. However, the barbarians did not come so soon as had been expected, and the time of Marius's consulship was expiring. When the next election drew near, Marius therefore repaired to Rome, leaving one of his officers in command of the army. It happened that there were many candidates of great worth for the consulship, but one of the tribunes, who had very great influence with the people, was gained over by Marius. In his speeches the tribune urgently advised the people to elect Marius for a fourth term as consul. Marius himself pretended to wish to decline the honour, whereupon the tribune called him a traitor to his country for refusing the chief command at a time of such danger. It was evident to all that the tribune was playing a part at the bidding of Marius. Nevertheless the majority, seeing that the times required a man of his energy and success, voted for him and gave him as a colleague Catulus Lutatius.

Hearing that the enemy was now getting near, Marius rapidly crossed the Alps, and established himself in a fortified camp near the river Rhone. In order that he might not be forced to fight against his better judgment on account of lack of provisions, he set to work to supply the camp with an abundance of stores. The carriage of these by sea, however, was tedious and difficult, because the mouths of the Rhone were choked up by banks of sand and mud, and the navigation was thereby made difficult. Marius therefore made his soldiers, who would otherwise have been idle, dig a great canal, into which he diverted much of the water of the river. This channel he caused to terminate at a convenient point on the seacoast. Thus he formed a deep and safe passage for his supply vessels.

As they approached, the barbarians divided

themselves into two bodies. The Cimbri directed their march so as to enter Italy from the north-east, where Catulus was stationed to oppose them. The other body, composed of the Teutones and Ambrones, marched along the seacoast against Marius. The advance of the Cimbri was somewhat delayed, but the other body rapidly traversed the space which lay between it and the Romans. They made their appearance before the camp of Marius in countless numbers, and, when they pitched their tents, the encampment covered a great part of the plain. In aspect they were hideous, and their language and the cries with which they challenged Marius to battle were unlike those of any people known to the Romans.

  Marius took no notice of these taunts. He kept his soldiers strictly within the lines of their entrenchments, and sternly rebuked those who made a show of their courage by their eagerness to leave the camp and fight in the open. Such soldiers, he told them, were traitors to the interests of their country, for the objects of the army now should not be to gain triumphs and trophies, but to ward off the threatening tempest of war and secure the safety of their land. The commanders and chief officers he especially addressed in such terms as these. As for the soldiers, he caused them to be stationed on the ramparts by turns, so that they might become used to the appearance of the barbarians, and to the sound of their savage shouts. He believed that familiarity would render the enemy less terrible to them, since he was of opinion that the imagination invests that which is unknown with fancied terrors. It proved indeed that the daily sight of the enemy not only lessened the alarm with which they were at first regarded, but that their boastings and insolent pride aroused the anger and the courage of the Romans. For the barbarians ravaged the country all around, and attacked the ramparts of the camp with such boldness that the Romans began to chafe under their inaction, and their impatient words were reported to Marius. 'Has Marius found us cowards,' said they, 'that he keeps us here like women under lock and key? Is he waiting for others to fight for Italy, intending to use us only as labourers to dig canals and scour mud from river-beds? Is it to this end that he has disciplined us with so many toils?'

Marius was pleased to hear his soldiers use such words as these. He quieted them by the assurance that he did not mistrust them, but that he was waiting for the time and place for victory which had been pointed out by certain oracles. He did in fact have carried about with him in a litter, and treated with great respect, a Syrian woman, who was said to have the gift of foretelling the future. Marius sacrificed according to her directions, while she assisted at the sacrifices clad in a purple robe fastened with a clasp, and holding a spear adorned with wreaths and ribands.

One matter which is reported is certainly wonderful. It is said that two vultures accompanied the army, and were always seen hovering over it before a victory. They were recognised by brass rings about their necks, for the soldiers had caught the birds, and, after fastening the rings upon them, had let them go. Ever afterwards the soldiers saluted the birds when they appeared hovering over the army, and rejoiced in the confidence of victory.

As Marius continued to keep quiet within his camp, the Teutones determined to attempt to take it by storm. But a number of them were killed and many wounded by the missiles hurled from the ramparts, so they abandoned the attempt and prepared to resume their march, expecting to cross the Alps without being attacked. Accordingly, laden with their baggage, they marched past the Roman camp. Some idea could now be formed of their numbers by the length of the column and the time it took for it to pass by. It is said that they marched past the camp for six days without any interruption. As they went by, the barbarians taunted the Romans, and asked if they had any messages to send to their wives in Rome.

As soon as the wild hordes had all passed by, Marius also broke up his camp and followed them. He always took care to keep them in touch, and chose strong places which he fortified for his camps, and in which his army passed the nights in safety. Thus the two armies moved on until they came to a place called Aquæ Sextiæ, which is but a short march from the Alps.

There Marius prepared for battle, and pitched his camp in a spot which afforded an excellent military position, but only a scanty supply of water. He did this advisedly, we are told, in order to incite his men to action. When many of them complained of thirst, he pointed to a river which ran close to the enemy's camp. 'There,' said he, 'is water which you must purchase with your blood.' 'If that be so,' answered the soldiers, 'lead us thither at once before our blood is quite dried up.'

To this request Marius replied in a gentler tone that he would indeed lead them thither, but that they must first fortify the camp. With some reluctance the soldiers obeyed his command. The servants of the army, however, being in great need of water, both for themselves and for their cattle, determined to have it even at the cost of fighting. Taking their pitchers and arming themselves with such weapons as came to hand, some with pickaxes, some with axes and some with swords and javelins, they rushed in crowds to the stream. The mob of servants encountered a small body of the enemy, some of whom were bathing in the hot wells which abound in this district, while others, having bathed, were eating their dinners. The disorder of the enemy enabled the Romans to cut off a number of them, and their cries brought others of their comrades running to their assistance.

Marius had now great difficulty in restraining the impetuosity of his soldiers, who were much concerned about their servants. Moreover, the Ambrones, who numbered thirty thousand, and were the best troops in the enemy's army, were by this time drawn up. Though they had eaten too freely and were somewhat flushed by wine, the barbarians did not advance in a wild or disorderly way. Clashing their arms at regular intervals, and shouting their name, 'Ambrones! Ambrones!' all together, they came on to the attack.

The Ligurians were the first of the Italians to

move against them, and when they heard the war-cry 'Ambrones!' they themselves echoed back the same shout, for the word was indeed the ancient name of their people. Thus the two bodies advanced against one another, shouting the same warcry and vying with one another as to which should shout it the louder.

It was necessary for the Ambrones to cross over the river to reach the enemy, and during the passage their ranks were thrown into some disorder. Before they could re-form upon the opposite bank, the Ligurians charged into them, and thus the battle began. Meanwhile the Romans came pouring down from the higher ground to support their comrades.

This attack upon the barbarians was pressed home so hard that they were soon thrown into disorder. Many were slain in a confused fight upon the banks of the river, and the stream itself was filled with the bodies of the slain. Those of the Ambrones who got back safely across the river did not dare to make any stand, and many were cut down by the Romans as they fled to their camp. Meanwhile the women in the barbarian camp seized swords and axes, and with hideous yells fell upon fugitives and Romans alike, the ones as traitors, the others as enemies. Mingling with the fighting men, they clutched at the shields of the Romans or seized their swords with their naked hands, and would not let go their hold until they were cut to pieces. Thus the battle was fought confusedly upon the banks of the river, rather in a haphazard way than according to any plans of the general.

Great numbers of the Ambrones were thus destroyed, and, when darkness was beginning to fall, the Romans retired. But their camp did not resound that night, as might have been expected after such a success, with songs of victory. There were no feasts and merrymakings in the tents, nor did the soldiers enjoy the greatest solace of the tired warrior, sound and refreshing sleep. Indeed, the night passed in dread and anxiety, for the camp was undefended by trench or rampart, and vast myriads of barbarians still remained unconquered. From their camp came horrible sounds of grief and rage, which seemed not like the sighs and groans of men, but like the howling and bellowing of wild beasts. The horrid din re-echoed from the mountains and the hollow river-banks, and filled all the plains with affrighting sounds. The Romans could not help feeling some terror, and Marius himself dreaded the chances of a confused night battle. However, the barbarians did not attack either that night or the next day, but spent the time in seeking to arrange their forces to the best advantage.

Meanwhile Marius, observing that the enemy's camp was overhung by wooded hills, sent one of his officers with three thousand men to lie in ambush there. He instructed them not to move until the battle was begun, and then to fall upon the enemy's rear. The rest of his troops he ordered to take their evening meal and to retire early to rest.

Next morning, at break of day, Marius drew up his army in front of the camp, and then ordered his cavalry to march down into the plain. As soon as the Teutones perceived this movement, they could not restrain themselves nor wait until the Romans had reached the plain. Arming themselves hastily, and thirsting to avenge their fallen comrades, they pressed up the hill to the attack. Marius at once sent officers through the whole of his army with orders to the troops to stand still and await the onset. He further ordered that, when the barbarians were within reach, the Romans should cast their javelins and then take to their swords, thrusting upon the enemies with their shields with all their strength. For he knew that the slope of the hill was so slippery that the foes, in struggling to keep their balance, could not put any great weight into their blows, nor would it be easy for them to keep in close order. Not only did Marius give these orders, but he was himself the first to put them into practice, for in activity he was inferior to none of his soldiers, and in resolute courage he excelled them all.

The firm and united charge of the Romans prevented the barbarians from ascending the hill, and little by little pressed them back into the plain. There the foremost ranks were beginning to form anew, when wild disorder showed itself in the enemy's rear. For the commander of the Roman ambush, having been warned by the noise which reached him that the battle was begun, dashed out of his hiding-place, and with loud shouts impetuously attacked the enemy's rear. Thus assailed in front and rear, the barbarians broke their ranks and took to flight. The Romans pursued, and either killed or took prisoners over one hundred thousand of the foes, and also made themselves masters of the enemy's baggage and tents. They afterwards voted that such of these as had not been plundered should be presented to Marius as a reward for his services in a time of such pressing danger.

After the battle Marius chose out from the arms and other spoils the finest specimens to grace his triumph. All the rest he caused to be piled in a great heap, in order to make a splendid sacrifice to the gods. Around stood the soldiers, crowned with laurel wreaths, while their general, clad in a purple robe girt in the Roman fashion, took a lighted torch. With both hands he raised it towards heaven, and was then just about to fire the sacrificial pile when horsemen were seen galloping towards him. Silence and expectation fell upon the assembly, but gave way to shouts of joy and exultant clashing of arms when the horsemen, leaping from their saddles, saluted Marius as consul for the fifth time, and handed him letters confirming his appointment. The officers thereupon brought their general fresh crowns of laurels, and amidst great rejoicings and loud acclaims he set fire to the pile and completed the sacrifice.

But there is something in life which will not long allow us to enjoy unmixed prosperity, but chequers human fortune with mingled good and evil. It may perchance be Fortune or some avenging deity, perchance Necessity or the very nature of things. Howsoever it be, but a few days had passed since this joyous sacrifice before dreadful news was brought to Marius of what had befallen his colleague Catulus. Like a cloud arising in a blue sky, the news threatened Rome with a fresh tempest.

Catulus, whose duty it was to oppose the advance of the Cimbri, had decided not to defend the passes of the Alps, because he feared that to do so he would have to weaken his force by splitting it up into a number of small bodies. He therefore withdrew his troops from the heights and descended into the plain of northern Italy, where he took up a position behind the line of the river Adige. Here he fortified posts on both sides of the river, across which he threw a bridge so that he might if necessary send supports to those of his troops who were stationed on the farther side.

The Cimbri, full of confidence in themselves and contempt for the Romans, advanced through the mountains with much bravado. In order to display their strength and daring rather than because there was any necessity for them to do so, they bore the snowstorms of the mountains without any covering. They climbed through snow and ice to the summits of the mountains, and then, seating themselves upon their broad shields, slid down the steep slopes over the great rocks.

When they reached the river, they examined the ford, and then proceeded to dam up the stream. For this purpose they worked with such strength and in such numbers that they seemed to tear up the hills in the neighbourhood like the giants of old. Whole trees were pulled up by the roots and, together with masses of rock and mounds of earth, were cast into the river. Moreover, the barbarians sent heavy timbers floating down the stream, which drove against the piles of the bridge and shook it so that it seemed likely to fall.

The Romans were terrified by all these things, and most of them left the main camp and began to retreat. Catulus then acted like a noble general, who preferred the reputation of his nation to his own. As he could not prevail upon his soldiers to stand, he ordered the standard of the eagle to be advanced, and, hastening to the van of the retiring troops, put himself at their head, so that the army might not seem to be flying, but to be following the general in retreat.

The fort on the other side of the Adige was taken by the barbarians, though there the Romans fought with a courage worthy of their race. Their valour aroused the admiration of the barbarians, who spared their lives and allowed them to go after they had sworn to certain conditions. The land was left defenceless, and the hordes of barbarians poured over it and ravaged far and wide.

Marius was now summoned to Rome. The senate had without hesitation voted him a triumph, and it was generally expected that he would celebrate it upon his arrival. He refused, however, to do so, perhaps because he felt that his soldiers and comrades ought to share in it. He then set out to join Catulus and, at the same time, sent a summons to his own army to join him. When the troops arrived, he crossed the river Po, and endeavoured to keep the barbarians from invading the regions south of that river.

The Cimbri declined his offer of battle. They

were waiting, so they said, for the Teutones, but it is doubtful whether they were really still ignorant of the fate which had befallen their comrades. At any rate, they treated those who brought the news of the defeat very cruelly. They also sent a demand to Marius for lands for themselves and their brethren, and for a sufficient number of towns for them to dwell in. Marius asked the ambassadors who brought this demand whom they meant by their brethren. He was told that they were the Teutones, whereupon all the Romans who were present at the interview burst out into laughter. Marius sneeringly answered, 'You need not worry about your brethren. They have land which they shall hold for ever, for we have given it them.' The ambassadors understood the point of this reply, and began to abuse him and to threaten him with the vengeance of themselves, the Cimbri, and of the Teutones also when they should arrive. 'They are with us already,' said Marius, 'and it is only fitting that you should embrace your brethren before you depart.' So saying, he ordered that the kings of the Teutones, who had been captured in their flight amongst the Alps, should be brought forward in chains.

After the ambassadors had reported this interview to their countrymen, the Cimbri at once advanced against Marius, who, however, remained quietly in his camp. It was at this time, so it is said, that he introduced an alteration in the spears used by the Romans. Previously the head had been fastened to the wooden shaft by two iron nails. Marius ordered that one of these should be withdrawn and a wooden peg, which would

CAIUS MARIUS

be easily broken, put in its place. He gave this order, designing that the spear when it struck the enemy's shield should, upon the breaking of the wooden peg, bend over on the single iron nail, and the end of the shaft drag along the ground and encumber the enemy so long as the head remained fixed in the shield.

The king of the Cimbri with only a few men now came riding up to the Roman camp, and challenged Marius to fix a time and a place to do battle for the possession of the country. Marius answered that it was not the custom of the Romans to take the enemy's advice about fighting, but nevertheless he was willing to oblige the Cimbri on this occasion. The adversaries then agreed that the battle should take place on the third day from that time upon the plain of Vercellæ, a situation which suited the Roman cavalry on the one hand, and on the other allowed full room for the great numbers of the Cimbri.

When the day came, the Romans prepared for the battle. Catulus with twenty-two thousand three hundred men occupied the centre, while the thirty-two thousand soldiers of Marius were divided between the two flanks. Meanwhile the infantry of the enemy advanced slowly from their fortified camp in a square formation, each side of which measured thirty stadia, while their fifteen thousand cavalry came on in splendid style. The horsemen wore helmets, shaped like the open-mouthed heads of hideous beasts, surmounted by lofty plumes of feathers, which added to the apparent height of the wearers. They also wore breastplates of iron and carried gleaming white shields. Their custom

MARIUS AND THE AMBASSADORS OF THE CIMBRI

in war was to hurl two javelins and then to close with their foes and use their big heavy swords.

On this occasion the cavalry of the Cimbri did not advance directly against the Romans, but turned off to the right, hoping to draw some of their foes little by little away from their supports before attacking them. The Romans generals saw the object of this manœuvre, but the soldiers were deceived. They raised a cry that the enemy was in flight and, regardless of their officers, rushed in pursuit.

Meanwhile, the barbarian army came on like a huge moving sea. As was to be expected, the movement of so many men raised a great cloud of dust. Hence it happened that Marius, rushing to the attack at the head of his men, missed the enemy entirely, and wandered for some time in the plain without knowing exactly where he was. By this time the barbarians had closed with Catulus, upon whose soldiers, therefore, fell the brunt of the fighting. Sulla was one of those who fought in this division.

He tells us that the heat of the day, and the fierce sun, which shone full in the faces of the barbarians, were a great aid to the Romans. For the Cimbri, being natives of a cool forest-covered country, were hardy in enduring cold, but the heat distressed them and made them sweat freely and labour in their breathing. Indeed, they were fain to shelter their faces from the sun with their shields, for the battle was fought in the summer season during the month now called August. The dust also favoured the Romans, for it hid from them the vast numbers of the enemy. So well were their bodies disciplined to toil and activity, that not one of the Romans was seen to sweat or heard to breathe heavily in spite of the excessive heat, although they closed with the enemy running at full speed.

The best soldiers of the barbarians were cut to pieces where they stood in their ranks, for, in order to prevent the line from being broken, those soldiers who were in the foremost rank had been fastened together by long chains passing through their belts. The others who fled were driven back to their encampments, where a most terrible scene was witnessed. For the barbarian women, who, clothed in black, were mounted upon the waggons in the camps, slew the men as they ran. Some killed their husbands, others their fathers or brothers. Then they strangled their little children and cast their bodies under the wheels of the waggons or the feet of the cattle, and, last, killed themselves. One woman, it is said, hanged herself from the pole of a waggon with her children tied to her feet with cords. Some of the men, too, fastened themselves to the horns or the feet of oxen and then goaded the beasts till the animals gored or trampled them to death. Many died in this manner, but nevertheless more than sixty thousand were taken prisoners, and more than twice that number are said to have been killed in the fight.

The most valuable part of the booty fell to the soldiers of Marius, but the military ensigns and spoils were carried to the tent of Catulus, who relied upon this fact as a proof that the victory had been won mainly by the soldiers under his command. A dispute arose concerning this point, and certain ambassadors who were present were chosen as arbitrators. The soldiers of Catulus pointed out to them that the dead bodies of the barbarians were pierced by spears upon the shafts of which the name of Catulus was inscribed. Nevertheless, Marius gained the whole credit for the victory, partly because of his previous success, and partly because of his higher rank, for Catulus was no longer consul. The proudest title which the people conferred upon Marius was that of 'The Third Founder of Rome.' They thought, too, that he should celebrate his triumph alone. He, however, shared the honour with Catulus, for he wished to show that he was not unduly elated by his victories. He knew, moreover, that the soldiers were unwilling that he alone should triumph and Catulus be deprived of the honour.

Though Marius was now fulfilling his fifth consulship, he was very anxious to be appointed a sixth time to the office. He therefore set himself to gain favour by courting the people. In this he went beyond what was befitting the rank and dignity of his position, and beyond what agreed with his own character, for, instead of being naturally easy and complaisant, he was in truth just the opposite.

It is said that the undaunted courage which he showed on the field of battle quite deserted Marius in civil rivalry and in the din of popular assemblies. There is a story told concerning the censure which fell upon him for giving the citizenship to a thousand people of a certain town. When complaint was made to Marius that his action was illegal, he answered, 'The law speaks in too quiet a voice to be heard above the clash of arms.'

Certain it is that though Marius was first in military matters, he found that he could not by his own abilities attain the highest position in civil affairs. This led him to pander to the many, in order to obtain their support; and, in order to remain the first man in Rome, he sacrificed all claim to be the noblest. Hence he came into sharp conflict with the aristocratic party in the state.

Out of all the members of that party he feared Metellus most. Not only had Metellus experienced the ingratitude of Marius in former time, but he was, moreover, a man of upright character, who was the natural foe of those who sought the favour of the people by dishonourable means and for their own selfish ends. Marius therefore plotted to get Metellus driven from Rome, and with this end allied himself with Glaucia and Saturninus, two bold and unscrupulous men, who had at their command a rabble of turbulent fellows. He also used his influence with the soldiers, and, it is said, spent large sums in bribery. By these means he secured his sixth consulship.

It was during this term of office that Marius drew upon himself most hatred, on account of the part he took in promoting many of the violent measures of Saturninus. One of these foul deeds was the murder of a rival candidate for the tribuneship. Having thus secured the office, Saturninus brought forward a certain measure to which was added a clause requiring that the members of the senate should take an oath to assent to any measure whatsoever which was voted by the people.

In the senate Marius pretended to oppose this proposal, and declared that he would not take the oath. He was, however, speaking falsely. His object was to entrap Metellus into declaring also that he would not take the oath, for Marius knew that his enemy would in no case go back upon his word. The perfidy succeeded; Metellus declared his determination not to take the required oath, and the senate separated. A few days later Saturninus summoned the senators, and pressed the oath upon them. Then Marius came forward amidst profound silence, for all were on the alert to see what he would do. In spite of his bold assertions in the senate, and with but a few words by which he hoped to cover the shame of his perfidy, he declared that he would take the oath. Thereupon the people were delighted and applauded loudly, but the nobles were cast down and looked upon Marius with hatred. However, through fear of the people, the other senators followed his example, until it came to the turn of Metellus. In spite of the entreaties of his friends, he would not swerve from his word. He refused to take the oath and withdrew from the Forum.

Thereupon Saturninus put it to the vote that Metellus should be placed under a ban and excluded from the use of fire, water, and house in the city. Some of the worst of the mob were indeed minded to murder Metellus, but those of more worth crowded around him in sympathy. He would not, however, suffer any civil strife to be raised on his account, and like a wise and prudent man quitted the city. 'If better times come, the people will invite me to return,' said he, 'while if things remain evil, I am better away.'

Marius had, however, purchased the support of Saturninus dearly, for he was now forced to wink at his supporter's excesses, even when it became evident that he was aiming at obtaining supreme power by bloodshed and murder. Though the chief men in the state came to Marius and urged him to take action against Saturninus, it was with difficulty that he could be prevailed upon to do so. At length, however, the senators and knights began to combine, and their indignation drove Marius to action. He drew out his soldiers into the Forum, and drove Saturninus and his followers to the Capitol. There thirst compelled them to surrender, for the water-pipes had been cut. Marius did everything he could to save the lives of the prisoners, but without avail, and as soon as they came down to the Forum, they were set upon and massacred. These events caused Marius to be hated by both the nobles and the people.

After the expiration of this consulship, Marius spent some time in Asia. He left Rome because he could not endure to witness the return of Metellus, for, in spite of his opposition, the people favourably received a measure for the recall of his enemy. In Asia he sought to stir up the kings to war, for he thought that by war alone should he renew his ascendency in the state.

When he returned to Rome, he built himself a house near the Forum, in order that those who wished

CAIUS MARIUS

to court his favour might have no difficulty in waiting upon him. Nevertheless, he found himself neglected in favour of others, for his want of affable manners and of aptitude for political affairs caused him to be passed over, like a weapon of war cast aside in times of peace. He was particularly chagrined at the popularity of Sulla, who founded his political conduct upon enmity to Marius, and who had risen to power on account of the hatred which the nobles bore to his rival.

One circumstance in particular threw Marius into a frenzy of rage and jealousy against Sulla. Bocchus, the Numidian king, received the title of 'Ally of the Romans,' and, in return, erected in the Capitol figures of Victory, by the side of which he placed gilded figures representing himself giving up Jugurtha to Sulla. So furious was Marius, that he began to make preparations to destroy the figures by force, and, as Sulla prepared to oppose him, civil strife between the two seemed to be upon the point of breaking out.

The conflict, however, was prevented by the Social War which suddenly burst upon Italy. In this struggle the most warlike and numerous of the Italian peoples combined against Rome, because they were refused the rights of citizenship. They were well supplied with war-like stores, their soldiers were brave and hardy, and their commanders showed such courage and skill that the war came near to overthrowing the supremacy of Rome.

The struggle was marked by many reverses and by many changes of fortune. On the whole, it detracted as much from the reputation of Marius as it added to the fame of Sulla. For Marius seemed both slow in forming his plans and also over-cautious and hesitating in carrying them out. It may be that age was beginning to quench his former fire, for he was now in his sixty-sixth year. Nevertheless, he won a great battle in which he killed six thousand of the enemy. He never allowed his foes to take him at a disadvantage, and when he was entrenched within his camp the insults and challenges of the enemy failed to provoke him to battle. It is said that when the most famous of the enemy's generals said to him, 'Come down and fight, Marius, if you are indeed a great general,' he replied, 'Not so, but do you, if you are a great general, make me fight against my will.'

Marius himself stated that his nerves were disordered, and that his body was incapable of bearing the fatigues of the campaign. Nevertheless, he endured the hardships of war to a degree beyond his physical powers. At last, however, his weakness forced him to give up the command.

After the Italians had given in, intrigue became busy in Rome about the choice of a commander for the war in Asia. Many sought the position, but everybody was surprised when the tribune Sulpicius, a bold and daring man, proposed that Marius should be made proconsul and entrusted with the prosecution of the war. The proposal met with a mixed reception. Some indeed were in favour of Marius, but others supported Sulla for the command, and mockingly advised Marius to go to the warm baths of Baiæ, near which he had a magnificent house, and look after his health. Marius, however, stirred by boyish emulation of Sulla, now endeavoured to throw off his age and infirmities. He went daily to the Campus Martius, where he exercised himself with the young men, and showed, though he was now very stout and heavy, that he was still active in arms, and had a firm seat in the saddle. Some were pleased to see the old warrior still full of martial ardour, but wise people regretted that greed for gain and glory did not permit him to be content with the vast wealth and high rank to which he had risen from poverty and obscurity.

The disease of civil war, which had long been rankling in the body of the state, at length broke out, mainly through the audacity of Sulpicius. This man was an admirer of Saturninus, and copied him in everything except that he considered his model lacking in boldness and promptitude. Certainly Sulpicius, who kept a kind of bodyguard of six hundred men about him, was prompt and bold enough himself. He even attacked the consuls with an armed force while they were holding a public meeting. One consul escaped, but his son was seized and murdered. The other consul was Sulla, who escaped by slipping into the house of Marius, which was the last place in which his pursuers, who ran past the place while he was within, expected him to take refuge. By such desperate means Sulpicius enforced his will and got Marius appointed to the command.

Marius now began to prepare to set out, and sent two of his officers to take over the troops who were at the time under the command of Sulla. His enemy, however, successfully incited the soldiers to resist. They fell upon the officers whom Marius had sent, and then, to the number of thirty-five thousand well-armed men, set out to follow their commander in an advance against Rome. Meanwhile Marius, in revenge, put to death many of the friends of Sulla who happened to be in the city. Then, in order to increase his forces, he offered freedom to the slaves if they would join him. But only three, so it is said, availed themselves of his offer.

When Sulla entered the city, Marius was only able to make a feeble resistance, and was forced to endeavour to seek safety in flight. He quitted Rome, and in the darkness became separated from his friends. He fled first to one of his farms, and then sent his son to the estates of his father-in-law to get provisions, while he himself hurried to Ostia, at the mouth of the Tiber, where one of his friends had provided a vessel for him. When he arrived at the port, he set sail without waiting for his son. Meanwhile, young Marius arrived at the estates and busied himself in getting the necessary things together. Daylight surprised him, however, before he had finished his task, and he narrowly escaped falling into the hands of the enemy. Some of their cavalry, thinking he might be at the place, came riding to the farm. When the overseer saw them coming, he hid young Marius in a waggon loaded with beans, yoked the oxen to it, and met the horsemen as he drove along the road to the city. In this manner Marius was taken to his wife's house, and then, making his way to the sea by night, escaped in a vessel to Africa.

The elder Marius sailed along the coast of Italy with favouring winds. He was especially anxious to avoid the neighbourhood of the town of Tarracina, because one of his enemies, Geminius, was a very powerful man there. He therefore ordered the sailors to keep clear of that place. They were willing enough to obey him, but, as it chanced, the wind suddenly changed and blew so strongly from the sea that the sailors feared that their ship would not weather the storm. Besides, Marius was sea-sick and ill, and the sailors, therefore, determined to make the land. They did so with great difficulty at a place not many miles distant from Tarracina. As the storm continued to increase in violence, and their provisions were almost gone, they landed there and wandered up and down, not knowing what to do or whither to go. They were indeed in great perplexity. Land and sea were alike hostile to them. They dreaded to meet any men, and yet they dreaded not meeting them, for they were by this time in dire want of food. At last the wanderers came across a few herdsmen who had no food to give the starving men. They recognised Marius, however, and told him to quit those parts at once, for only a little while ago a body of horsemen had ridden by that very spot in search of him.

Marius was now in the greatest difficulties and his companions were ready to faint with hunger. In order to hide themselves they left the road and plunged into the recesses of a thick wood, where they passed the night in great anxiety. The next day found Marius sorely distressed for want of food, and he determined to drag himself down to the seashore while he had still strength enough to do so. On the way he begged his companions not to desert him. He sought also to encourage them by telling them to wait for his last hope, which he based upon an old prophecy. For he said that, when he was very young and lived in the country, an eagle's nest, with seven young ones in it, once fell into his lap. His parents consulted the diviners about this strange occurrence, and were told that it signified that their son would become the greatest of men, and that he would seven times hold the highest office in his country.

The starving wanderers had arrived at a distance of about two and a half miles from the sea, when at the same time they espied on the landward side a troop of horse a long way off making towards them, and, seaward, two vessels sailing near the shore. They ran down, therefore, with all the speed and strength they had left, to the seashore, plunged into the water and swam to the ships. The stepson of Marius reached one of them, and was taken over to an island opposite. Marius, who was very stout and heavy, was meanwhile with difficulty borne along above the water by two servants, and put on board the other vessel. By this time the horsemen had ridden down to the water's edge. There they shouted loudly to the sailors, ordering them either to put ashore immediately or else to throw Marius overboard. The fugitive with tears implored the sailors to save him, and at last the masters of the vessels, after changing their minds more than once, shouted a refusal to give him up.

The soldiers now rode away in anger. But the crew of the vessel which Marius had reached soon repented of their decision, for they feared the danger of protecting the fallen man. They therefore made for the land at a point where the mouth of a river overflows and forms a marsh. There they advised Marius to go ashore and rest himself, while they waited for a favourable wind. They assured him that the sea breeze would fall, and a favouring wind arise from the land at a certain hour of the day. Marius believed them, and the sailors helped him ashore, where he seated himself upon the grass, little dreaming of what was to befall him. For the sailors, unwilling to give him up and yet fearing to protect him, at once hurried on board their ships, weighed anchor and sailed away.

Marius was thus left alone and deserted by everybody. For some time he sat there on the shore silent and stupefied. Then, recovering himself at last, he rose and walked sadly forward along wild and winding paths till, by scrambling over deep bogs and ditches full of muddy water, he came to the hut of an old man who worked in the marsh. Marius threw himself at the stranger's feet, implored him to save him, and promised, if the present danger were escaped, to reward him far beyond his greatest hopes. The cottager replied that his hut would afford Marius shelter, if that was all he required, but that, if enemies were seeking his life, he would show him a safer hiding-place. He then led Marius through the fens down to the river, where he hid him in a hollow under the river-bank, and covered him over with reeds and rushes.

Marius had not been long in this hiding-place before he was disturbed by the sound of loud noise and wrangling coming from the cottage. His enemy,

Geminius, had sent out a number of men to scour the country in search of him, and one party of the pursuers had just come that way and were loudly threatening the cottager for having helped an enemy of the Romans.

Marius now thought it unsafe to remain in the cave. He therefore stripped himself and plunged into the slimy water of the bog. By doing so he did not escape, but in fact revealed himself to his pursuers. They pulled him out of the bog, naked and covered with mire, and bore him off to the town of Minturnæ, where they handed him over to the magistrates.

A proclamation had been made through all the towns in those parts that strict search should be made for Marius, and that he should be put to death wherever found. The magistrates of Minturnæ, however, thought it well to deliberate about the matter before carrying out the order. They therefore sent Marius under a guard to the house of a woman named Fannia. Now, in the time of his sixth consulship, Marius, in a law-suit which came before him, had inflicted a fine upon this woman as a mark of disgrace. It might therefore have been expected that she would have been filled with resentment against him. Fannia, however, rose above such feelings, and did all she could to comfort and encourage the prisoner.

The magistrates of Minturnæ having deliberated upon the fate of Marius, decided that he should be put to death. None of the citizens would undertake to do the deed, but a barbarian horse-soldier was induced to do so, and took a sword with the intention of killing the prisoner. Now it happened that the room in which

Marius lay was somewhat dark, and it is said that when the assassin entered a light seemed to gleam from the eyes of Marius through the gloom, while his deep voice blared out, 'Darest thou kill Caius Marius?' Thereupon the soldier was smitten with terror. Throwing down his sword, he fled from the room crying, 'I cannot kill Marius.' This turn of events deeply impressed the people of the city, and they began to ask whether it was not right that they should aid the man who had saved Italy, rather than put him to death. 'Let the exile go,' said they, 'and await his fate in some other place. And for our part, let us implore the gods to pardon us for refusing shelter to the poor naked wanderer.'

Impelled by such feelings they conducted Marius down to the seacoast. There he set sail and was carried by the wind to the island upon which his stepson and some friends had taken shelter. Together they then sailed for Africa, but, being obliged to put in for water on the coast of Sicily, they had a very narrow escape. The Roman governor of the island was on the lookout for the fugitives, and nearly succeeded in capturing Marius when he landed. Indeed, sixteen of the watering party from the ship were slain.

Soon after this escape Marius learnt for the first time that his son had managed to make his way to Africa, and was gone to seek aid from the King of Numidia. The news encouraged him to press on for Africa, and he landed in the neighbourhood of Carthage. As the Roman governor of the district around had never been either injured or favoured by Marius, it was expected that he would feel sufficient compassion for the exile to give him some aid. But, immediately after he landed, the fugitive was met by an officer, who delivered this message: 'The governor of Libya forbids you, Marius, to set foot in this province, and warns you that he will treat you as an enemy if you disobey this command.' Sorrow and anger at this reception for a time deprived Marius of the power of speech. He stood a long time silent, staring fixedly at the officer. When, at last, he was asked what reply he had to make to the message of the governor, Marius answered with a deep sigh, 'Tell him that you have seen Caius Marius an exile sitting amidst the ruins of Carthage!' a speech in which he fittingly compared his own fallen fortunes with the fate of the city.

Meanwhile, the King of Numidia had been in doubt how to act. He treated young Marius and his companions with honour certainly, but he kept them about him, on one pretext or another, whenever they proposed to depart, so that it appeared that he was detaining them with no good object towards them. By the aid of one of the women about the court, however, they succeeded at last in escaping, and made their way down to the coast. There young Marius embraced his father, and together they left the mainland for an island at no great distance from it. Their departure was timely, for no sooner had they set sail than they saw a body of horsemen, sent by the king to seize them, riding down to the shore.

Meanwhile, Sulla had left Rome in order to command the army in the war against Mithridates. While he was absent, the two consuls, Octavius and

**THE EXILED MARIUS
AMIDST THE RUINS OF CARTHAGE**

Cinna, quarrelled, and civil war broke out between them. Octavius got the better of the struggle and deposed Cinna from his office. But the defeated consul determined to continue the contest, and collected troops in Italy in order to make war upon his rival.

When Marius heard this news, he resolved to take advantage of the strife in order to return to Italy. He knew that Cinna was the enemy of Sulla, and was disposed to make changes in the government. Marius therefore hoped to establish his position once again by an alliance with Cinna.

As soon as he had landed in Italy, Marius proclaimed freedom for such slaves as would join him. He also persuaded the most stalwart of the freemen who, attracted by his fame, flocked down to the seashore upon hearing the news of his arrival, to enrol themselves with him. By these means he succeeded in a few days in gathering a considerable force, and in manning forty ships. He then sent a message to Cinna, recognising him as consul and offering to obey him in all things. Cinna gladly accepted the proffered aid, named Marius proconsul, and sent him the insignia of that office. The returned exile, however, declared that such signs of honour did not become his fallen fortunes. He dressed himself in mean robes; his disordered hair, uncut since his exile, streamed over his shoulders; and he walked with a slow and measured gait which might, indeed, well agree with his age, for he was now about seventy years. But, in truth, his dress and his halting gait were means by which he hoped to awaken the pity of the people. Despite his abject look and garb, a more than usually terrible expression of face belied his pretended humility, and showed that his pride was infuriated rather than humbled by the buffets of fortune.

After Marius had met Cinna, he at once began his operations, and very soon completely changed the aspect of affairs. His fleet cut off the enemy's convoys, he plundered their store-ships and made himself master of their food supplies. Then, sailing along the coast, he captured the seaports one by one. At last Ostia itself, the port of Rome, was treacherously betrayed to him. He plundered the town, killed most of the inhabitants, and then threw a bridge across the Tiber to prevent the carrying of any provisions to Rome by way of the sea. Next, he marched against Rome itself, and took up his position on the hill called Janiculum.

Meanwhile, the cause of Octavius suffered less from his lack of ability than from his scrupulous observance of the laws. Thus, for example, he refused to grant freedom to the slaves as the price of their support. He depended, too, much upon diviners and soothsayers, and spent more of his time with them than with men of military and political abilities. At last, the consul was dragged from the tribunal and murdered by some persons employed for that purpose.

The senate assembled while affairs were in this condition, and, despairing of defending the city, sent some of their members to Cinna and Marius, inviting them to come into the city, but beseeching them to spare the inhabitants. Cinna received them seated in his chair of state as consul, and returned them a smooth answer. Marius stood by the consul's chair but said not a word, and the gloom upon his brow and the menace in his eye revealed his intent to fill Rome with blood.

The two generals then moved forward towards the city. Cinna entered the city with a strong guard, but Marius stopped at the gates. He pretended unwillingness to enter, declaring that, as he was a banished man, the law forbade his return. 'If the country needs my services,' said he, 'the law by which I was driven into exile must first be repealed.' The people were therefore assembled for this purpose.

Very soon, however, Marius threw off the mask, and, when only a few of the tribes had given their votes, he entered the city with his bodyguard, a company made up of slaves who had joined his standard. This band of scoundrels murdered all whom Marius, by the slightest word or sign, singled out for destruction. Indeed, when a certain senator of high rank saluted Marius, and the salutation was not returned by their leader, they immediately fell upon the man and killed him. After this time the bodyguard regarded the failure of Marius to return a salute as a sentence of death, so that the very friends of their general were in terror of their lives when they went to pay their respects to him.

When great numbers had been butchered, Cinna's thirst for blood began to be satiated. But the frenzy of Marius seemed to increase and his appetite for vengeance to be sharpened by indulgence in bloodshed.

He continued to slay all upon whom fell the slightest shadow of his suspicion. Every road was beset by his soldiers, and every town was full of his assassins employed in hunting out the wretched victims of his vengeance.

Dread of his resentment broke down the bonds of friendship and the ties of hospitality, so that there were very few who did not betray the fugitives who sought shelter with them. On this account the conduct of the slaves of Cornutus is the more worthy of high admiration. They hid their master within his house, and then, taking up a dead body from among those which lay in the street, they put their master's ring upon the finger of the corpse, which they then hanged by the neck. This they showed to Marius's assassins as the body of their master, and afterwards they prepared it for the funeral and buried it in his name. No one suspected the trick, and after the most severe danger had passed, the slaves safely conveyed their master out of the country.

Mark Antony, the orator, also had a faithful friend, but this did not avail to save his life. He took refuge with a man in poor circumstances, who, wishing to entertain his distinguished visitor as well as he could, often sent into a neighbouring town to get wine for him. The wine-seller noticed that the servant who came to fetch the wine was very particular about the quality, and insisted upon having the best. His curiosity was aroused, and he asked the servant why his master was no longer satisfied with the ordinary new wine which he was accustomed to buy, but demanded the best and dearest quality. The foolish servant told him, in confidence as a friend, that the wine was wanted for Mark Antony, who lay hid in his master's house. Directly the servant was gone, the wine-seller hastened to Marius, whom he found at supper, and told him that he could put Mark Antony into his hands. Marius clapped his hands with joy, and but for the persuasions of his friends would himself have hastened to the spot. In his stead he sent an officer with a body of soldiers and ordered him to bring the head of Antony. When the troop arrived at the house, the officer stood at the door, while at his command the soldiers climbed by a ladder to the room of Antony. The orator, however, met them with such moving appeals to spare his life, that the intending assassins could not find it in their hearts to lay hands upon him. They stood before him with downcast eyes, till at last the officer, wondering at the delay, burst into the room. He, upbraiding his men for their weakness, with his own hand struck off Antony's head.

Catulus, the former colleague of Marius, who had shared in their joint triumph over the Cimbri, sought by every means to put a stop to the slaughter, but found his prayers and intercessions vain. Sickened with the horror of the time, he shut himself up in a small closed chamber, and allowed himself to be suffocated by the fumes arising from a charcoal fire.

The bodies of the slain were thrown out into the streets and trodden under foot. In this horror of bloodshed, the conduct of the bodyguard of Marius was especially atrocious, for they wreaked their vengeance not only upon men but upon helpless women and children. Indeed, their violence and crime went beyond all bounds, until at length Cinna and one of his officers were revolted by their cruelty. They took counsel together, and falling upon the guards while the ruffians slept cut them off to a man.

At this time a sudden change happened in affairs. News came that Sulla had finished the war against Mithridates, and, having reduced the provinces, was returning to Rome with a great army. The intelligence brought a brief respite from the horrors of slaughter, and during this period Marius was chosen consul for the seventh time. But by this time his violent passions and the vicissitudes of his life had worn him out, and his faculties were failing him. He trembled at the thought of the approaching conflict. He could not but reflect that he had now to deal not with Octavius or with some desperate leader of a petty rising, but with Sulla, the conqueror of Mithridates, and the man who had before driven him into exile. Torn by these anxieties and unable to bear the suspense of awaiting the approach of his enemy, he had recourse to wine, and indulged in excesses by no means suited to his years. At last, when certain news came by sea of the approach of Sulla, he fell into a fever of which he died. Some, however, say that he died of the excess of his ambition, which threw him into a frenzy in which he imagined himself to be carrying on the war against Mithridates and shouting orders to his troops.

Thus died Caius Marius at the age of seventy, distinguished by the unexampled honour of seven consulships, and possessed of more than regal wealth. Yet he died in all the misery of an unfortunate wretch.

His death happened on the seventeenth day of his seventh consulship, and was hailed with joy by the citizens, who trusted to be freed by it from the most hideous of tyrannies.

JULIUS CÆSAR

The birth date of Caius Julius Cæsar, the greatest man of the ancient world, is generally given as 100 B.C. If so, Cæsar must have filled a number of public offices two years earlier than the law allowed. Some historians, therefore, consider that he was probably born in 102 B.C. Cæsar is remarkable among great men for the marvellous variety of his powers. He ranks among the greatest statesmen and generals of the world. But that is not all. He was also a great administrator, a great orator, and a great writer. In spite of natural weakness of body and the distressing malady from which he suffered, the labours of the camp and the council did not exhaust his energies or suffice to occupy his time. Throughout his life he found leisure for literary pursuits, and the purity of his style was famous among the Romans themselves. The only works of Cæsar which survive to our time are his **Commentaries***, which tell the story of the first seven years of the Gallic War and of a part of the civil war against Pompey and his party. The chief charge brought against Cæsar is that of inordinate ambition and of seeking to make himself king. No doubt Cæsar, with his clear-sighted wisdom, did indeed see that the wide extension of the dominions of Rome had, by his time, made good government impossible by the system which had served well enough when the rule of*

Rome did not extend beyond Italy. He saw that it was necessary for the supreme rule to be in the hands of one man, and there can be no doubt that he, above all others, was the man endowed with the gifts necessary to found the new system. It may, however, well be doubted whether Cæsar cared much about receiving the actual title of rex, or king. It was not like his broad, clear-visioned intellect to be concerned greatly about an empty title.

The first act of the civil war, when, by crossing the Rubicon, Cæsar practically declared war upon Pompey, was undoubtedly forced upon him by the instinct of self-preservation. The bloody massacres of Marius and Sulla were too recent to permit Cæsar to doubt that obedience to the senate would mean his accusation and death. He had either to fight or to die.

It is a great and enduring honour to Cæsar, greater in a moral sense than his victories and conquests, that he used his triumph over the party of Pompey with extraordinary mercy in comparison with others. Had Cæsar been a Marius or a Sulla, few or none of the conspirators, Brutus, Cassius, and the rest, would have survived the ruin of their party to plot against him and to compass the great dictator's death.

Cæsar was murdered on the Ides, the 15th, of March 44 B.C. But though he perished, the system of government he had begun survived, and the Roman Republic passed into the Roman Empire.

Almost the whole of the material of Shakespeare's play of **Julius Cæsar** is taken from Plutarch's Lives of Julius Cæsar and of Brutus. It is of great interest to

JULIUS CÆSAR

observe how the genius of Shakespeare deals with the material supplied by Plutarch's narrative and gives it a living, dramatic form.

WHEN Sulla had established himself as master of Rome, he put to death a great number of the relatives and supporters of his rival and enemy, Caius Marius. Now Cæsar's aunt was the wife of Marius, and Cæsar himself had married the daughter of one of the bitterest enemies of Sulla. Nevertheless, he was overlooked in the great number of those whom the dictator proscribed. When, however, Cæsar presented himself as a candidate for the priesthood, Sulla prevented his obtaining the office, and was further minded to have him put to death. As Cæsar was still very young, some one said to the dictator that there was no need to take the life of such a boy. Thereupon Sulla replied that those men must indeed be lacking in insight who did not see in this boy more than one Marius.

When this saying was reported to Cæsar, he deemed it prudent to go into hiding, and for a time wandered about in the country of the Sabines. There he fell sick, so that he had to be carried about from place to place in a litter. In this condition he was one night found by a party of soldiers sent by Sulla to scour the country and to drag proscribed persons from their hiding-places. Cæsar, however, by bribing the officer in command, prevailed upon him to let him go.

Cæsar then hastened to seek safety at sea. In

the course of his voyages he was captured by pirates, who had beset the neighbouring seas with a number of galleys and other vessels. The pirates set a ransom of twenty talents upon their prisoner, whereupon Cæsar laughed, for their demand showed that they did not know who he was. Of his own accord he promised them fifty talents. He then sent his people to different cities in order to raise the money, and himself remained, with only one friend and two servants, among these ruffian pirates, who looked upon murder as a mere trifle. Cæsar, however, treated them with contempt. When he had a mind to sleep, he was wont to send to tell them to keep silence. Thus he lived among them for thirty-eight days, rather as though they were his guards than he their prisoner. He moved among them perfectly fearless and unconcerned, joined in their exercises and sports, recited to them poems and orations which he had composed, and did not scruple to call them blockheads when they gave no sign of admiration. Indeed, he did not hesitate to tell the pirates that some day he would crucify them. His captors laughed at these threats, which they looked upon as jests.

When at length the money for his ransom had been brought and he was released, he set himself to man some vessels in a neighbouring port, and sallied out to seek the pirates. He found their ships still lying at anchor near the place of his captivity, and attacking them captured the money and most of the pirates and clapped them into prison. Then, as the Roman officer in that region, having his eye upon the money, delayed in punishing the robbers, Cæsar took the matter into his own hands, and crucified them all, as he had before threatened to do when they thought he was in jest.

When the power of Sulla began to decline, Cæsar's friends pressed him to return to Rome. First, however, he went to Rhodes, in order to study rhetoric under a famous teacher of that place of whom Cicero was also a pupil. Cæsar had great natural talents as a speaker, and was not without ambition to cultivate them. Hence he became second only to Cicero among the orators of Rome, and might indeed have been the first had he not preferred to be pre-eminent in arms rather than in eloquence.

When he returned to Rome, the eloquence which he displayed in many cases procured him a considerable amount of influence, which was increased by his engaging manners and conversation. Moreover, he kept an open table and spent money freely, so that he became very popular and thus gained office. Those who were envious of him imagined that his resources would soon fail, and therefore made light of his popularity as something which would not last.

Cicero seems to have been the first who suspected something dangerous to the established order of government from Cæsar, and to have seen that deep designs of ambition lay beneath his smiling affability. 'I perceive,' said he, 'a tendency towards absolute rule in all he designs and does; yet, on the other hand, when I see him arranging his hair so carefully and scratching his head with one finger, I can hardly credit such a man with the vast design of overthrowing the Roman commonwealth.'

Many people, who observed the vast sums which Cæsar expended, thought that he was purchasing short and fleeting honours very dearly. In truth, however, he was preparing the way to gain the greatest things to which a man can aspire at a cost small in comparison with their importance. He is said to have been in debt to the amount of one thousand three hundred talents before he obtained any public employment whatever. When he was appointed to superintend the Appian Way, he spent large sums of his own money on the work. Again, when he held the office of ædile, he exhibited a great gladiatorial show in which six hundred and forty gladiators took part. In addition to this, he provided other amusements in the theatre, and processions and public feasts which far outdid anything that the most ambitious of his predecessors had attempted.

Cæsar's growing popularity and his efforts to revive the party of Marius greatly alarmed many of the senate, who believed that he was aiming at obtaining the sole rule in Rome. He was indeed accused of this in the senate, but defended himself so well that the decision went in his favour.

While affairs were going on thus, the chief pontiff of Rome died. Though the office was sought by two of the most distinguished men in Rome, who had, moreover, great interest with the senate, Cæsar did not hesitate to offer himself as a candidate for the position. The prospects of the competitors seemed fairly equal, and one of his rivals therefore sent privately to Cæsar and offered him large sums of money to withdraw from the contest. Cæsar, however, replied that he would rather borrow in order to win the election still larger sums than those offered.

When the day of election came, his mother, her eyes filled with tears, accompanied him to the door. Embracing her, Cæsar said, 'My dear mother, you will to-day see me either chief pontiff or an exile.' The contest was very keenly fought, but in the end Cæsar was successful, much to the alarm of the senate and many of the principal citizens.

After he had served as prætor at Rome, the government of Spain was allotted to him. He found himself, however, in difficulties. His debts were so great and his creditors so troublesome and clamorous that he was obliged to apply for help to Crassus, the richest man in Rome. Crassus undertook to answer the most pressing of the creditors, and, by becoming security for eight hundred and thirty talents, enabled Cæsar to set out for his province.

It is said that when Cæsar was crossing the Alps on his journey, one of his friends said, as they were passing through a little town, 'I wonder if there are any disputes about office, and whether there is envy and ambition, such as we see at Rome, in this paltry little place.' Thereupon Cæsar, speaking very seriously, said, 'I assure you that for my part I would rather be first in this village than second in Rome.'

Again, we are told that when he was in Spain

he spent some of his leisure in reading the history of Alexander the Great. It was noticed that he was greatly affected by his reading, and that, after sitting some time in thought, he burst into tears. His friends, greatly wondering, inquired the reason, whereupon Cæsar exclaimed: 'Do you not think I have sufficient cause for concern when Alexander at my age ruled over so many conquered lands, while I have not a single glorious achievement of which to boast?'

Inspired by this desire for fame, Cæsar immediately upon his arrival applied himself diligently to business. He raised ten new cohorts in addition to the twenty which he received with his government, and with these penetrated to the shores of the western ocean and conquered peoples who had not hitherto come under the Roman sway. Nor was his success in peace less than in war. He composed differences between the various cities and removed occasions of quarrel between the people, so that he left the province with a great reputation. Meanwhile he had acquired much wealth for himself, and enriched his soldiers with booty.

On his return to Rome, which happened at the time of the election of consuls, he found himself in a difficulty, for while those who wished for a triumph were obliged to remain without the walls, those who sought the consulship were required to appear in person in the city. He therefore applied to the senate for permission to stand for the consulship without presenting himself within the walls. The proposal, however, was strongly opposed by Cato, who, seeing that the request was likely to be granted, spun out the debate until it was too late

JULIUS CÆSAR

for anything to be decided that day. Cæsar therefore determined to give up the triumph, and to stand for the consulship.

As soon as he had entered the city, Cæsar set himself to reconcile the enmity between Pompey and Crassus, two of the most powerful men in Rome. His success in making them friends secured the interest of both for himself. He walked to the place of election between them, and under the influence of their friendship he was elected consul with special honours.

He then at once proposed measures such as would have been expected rather from a tribune of the people than from a consul. Thus he brought forward bills for a division of lands and for a distribution of corn, both of which measures were wholly intended to please the plebeians. A part of the senate strongly opposed these proposals, whereupon Cæsar with great warmth protested that their opposition drove him against his will to appeal to the people. Accordingly he did apply to them, and, with Crassus standing on one side of him and Pompey on the other, asked whether they approved of his laws. They replied that they did, whereupon Cæsar further asked for their assistance against those who threatened to oppose them with the sword. Again they assented, and Pompey added, 'Against those who come with the sword, I will bring both sword and buckler.'

To strengthen still further his alliance with Pompey, Cæsar gave him his daughter Julia in marriage, and soon after Pompey filled the Forum with armed men and so secured the passing of the laws which Cæsar had proposed. At the same time the government of Gaul was decreed to Cæsar for five years, and to this was added Illyricum, with four legions.

The wars which Cæsar waged in Gaul, and the many glorious campaigns in which he reduced that country into submission to Rome, present him in a fresh light. We have to deal, as it were, with a new man. We behold him as a warrior and general not inferior to the greatest commanders the world ever produced. For he surpassed some in the difficulties of the scene of war, others in the extent of the lands he subdued, others in the numbers and strength of those he overcame, others in the savage manners and treacherous dispositions he civilised, others in his mercy to his prisoners, others in his bounty to his soldiers, and all, in the number of the battles which he fought and of enemies that fell before him. For in less than ten years of warfare in Gaul, he carried eight hundred cities by assault, conquered three hundred nations, and at different times fought pitched battles with three millions of men, of whom one million were slain and another million made prisoners.

Moreover, such was the affection which Cæsar inspired in his soldiers, and such was their devotion to him, that they who under other leaders were nothing above the common, became under him invincible and capable of meeting the utmost danger with a courage which nothing could resist, and which was displayed in such instances as the following:

One of Cæsar's legionaries, after boarding one of

JULIUS CÆSAR

the enemy's ships in a sea-fight near Marseilles, had his right arm smitten off by a sword-cut. But, dashing the buckler which he bore upon his left arm in the faces of his foes, he vanquished them and captured the vessel.

Another soldier in the midst of battle had one eye shot out by an arrow, his shoulder pierced by a javelin, his thigh transfixed by another, while upon his shield he received a hundred and thirty darts. He called out to the enemy, and upon two of them, who thought he was about to surrender, approaching, he smote one so sorely that his arm was lopped off, and the other he wounded in the face. Then, his comrades rushing to his aid, he came off with his life.

Again, in Britain, it chanced that some of the vanguard got into difficulties in a deep morass, and were attacked there by the enemy. Then a private soldier, in the sight of Cæsar, threw himself into the midst of the assailants, and by dint of extraordinary acts of valour drove them off and rescued his comrades. He then with much difficulty, partly by wading and partly by swimming, crossed the morass, but in so doing lost his shield. Cæsar and those around him ran to meet the soldier when he got to land with shouts of joy, but he, with signs of deep distress, threw himself at Cæsar's feet and besought pardon for the loss of his shield.

In Africa it chanced that one of Cæsar's ships was taken by the enemy, and all on board were put to the sword except one officer, who was told that he would be given his life. 'It is the custom,' said he, 'for

Cæsar's soldiers to give quarter, but not to take it,' and immediately plunged his sword into his own breast.

This courage of his soldiers was cultivated in the first place by the generous manner in which Cæsar rewarded his troops and by the honours which he paid them. For he did not heap up riches in his wars in order to live in luxury. He poured the wealth, as it were, into a common bank, to serve as prizes for distinguished valour. Another thing that helped to make his soldiers invincible was the fact that Cæsar himself always took his full share in danger, and did not shrink from any labour and fatigue.

His soldiers were indeed not surprised at his exposing himself to danger, for they knew his ardent love of glory. But they were astonished at the patience with which he underwent toils and fatigues which appeared beyond his strength, for he was of slender build, fair in complexion and delicate in constitution, being subject to violent headaches and to epileptic fits. Yet he did not make these infirmities an excuse for indulging himself. On the contrary, he sought a remedy for them in warfare, and endeavoured to strengthen his constitution by long marches, simple food, and living largely in the open air. Thus he fought against his bodily weakness and strengthened himself against the attacks of his malady.

He generally took his sleep upon the march, either in a chariot or a litter, in order that rest might not cause any loss of time. In the daytime he visited the cities, castles, and camp attended by a servant, whom he employed to write from his dictation, and followed by a soldier, who carried his sword. In this way he was able to travel so fast that he reached the Rhone in eight days from the time of setting out from Rome.

In his early years he was a good horseman, and acquired such a mastery of the art of riding that he could sit his horse at full speed with his hands behind him. In his expedition into Gaul he was accustomed to dictate letters to two secretaries at the same time as he rode on horseback. Moreover, he showed himself indifferent to the pleasures of the table and careless of discomfort. 'Honours to the great and comforts for the infirm,' said he, giving up the only room in a poor hut where he had sheltered to one of his weaker followers, while he himself slept under a shed at the door.

Cæsar's first expedition in Gaul was against the Helvetians and the Tigurini, who, having burnt twelve of their own towns and four hundred of their villages, set out to march through that part of Gaul which was subject to Rome, in order to invade Italy. They were brave and warlike peoples and formidable in numbers, for they mustered in all three hundred thousand, of whom one hundred and ninety thousand were fighting men. Cæsar sent his chief lieutenant against the Tigurini, who were defeated by him near the river Saone.

The Helvetians suddenly attacked Cæsar as he was on the march, but, notwithstanding the surprise, he was able to take a good position and to draw up his men in order of battle. His horse was then brought to him, but he sent it away. 'I shall need my horse for the pursuit when I have won the battle,' said he, 'but at present let us attack the enemy on foot.' The enemy was not driven from the field without a long and severe combat. The Romans met with their chief difficulty when they came to the enemy's rampart of chariots, for then not only did the men make a determined stand, but even the women and children fought till they were cut to pieces. So stubborn was the resistance that the battle lasted till midnight.

Cæsar followed up this great victory by a very wise act. He collected the surviving barbarians, who were in number about one hundred thousand. These he obliged to settle again in the lands they had abandoned and to rebuild the cities they had burnt, in order that the lands might not be left to be seized by the Germans.

Cæsar's next war was in defence of Gaul against these Germans, who proved themselves very troublesome neighbours to the peoples he had subdued. He found, however, that some of his officers shrank from this expedition, especially some of the young nobility who had followed Cæsar in the hope of both living in luxury and making their fortunes. The general therefore called them together, and before the whole army told them that, since they were so unmanly and spiritless, they were at liberty to depart. 'For my part,' he continued, 'I will march against the barbarians with the tenth legion only, for these Germans are not better men than others I have conquered, nor am I a worse general than Marius, who defeated them aforetime.' Upon this some of the tenth legion sent a deputation to thank Cæsar for the honour he proposed to do them, while

JULIUS CÆSAR

the other legions laid the whole blame for backwardness upon their officers. In the end all followed him in good spirits, and after several days' march arrived within twenty-five miles of the enemy.

The approach of Cæsar broke down the confidence which the German king, Ariovistus, had felt. He had never dreamt that the Romans would march to attack him, but had expected, on the contrary, that they would not dare to stand against him when he went in quest of them. Moreover, he saw that his men were dispirited by the bold move of Cæsar and by the prophecies of their diviners, who warned them not to give battle until the new moon.

Cæsar was informed of the discouraged state of the enemy, and found that they kept close within their camp. He therefore thought it better to attack them while they were thus dejected, than to sit still and bide their time. Accordingly he attacked their defences and the hills upon which they were posted. The attack roused the Germans to fury, and they rushed to meet the Romans in the plain. They were, however, utterly routed, and were pursued by Cæsar as far as the river Rhine so fiercely that the whole distance of nearly forty miles was strewn with dead bodies and scattered weapons. The number of killed is said to have been eighty thousand, Ariovistus himself narrowly escaping across the river with a few of his troops.

Having thus ended the war, Cæsar left his army in winter quarters, and journeyed to that part of his province of Gaul which lay on the southern side of the

Alps, and which is separated from Italy by the river Rubicon. His object was to keep affairs in Rome under his observation and to maintain his interests in the city. Many came thence to pay their respects to him, and all he sent away satisfied, some with presents, others with hopes of future benefits. Thus, throughout his wars, he gained over the citizens of Rome by means of the money which he obtained from the enemies whom he conquered by the use of the Roman arms.

When Cæsar received news that the Belgæ, who were the most powerful people in Gaul and whose territories made up a third part of the whole country, had collected a great army and broken out into rebellion, he marched against them with marvellous speed. He found them ravaging the lands of those Gauls who were allies of Rome. The main body made but a feeble resistance to him, and was defeated with such terrible slaughter that lakes and rivers were choked with bodies, and the soldiers crossed them over bridges of corpses.

Then Cæsar led his army against the Nervii, who dwelt in a densely wooded country. These people, having hidden their families and their valuables in the depths of a great forest far from the enemy, marched, to the number of sixty thousand, against the Romans. They came upon Cæsar as he was fortifying his camp, and when he was quite unprepared for their attack. The Roman cavalry was first of all routed, and then the barbarians surrounded the twelfth and seventh legions, which lost all their officers in the fight. Probably not one Roman would have survived the battle had not Cæsar snatched a buckler from one of his men and thrown himself into the combat, while the tenth legion, which was posted on the heights above, rushed to support their general when they saw his danger. But though the Romans, encouraged by Cæsar's bold action, fought with superhuman courage, they could not make the Nervii turn their backs. They stubbornly held their ground and were hewn to pieces where they stood, so that it is said that, of the sixty thousand, not five hundred survived the fight.

When the news of this great victory reached Rome, the senate decreed that sacrifices should be offered and festivities kept up for fifteen whole days, a longer term of rejoicing than had ever before been known. As for Cæsar, when he had settled the affairs of Farther Gaul, he again crossed the Alps and passed the winter near the river Po, in order to watch over his interests in Rome. Thither came the greatest and most illustrious people in the state to pay their court to him, among them being over two hundred senators. Pompey and Crassus were of the number, and among these three it was settled that Pompey and Crassus should be consuls for the next year, and that in return they should procure for Cæsar a further term of five years in his government, together with supplies for his needs from the public treasury.

Upon his return to his army Cæsar found that another furious war had blazed out, for two German peoples had crossed the Rhine to make conquests in Gaul. When Cæsar marched against them, however, they sent messengers to ask for a truce, and this he granted. Nevertheless, they treacherously attacked him when he was on the march with only eight hundred horse, who, on account of the truce, were quite unprepared for the onslaught. But even with this small force Cæsar beat off the cavalry of the enemy, who numbered five thousand men.

Next day the Germans sent messengers to express their regret for the attack. These envoys Cæsar seized, for he thought it foolish to stand upon honour with so treacherous a people, and then marched against the enemy. Four thousand of them were killed in the fight, and the few who escaped recrossed the Rhine, where they were sheltered by another German tribe. Cæsar seized upon this as a pretext to attack the latter people, but his real motive was the desire of having the glory of being the first Roman to cross the Rhine in a hostile manner. For this purpose he threw a bridge across the river, which in that place is a wide rushing stream which bears down upon its waters many great trunks of trees. To ward off the shocks from these upon the supports of the bridge, Cæsar drove great piles into the river bed, which stopped the trees and also served to break the force of the current. He carried out this great work, and finished the bridge in the astonishingly short space of ten days.

His crossing was not opposed by the enemy, who retired into the depths of their forests. Cæsar laid waste their lands with fire, and then returned into Gaul after an absence of only eighteen days in Germany.

But Cæsar's daring spirit of enterprise was most fully displayed by his expedition into Britain. For he

JULIUS CÆSAR

was the first to sail a fleet upon the western ocean, and, embarking his army on the Atlantic, to carry war into an island the very existence of which was doubted. For some writers had represented it as so incredibly vast in size that others declined to believe that there was such a place, and declared both name and place to be fictitious. Yet Cæsar endeavoured to conquer it, and to extend the bounds of the Roman Empire beyond the limits of the habitable world. He twice sailed to Britain from the opposite shores of Gaul and fought many battles, which brought more suffering to the Britons than profit to the Romans, for there was nothing worth taking from people so poor and living in such a state of misery. Cæsar, however, did not finish the war as he had hoped; he only received hostages from the king and fixed a tribute which the island was to pay, and then returned to Gaul.

There he found news awaiting him of the death of his daughter, the wife of Pompey. Both father and husband were deeply affected by her death. It was also a matter of great concern to their friends, for her life was a great support to the alliance between Cæsar and Pompey, upon which the peace of the state so largely depended.

As Cæsar's army was now very large, and as there was, moreover, a scarcity of food in Gaul, he was forced to divide it when he went into winter quarters. When this was done, he himself, according to custom, set out towards Italy. But he had not gone long before the Gauls rose again in rebellion, raised considerable armies, and fiercely attacked the scattered Romans in their quarters.

The strongest body of the insurgents attacked two of Cæsar's officers in their camp and cut off the whole party. Then with an army of sixty thousand men they besieged a legion under Quintus Cicero. The Romans made a spirited resistance, but they suffered very heavy losses, so that they were near being taken.

Cæsar was a long way off when he received news of the danger which threatened the legion. He returned with great speed, and, having collected troops, not more than seven thousand in number, marched to the relief of Cicero. Thereupon the Gauls, who had intelligence of his movements, raised the siege and marched to meet him in full confidence of victory, for they knew how small his force was. Cæsar, in order to deceive them, pretended to retreat hastily before them, until he came to a place which offered advantages to a small force resisting a large one. There he fortified his camp, and, in order to increase the self-confidence of the Gauls, he ordered his men not to attack but to shelter themselves behind a great rampart and strongly barricaded gates. Cæsar's devices succeeded as he had hoped. The Gauls, despising an enemy which seemed so much afraid of them, confidently advanced to the attack in a disorderly rabble. Then Cæsar suddenly burst out of the camp, and destroyed the greater part of them. This success laid the spirit of revolt for the time, though Cæsar, as a measure of precaution, spent the whole of the winter in Gaul, visiting all the camps and keeping a vigilant eye upon any movement among the people.

Still later than these events, however, the embers of hatred to Rome, which had long smouldered in

JULIUS CÆSAR

the more distant parts of the country and among the most warlike peoples, blazed out into one of the most dangerous and greatest wars that ever happened in Gaul. The difficulties of the Romans were increased, too, by the severity of the season in which the outbreak occurred. Ice covered the rivers and snow the forests, while the roads lay hidden beneath the snow or beneath the frozen flood-water which spread far and wide across the land. It seemed impossible, therefore, for Cæsar to march against the insurgents. Nevertheless, immediately he received the news he struck swiftly. Covering with his whole army great distances at a speed which would have been remarkable for a single courier, he appeared in the lands of the enemy, ravaging the country, destroying the forts and storming the cities. So he went on, until a people who had been hitherto loyal to the Romans joined in the revolt. Then he was obliged to retreat, until he came to a region where the people remained steadfast to their alliance with Rome. There he made a stand, and although surrounded by a vast army, he totally defeated the enemy. Many of the foes who escaped from the battle took shelter in the town of Alesia. Though it seemed impossible to take the place on account of the strength of the walls and the great number of soldiers by which it was defended, Cæsar immediately formed the siege of the town.

While he was thus engaged, he was exposed to the most extraordinary peril. Three hundred thousand of the bravest men in Gaul marched to the relief of Alesia, while within it was a garrison of seventy thousand soldiers. Then Cæsar accomplished the most marvellous of all his feats of war and generalship. He built two lines of fortification around the town, from the inner one of which he carried on the siege, while the outer one was a defence against the relieving army. He successfully accomplished the feat of defeating the latter army, while he maintained the siege and forced the town to surrender.

By this time the rivalry between Cæsar and Pompey had become very severe, the more so as Crassus, who alone might have entered into the lists against them, had been slain in the Parthian War. It is true that Pompey had not for any long time felt any fear of Cæsar, but had rather despised him, as one who could be pulled down as easily as he had been set up. But Cæsar had long been bent upon the ruin of Pompey, who, he plainly saw, alone stood between him and the mastery of Rome. Like a competitor in the games, he had therefore retired to a distance to train himself for the contest. The long service and glorious achievements in Gaul had provided him with a devoted army, and he himself had gained a fame which rivalled that of Pompey.

The misgovernment at Rome, the open corruption and bribery, the anarchy and bloodshed in the city, and especially some of the acts of Pompey, furnished Cæsar with sufficient pretexts for action in accordance with his designs.

The disorders in the state were such that wise men thought it would be well if they ended in nothing worse than the establishment of a monarchy, and Pompey was hinted at as the man likeliest to remedy matters with the gentlest hand. For his part, Pompey, though he declined the honour of being made dictator, nevertheless acted in such a way as tended to bring all power into his hands. The senate was persuaded to declare him sole consul, he was continued in his governments of Spain and Africa, which he ruled by means of his lieutenants, and he was allowed a thousand talents a year for the maintenance of his troops.

Thereupon Cæsar applied for another consulship, and for the continuance of his commission in Gaul, in order that he might be on the same footing as Pompey. The supporters of the latter, however, strongly opposed these demands, while Cæsar, by a lavish use of the treasures he had amassed in Gaul, busied himself in greatly strengthening his party in the city. Pompey was alarmed by the rapid increase in the influence of his rival. He began to exert himself openly to get a successor to Cæsar appointed to the rule of Gaul, and he also demanded back the legions which he had formerly lent to Cæsar for his wars.

Cæsar returned the legions, and the officers who led them back spread reports which filled Pompey with vain hopes which proved his ruin. They said that Cæsar's victorious legions would declare for Pompey directly they arrived in Italy, so much did they hate Cæsar because he hurried them ceaselessly from one expedition to another. Such confidence did Pompey repose in these assurances that he neglected to levy troops. He contented himself with making speeches and decrees, for which Cæsar cared nothing. It is said that a centurion in Cæsar's army, who had been sent by his general to Rome, waited at the door of the senate-house to learn the decision of the senate concerning Cæsar's commission in Gaul. He was told that a longer term would not be given. Thereupon, clapping his hand upon his sword, he cried, 'This, then, shall give it.'

Indeed, Cæsar's demands appeared very just and reasonable. He offered to lay down his arms if Pompey would do the same, and he pointed out that to deprive him alone of his government and legions was to leave Pompey absolute master of the state. The senate, however, was strongly opposed to Cæsar. Few voted that Pompey should dismiss his forces, while almost all called upon Cæsar to lay down his arms. Even when Cæsar made still more moderate proposals than at first, they were rejected, and Antony and Curio, two of his friends, were driven with ignominy from the senate-house. Indeed, in such danger did they believe themselves to be, that, disguised as slaves, they escaped in hired carriages to Cæsar's quarters. He did not fail to use the plight to which men of such distinction in the state had been reduced, merely through friendship to him, to exasperate his troops against the party of Pompey.

Cæsar at this time had with him not more than three hundred horse and five thousand foot. He sent orders for the rest of his troops, who lay on the other side of the Alps, to join him. But for his present purposes he considered that swiftness and boldness of action were more necessary to his success than numbers. He therefore, without waiting for further forces, set out

JULIUS CÆSAR

secretly for the Rubicon, the little stream which divided his government of Cisalpine Gaul from Italy. As he approached the river, his mind was disturbed by the greatness of the enterprise. He stood still for a time revolving in his mind the arguments on both sides, and talking with his friends about the calamities which his passage of the river would let loose upon the world. At last, impelled by a sudden impulse, he bade adieu to his reasonings, and crying out, 'The die is cast,' crossed the river. So fast did he travel during the rest of the night that before daylight he reached Ariminum and took it.

Now war by sea and land had opened wide its gates, for Cæsar, by going beyond the bounds of his province, had broken the laws and declared war upon the state. Terror seized upon the land, whole cities were broken up, and their peoples sought safety in flight. Most of this tumultuous human tide flowed into Rome, and increased the wild confusion which reigned in the city. Pompey, though his forces were not inferior in numbers to those of Cæsar, was borne along in the general panic. He left Rome, having first issued orders to the senate, and to every man who preferred liberty to tyranny, to follow him. The consuls fled with him, and most of the senators, snatching up such of their property as lay next to hand, joined in the frenzied flight. Indeed, so blind was the panic, that even some of those who had before been well disposed to Cæsar now joined in the rush from the city. Cæsar continued his advance and laid siege to Corfinium, wherein lay thirty cohorts of Pompey's troops. Their commander in despair ordered his physician to give him a draught of poison, which he immediately drank. In but a little while, however, he regretted his action, for he heard of the extraordinarily merciful way in which Cæsar was treating his prisoners. Thereupon his physician removed his fears, for he was able to assure him that the draught was a sleeping potion, and not a deadly poison. Rejoicing greatly, the officer went to Cæsar, who took him by the hand and pardoned him. The news of Cæsar's clemency gave great relief in Rome, and many of those who had fled now ventured back again.

The thirty cohorts at Corfinium, and others whom Pompey had left in garrison at various places, were added to Cæsar's army, and he now felt strong enough to march against his rival. Pompey, however, did not await his attack. He retired to Brundisium, and thence sent the consuls across to Greece with part of the army. Thither he himself followed with the rest upon the approach of Cæsar, who was prevented from pursuing farther by lack of ships. Cæsar, therefore, returned to Rome with the glory of having subdued the whole of Italy without bloodshed in sixty days.

He found the city in a more orderly condition than he expected. One of the tribunes, indeed, opposed him. Cæsar proposed to take money for his needs from the public treasury, whereupon the tribune alleged that it was contrary to the law. Thereupon Cæsar exclaimed, 'War and laws do not flourish together, and indeed war will not brook much liberty of speech. You and all whom I find stirring up a spirit of faction against me are at my disposal.' Moreover, as the keys of the treasury were not produced, he sent for workmen to break open the doors. The tribune again strove to prevent his bursting into the treasury, but was silenced by a threat of death. 'And this,' said Cæsar, 'you are aware it is easier for me to do than say.'

His first movement was to Spain, whence he was resolved to drive Pompey's lieutenants and to add their troops to his own before setting out against their master. In the course of this expedition he was often in danger from ambushes, and his army had to contend against famine. Nevertheless, he waged war by battle, pursuit and siege, till he forced the camp of his enemies and added their troops to his own.

Upon his return to Rome he was declared dictator, and, while he held that office, he recalled the exiles, restored to their honours the children of those who had suffered under Sulla, and relieved the debtors. He then laid down the dictatorship, after holding it for only eleven days. Then, having caused himself and one of his supporters to be declared consuls, he left Rome in order to continue his war against Pompey.

So fast did he march to Brundisium that only a part of his troops could keep up with him. He therefore embarked with only six hundred chosen cavalry and five legions. He crossed the Ionian Sea early in the month of January, made himself master of two towns, and then sent back his ships to bring over the remainder of his soldiers.

Meanwhile these war-worn troops, heavy with the fatigue of marching and wearied of the succession of foes they had to encounter, marched discontentedly towards Brundisium. They cried out upon Cæsar, saying, 'Whither will this man lead us, and where is the end of our labours? Are we to be harassed for ever as though our limbs were hard as stone and our bodies strong as iron? Our very shields and breastplates cry out for rest, for iron itself yields to repeated blows. Our wounds should teach Cæsar that we are mortals, and yet he would expose us to the rage of winter upon the sea, though even the gods cannot clear the wintry seas of storms.'

With such complaints they marched slowly to Brundisium. But when they arrived and found their general gone, the wonderful power which Cæsar had over them was revealed. They changed their tone, blamed their officers for not having hastened the march, and sitting upon the cliffs strained their eyes across the seas in search of the transports that were to take them to share the dangers and labours of their general.

Meanwhile Cæsar lay in the town which he had seized, lacking sufficient troops to make head against the enemy, and full of anxiety at the delay of the rest of his army. In his difficulty he took an astonishing and daring course. The sea was covered with the fleets of the enemy, yet he resolved to take the risk of sailing secretly to Brundisium to bring up his missing legions. By night, therefore, dressed in the habit of a slave, he went on board a little vessel of twelve oars, and throwing himself down as though he were a person of no account, sat in silence. The boat dropped down the river for the sea. At that place the outfall is generally easy, because the land wind which rises in the morning beats down the waves where sea and river meet. But, by ill-fortune, a strong sea wind blew that night, so that the opposing waters were lashed into fury. Wave dashed against wave in tumult, and the pilot, despairing of making good the passage through the boiling eddies, ordered the mariners to turn back. Thereupon Cæsar arose and discovered himself to the astonished pilot. 'Go forward, my friend,' said he. 'Fear not, thou carriest Cæsar and his fortune.'

The sailors forgot their fears, and, plying their oars manfully, endeavoured to force the boat along against the furious waves. But at the mouth of the river the storm was so violent and the water poured so fast into the vessel that Cæsar, though with reluctance, was obliged to permit the pilot to put back. When he returned to the camp, the soldiers met him in crowds, complaining loudly that he had not enough confidence in them to be assured of victory by their aid alone, and that, in his distrust of their support, he had exposed himself to such peril.

Soon after this Antony arrived with the troops from Brundisium, and Cæsar in high spirits then offered battle to Pompey. His rival was strongly encamped, and was abundantly supplied with provisions both by way of sea and land, while Cæsar from the first had but little food, and later on suffered from great scarcity. His soldiers, however, found relief from their hunger in a root which grew in the neighbouring fields, and which they prepared in milk. Sometimes they made a kind of bread from it, and throwing it amongst Pompey's

CÆSAR AND THE PILOT

JULIUS CÆSAR

outposts declared that they would maintain the siege while the earth continued to produce such food.

Pompey would not suffer this bread to be shown nor these speeches to be reported in his camp, for his men were already discouraged. They shuddered, indeed, at the hardihood of Cæsar's troops, who seemed as insensible to fatigue as so many wild beasts. Skirmishes around Pompey's entrenchments frequently took place, and in all save one Cæsar had the advantage. That one, however, promised disaster for his cause, for his troops were driven back in such hurried flight that his camp was in danger of being taken. Pompey himself headed the attack, and none could stand before him. He drove Cæsar's troops upon their own lines in utter confusion, and their trenches were filled with dead.

Cæsar ran to stay the flight, but it was beyond his power to rally the fugitives. He seized hold of the standards in order to recall his soldiers to a sense of discipline, but the standard-bearers then cast their ensigns away, so that no less than thirty-two were taken by the enemy. Indeed, Cæsar narrowly escaped with his life in the panic. He laid hold of a tall, strong fellow who was running past him and tried to make him stand and face the enemy. Thereupon the fugitive, mad with fear, raised his sword to strike his general, but the blow was prevented by Cæsar's armour-bearer, who struck off the soldier's arm.

That day Cæsar so completely despaired of his affairs that after Pompey, either through too great caution or some accident, caused the retreat to be sounded without giving the finishing stroke to his great success, Cæsar said to his friends, 'This day victory would have been with the enemy if their general had known how to conquer.' That night, when Cæsar sought repose in his tent, was the most full of anxiety of any in his life. He reflected that his generalship had been bad in neglecting to carry the war into the fertile lands near him, and in confining himself to the seacoast, where the fleets of the enemy cut off his supplies, with the result that he, rather than Pompey, suffered the difficulties and scarcity of a siege. Therefore, after a night thus disturbed by his sense of the difficulty and danger of his position, he broke up his camp in order to march into Macedonia. He considered that Pompey, if he followed him, would lose the advantage he now had of receiving supplies; while, if his rival sat still, Pompey's lieutenant in Macedonia might easily be crushed while left unsupported.

His enemies were greatly elated by Cæsar's retreat. They looked upon it as an acknowledgment that he was beaten, and Pompey's officers and men wished to pursue him closely. But Pompey was unwilling to stake all upon the hazard of immediate battle. He himself was well provided with all necessary stores, and he therefore thought that time was on his side, and that, by dragging out the war, he could break down such vigour as remained in Cæsar's army. For the best of that general's soldiers were indeed veterans of the staunchest valour in battle, but age had rendered them less fitted for the wearisome labours of war, for long marches and the making of encampments, for attacking walls, and for standing whole nights on guard under arms. It was said, too, that a disease due to the lack of proper food was raging among them. Moreover, Pompey's chief consideration was that Cæsar was so poorly supplied with money and provisions that it seemed likely that his army would soon break up of itself.

Such were Pompey's reasons for avoiding a battle, but none of his officers, save one, approved of his opinion. All the rest reproached and upbraided him, and hinted that his inaction was due to the kingly state in which he found himself, with so many officers of high rank paying him court. Stung by these reproaches, Pompey, against his own judgment, went in pursuit of Cæsar with the intention of bringing on a battle. Meanwhile Cæsar had continued his retreat with difficulty, for, being looked upon as a beaten man, he was everywhere refused provisions. However, he took a certain town where his troops obtained plenty of food and wine, and, the disease which had oppressed them disappearing as if by magic, they marched on with renewed vigour. Thus the two armies entered the plain of Pharsalia and encamped over against one another. Pompey now returned to his former opinion as to the wisdom of postponing battle, and some unlucky omens and an alarming dream strengthened his views. His officers, however, were so foolishly confident of victory, that some disputed about the offices which should be theirs when they returned in triumph to Rome, while others sent to the city to secure houses suitable for men of the high rank to which they expected to be raised.

Especially were the cavalry impatient for battle, in the pride of their splendid armour, their well-fed horses and their own handsome persons, and in the confidence in their numbers, for they were seven thousand against Cæsar's one thousand. In foot-soldiers, too, Pompey had a great advantage, for he had forty-five thousand to oppose to twenty-two thousand who followed his rival.

Cæsar now assembled his soldiers, and told them that two more legions were coming to join them and were at no great distance, while fifteen other cohorts lay round about Megara and Athens. He then asked whether they would wait for these troops or whether they would risk a battle without them. His soldiers cried aloud, 'Let us not wait, but do you rather contrive some plan to make the enemy fight as soon as possible.'

Cæsar then offered sacrifices, and the soothsayer announced that a decisive battle would be fought within three days. Cæsar then asked if he saw any sign favourable to his success. 'You,' said the soothsayer, 'can answer that question better than I. The gods announce a complete change in the state of affairs. If, then, you consider your present condition a happy one, prepare for a worse; but if not, you may expect a better.'

The night before the battle there was a strange appearance in the sky. About midnight Cæsar was going his round to inspect the watches when a fiery torch was seen in the heavens. It seemed to pass over Cæsar's camp, and then, flaming out with great brightness, to fall in the midst of Pompey's army. In the morning, too, when the guard was relieved, a great tumult was observed in the enemy's camp. Cæsar, however, did not expect a battle that day, and therefore ordered his soldiers to break up their camp.

The tents were already struck when the scouts came riding in with news that the enemy was coming down to battle. Cæsar was filled with joy at the news, and, after offering prayers to the gods, arranged his army in three divisions. He himself had the right wing, where he intended to fight in the tenth legion.

Cæsar was struck by the number and splendid appearance of the enemy's horsemen, who were posted over against him. He therefore brought round six cohorts of his horse from the rear without the movement being observed. These he stationed behind his wing, and gave them instructions as to what they should do when the enemy's cavalry charged. The whole strength of Pompey's horsemen was brought to bear against Cæsar's wing, with the design of breaking up that part of the army where he commanded in person by the shock of an irresistible charge.

When the signal for battle was about to be given, Pompey ordered his foot-soldiers to stand in close order, and not to move to meet the enemy's attack until they were within cast of a javelin. Here, Cæsar says, his rival was wrong, because the swift charge fires a soldier's courage, and lends force to his blows.

As Cæsar was going into action with his phalanx, he espied a valiant and veteran centurion urging on his troop to play the men that day. Cæsar hailed him by name and cried: 'How do we stand for victory, Crassinus?' The centurion stretched out his right hand. 'A splendid victory is ours, O Cæsar!' he cried, 'and whether I live through the day or not, of this I am sure, that I shall earn your praise.' First of all the host, Crassinus, with his hundred and twenty soldiers following, burst upon the enemy, cut his way through the front ranks, and was fiercely driving the foe back, when a sword-thrust in the mouth, so shrewd that the blade came out at the back of his neck, laid him low.

When the infantry had come into close action and were fighting hotly, Pompey's cavalry advanced boldly from his left, and extended their squadrons to envelop Cæsar's right. But at once the six cohorts whom Cæsar had stationed behind his infantry came up at a gallop to meet the charge. They did not, as was the custom, hurl their javelins at the enemy from a distance. Nor did they, when they came to close quarters, strike at the legs and bodies of their foes. But they aimed their thrusts at their enemies' eyes and wounded them in their faces, as Cæsar had ordered them before the battle. For he judged that Pompey's gay young horsemen, unused to war and wounds, and proud above all things of their handsome looks, would dread exceedingly blows directed at their faces, and that their ranks would thus be broken as much from fear of the disfiguring wounds as from the terror of the combat.

The event fell out as Cæsar had expected. The gallants could not bear to look upon the spear-points pointed at their faces and the gleam of the swords flashing in the thrust at their eyes. They turned away

JULIUS CÆSAR

their faces or covered them with their hands, broke into shameful flight, and, by their flight, ruined the whole cause of their army. For Cæsar's cohorts of horsemen then swept round the enemy's infantry on that wing, charged them in front and rear, rode them down and cut them to pieces.

When Pompey from the other wing saw the rout of his cavalry, he forgot that he was Pompey the Great and became like one possessed. Without a word he left the battlefield, went to his tent, and there sat down to await the issue of the fight. At length, when his whole army was broken and dispersed and the victors were attacking the ramparts of his camp, he seemed to come to himself. 'What, into my camp too!' he cried, and, laying aside the signs of his rank as general, donned humble garments and fled from the camp. He made his way safely to Egypt, but there, as he was landing from his boat, he was treacherously murdered by a centurion who had formerly served under him. When Cæsar entered the camp of his rival, and saw the number of those who lay dead and the slaughter that was still going on, he said, with a sigh of regret, 'Alas! that cruel necessity has brought this about; but, alas had I dismissed my troops I should myself have been condemned as a criminal.'

Cæsar took most of the infantry who were made prisoners into his own legions. Moreover, he pardoned many persons of rank and importance, amongst whom was that Brutus who afterwards killed him. Cæsar is said to have shown much concern when Brutus could not be found after the battle, and to have been overjoyed when he found that he was unhurt.

The victor soon went in pursuit of Pompey and arrived at Alexandria. There the head of his great rival, which had been cut off after the murder, was brought to him. But the conqueror turned away in abhorrence from the sight, and ordered that the murderer should be put to death. Such of Pompey's friends and supporters as were captured wandering about the country and were brought to Cæsar, met with a welcome from him, were loaded with favours and taken into his own service. He wrote to his friends at Rome, saying that the chief satisfaction he derived from his victory was the pleasure of pardoning every day some one or other of his fellow-citizens who had fought against him.

In Egypt, Cæsar became engaged in a dangerous war, which some have blamed him for undertaking needlessly. Others, however, accuse the servants of the ruler of Egypt of causing the war. For a servant of Cæsar's, a prying and suspicious man, discovered that two officers at the Egyptian court were plotting to kill his master. When Cæsar heard of this he planted his guards about the hall. One of the plotters was killed, but the other, who was the general of the army, escaped. His soldiers supported him, and thus Cæsar was drawn into a difficult war, for he had but a few troops with which to subdue a great city and a large army.

His first great difficulty arose from a lack of water, for the enemy stopped up the aqueducts from which he drew his supply. When he had surmounted this by digging wells, he was faced with the necessity of burning his ships in the harbour to prevent their falling into the enemy's hands. And in a sea-fight near the island of Pharos he was in the most imminent danger. For, seeing his men hard pressed, he jumped from the mole into a small boat in order to go to their assistance. From all sides the Egyptians hastened to attack him. In order to escape, Cæsar was obliged to jump from the boat, which soon after sank. With great difficulty he managed to escape to his own galley by swimming. But, imminent though his danger was, Cæsar contrived to save some valuable documents which he had with him by holding them above water with one hand, while he swam with the other. In the end Cæsar triumphed. He won a great victory over the Egyptians, and then established Cleopatra as queen over the country.

He next marched by way of Syria into Asia Minor, where he found that the governor whom he had appointed had been defeated, and that all the kings and rulers of Asia had been stirred up against the Romans. With three legions Cæsar attacked their forces, and overthrew them with utter ruin in a great battle near Zela. He expressed the rapidity of his success by the brevity of the message in which he announced the victory to his friends in Rome: *Veni, vidi, vici;* (I came, I saw, I conquered).

After this extraordinary success he returned to Italy, and arrived in Rome just as the year of his second dictatorship was expiring. He was declared consul for the ensuing year, and after some interval prepared for another campaign against the remnants of Pompey's party, two of the leaders of which, Cato and Scipio, had escaped to Africa after the battle of Pharsalia, and there raised a considerable army. Cæsar first crossed over to Sicily, and to show his intention of brooking no delay, had his tent pitched on the seashore almost within wash of the waves, although it was the winter season. When a favourable wind sprang up, he embarked three thousand foot and a small body of horse, and landed them secretly and safely on the African coast. He then returned to bring on the remainder of his troops, who were greater in number, but had the good fortune to meet them at sea, and to lead them safely to his African camp.

Cæsar was often in difficulties during this war, mainly through the number of the African cavalry, who were extremely well mounted. By swift and sudden incursions they commanded the whole coast and prevented Cæsar from receiving provisions and forage by sea. Hence he was often obliged to fight to obtain food. He was even forced to give his horses seaweed for fodder, merely washing out the salt and mixing it with a little grass to make it more palatable.

One day Cæsar's cavalry, having no special duty to perform, left their horses to the care of boys and sat watching an African who danced and played upon the flute for their amusement. Suddenly the enemy burst upon them, killed some and drove the others in a confused mob into their camp. Had not Cæsar and one of his officers come to the rescue and rallied the fugitives, the war would have been over in that hour. On another occasion the enemy again had the advantage, and again Cæsar stopped the fight. It was in this fight that he caught by the neck a standard-bearer who was running away, and twisting him round, said, 'Look this way, my man, for the enemy.'

Scipio, flushed with these early successes, sought to come to a decisive action with Cæsar. He marched to a camp by a lake near Thapsus in order to raise fortifications there and make it a place of arms. While he was raising his walls and ramparts, Cæsar advanced with marvellous rapidity through a country very difficult for troops on account of woods and rough mountain passes, and surprised him at the work. Scipio's army, taken in front and rear, was utterly broken and put to flight. Then, acting upon the flood-tide of success, Cæsar attacked the two other camps of the enemy, which were at no great distance, and captured both. Thus, in a small part of a single day, he took three camps and killed fifty thousand of the enemy with a loss to his own army of only fifty men.

A number of officers of high rank escaped from the battle. Some of them killed themselves when they were afterwards taken, and a number were put to death. Cæsar was especially anxious to take Cato alive, and therefore hastened to the place where he had been stationed. But when he approached the town he learnt that Cato had put an end to his life. He was plainly disturbed at the news, and when his officers sought to know the reason of his uneasiness he exclaimed, 'Cato, I envy thee thy death, because thou hast denied me the glory of giving thee thy life.'

After his return to Rome Cæsar spoke in glowing words of the victory he had won, and celebrated great triumphs for his victories over foreign peoples.

About this time a count was taken of the citizens of Rome, and it was found that their number had been reduced from three hundred and twenty thousand to a hundred and fifty thousand. Such was the dreadful loss which the civil war brought upon the city, to say nothing of the misery it inflicted upon the rest of Italy, and upon all the provinces under the Roman sway.

Cæsar was now made consul for the fourth time. The first thing of importance which he undertook was to march into Spain, where the sons of Pompey, though young, had collected a large force. The great battle which put an end to the war was fought under the walls of Munda.

At first Cæsar's men were hard pressed, and appeared to fight with but little vigour. He therefore ran through the ranks amidst the clash of swords and spears, crying, 'Are you not ashamed to let your general be taken captive by boys?' The reproach stung his soldiers to desperate efforts. At length the enemy turned and fled, and more than thirty thousand were slain. Cæsar lost but one thousand, but the loss included some of the best of his troops. Concerning this battle he said to his officers, as he left the field, that he had often fought for victory, but never before for his life.

This was the last of Cæsar's wars, and the triumph in which he celebrated it gave more pain to the people of Rome than any act he had hitherto taken. For he did not now mount the triumphal car to celebrate victory over foreign kings and generals, but to glory in the ruin of the children and the destruction of the race of one of the greatest men that Rome had ever produced. It seemed to all that he was triumphing over the calamities of his country, and rejoicing in the miseries of a civil war which nothing but stern necessity could justify in the sight of gods or men. But the Romans saw no escape from ceaseless internal wars and troubles unless they took Cæsar for their sole master, and they therefore created him dictator for life. His friends and enemies now vied with each other in paying him the most extravagant honours, the latter perhaps because they hoped that the very extravagance of their decrees in his favour would turn many of the people from him. Certainly Cæsar's own actions at this time were above reproach. He not only pardoned most of those who had fought against him, but on some of them he bestowed offices and honours. He also caused the statues of Pompey which had been thrown down to be erected again. Concerning this the orator Cicero said, that by raising Pompey's statues, Cæsar set up his own. Though his friends pressed him to have a bodyguard, Cæsar refused. 'Better die once,' said he, 'than live in constant fear of death.' Indeed, he considered the affection of the people his greatest safeguard, and therefore sought to please them by feasts and gifts of corn. Similarly he gratified the soldiers by placing them in pleasant colonies. The most notable of these were at Carthage and Corinth, cities which he caused to be rebuilt. Thus it fell out that these two famous cities, which had been destroyed at the same time, were restored together.

So great were Cæsar's abilities, so vast his ambition, that he was by no means ready, now that he was master of the world, to sit down and enjoy the glory he had won. Rather was his appetite whetted for still further achievements. In this spirit he formed the vast design of waging war against the Parthians and of making a circuit, after he had subdued them, of the whole northern boundary of the Empire, and of extending its limits to the ocean throughout his course.

During the preparations for this expedition he attempted to dig a canal through the Isthmus of Corinth. He planned also a canal from Rome to the sea, the draining of a wide extent of marsh-land, the embankment of certain parts of the seashore, the removal of obstructions to navigation, and the building of a number of harbours.

These designs, however, he did not live to carry out. But he did complete a work of great usefulness in reforming the calendar and correcting the reckoning of time. The change, useful and necessary though it was, was disliked by some.

The matter which most of all excited hatred against Cæsar, and which led at last to his murder, was his desire for the title of king. This first offended the multitude, and it also gave his enemies a plausible excuse for their hatred. Those who, to curry favour with him, sought to procure him the title, spread among

JULIUS CÆSAR

the people the statement that it appeared from the Sibylline Books that the Romans would never conquer the Parthians except under the leadership of a king. One day, when Cæsar was returning from Alba to Rome, some of his followers ventured to salute him with the regal title. Cæsar, however, saw that the people standing about were much disturbed by this compliment. He therefore assumed a look of anger and exclaimed, 'I am not called king, but Cæsar.' Thereupon a deep silence fell upon the people, and the dictator passed on, by no means well pleased.

At another time, when the senate had decreed certain extravagant honours to him, the consuls and other great officers of state went to acquaint him with the decree. Cæsar declared that there was more need to retrench his honours than to increase them. But in spite of this answer, he gave great offence because he did not rise to receive the consuls, as was due to their office, but remained seated. Not only the senate, but also the people were displeased by this haughty reception, and Cæsar saw his mistake. He sought to make his malady an excuse, saying that those who suffer from epilepsy are liable to find their faculties fail them when they speak standing, through trembling and giddiness overcoming them. But the truth seems to be that Cæsar himself did intend to rise to greet the consuls, but was restrained by one of his flatterers, who laid hold of him and said: 'Why do you not remember that you are Cæsar? Let them pay their court to you as to their superior.'

Other causes of offence were afterwards added. It was the custom at the feast of the Lupercalia for many of the young nobles and magistrates to run, stripped of their togas, through the city, and to strike those whom they met with strips of hide to cause sport and laughter, many women of rank putting themselves in the way of the runners and holding out their hands like scholars to their master. On this occasion Cæsar, wearing a triumphal robe, sat upon a golden chair to view the spectacle.

Among those who ran was Mark Antony, for he was consul. When he came into the Forum, the crowd made way for him. He then approached Cæsar and offered him a diadem wreathed with a crown of bay. Thereupon there was some applause, but it was slight, and came only from some few who had been placed there for the purpose. But when Cæsar refused the proffered crown, all the people applauded loudly. Antony again offered it, and a few clapped their hands, but when Cæsar once more put it from him the applause was again general. The trial of the people's feelings having thus shown their dislike to the emblems of kingship, Cæsar rose and ordered the diadem to be taken away and placed in the Capitol.

A few days afterwards the statues of Cæsar were found to be adorned with royal crowns. Thereupon two of the tribunes went and tore off the diadems, and, having discovered those persons who first saluted Cæsar as king, carried them off to prison. A crowd followed the tribunes, applauding and clapping their hands and calling them Brutuses, because of that Brutus who put down the power of the kings and placed the government in the hands of the senate and the people.

JULIUS CÆSAR

Cæsar was very angry at these proceedings, rated the tribunes soundly with jeering speech, and deprived them of their offices.

In this state of affairs the minds of many turned towards Marcus Brutus, who on his father's side was said to be descended from the ancient Brutus. Many sought to stir him up against Cæsar, and Cassius, who cherished a private hatred against the dictator, was especially active in doing so. Thus a plot against the life of Cæsar, as being one who sought the kingly power, grew up.

It seems, from the death of Cæsar, that fate is not so much a thing which gives no warning as something not to be escaped, for his death was foretold by many wondrous signs and portents. Perhaps, in connection with so great an event, it is not worth while to mention the lights which appeared in the heavens, the strange noises heard from various quarters in the air, and the solitary birds that appeared in the Forum. But one philosopher tells of more wondrous happenings; of warriors of fire seen contending in the air; of a flame that burst forth from the hand of a soldier's slave but left it unconsumed; of a victim which Cæsar sacrificed and which was found to be without a heart.

Other stories are told by many. It is said that a certain seer warned the dictator of a great danger that threatened him upon the Ides of March. When the day arrived, we are told that Cæsar saw the seer as he was going to the senate-house, and called out to him, with a laugh, 'Well, the Ides of March are come'; whereupon the other answered quietly, 'Yes, but not gone.'

The evening before his murder Cæsar supped with one of his friends, and according to his custom signed a number of letters while he was reclining at the table. While he was thus employed, the talk happened to turn on what kind of death was the best. Before any one else could give an opinion Cæsar cried out, 'A sudden one.'

It is said that as he lay in bed the same night all the doors and windows of the room flew open at the same moment. Cæsar was startled by the noise and by the bright moonlight which fell upon him, and looking at his wife Calpurnia, he saw that she lay in a deep sleep, but heard her uttering broken words and inarticulate groans. She was indeed dreaming that she held the body of her murdered husband in her arms and that she was weeping over him.

However that may be, the next day Calpurnia besought Cæsar not to go out, but to put off the meeting of the senate if possible. She further implored him, that even if he paid no attention to her dreams, he would, at least, by sacrifices and other means of divination, seek information as to his fate.

It seems that Cæsar himself felt some fear, especially as he had never before found any womanish superstition in Calpurnia, and now saw that she was much disturbed. He therefore caused a number of sacrifices to be made, and as the diviners found the

JULIUS CÆSAR

omens unfavourable, he sent Antony to dismiss the senate.

In the meantime Decimus Brutus came in. He was in such great favour with Cæsar that he had been appointed his second heir, but nevertheless he had joined in the plot with the other Brutus and Cassius. This man feared that, if Cæsar escaped that day, the plot might be discovered. He therefore laughed at the diviners, and told Cæsar that he would be greatly to blame if he insulted the senate by such a slight. 'They are met together at your bidding,' said he, 'and are all of one mind to pass a decree declaring you king of all the provinces outside Italy and granting you the right to wear the diadem in all those parts by land and sea. But if you send to tell them, when they are taking their seats, to begone and come again some other day when Calpurnia may chance to have had better dreams, what do you expect will be said by those who envy you? If, however, you are firmly resolved to look upon the day as ill-omened, at least go yourself and address the senate, and then adjourn the meeting.' So saying, he took Cæsar by the hand and led him forth. The dictator had gone but a little way from the door, when a certain slave strove to get near enough to speak to him, but could not do so by reason of the crowd that pressed around him. The slave therefore made his way hurriedly into the house, and begged Calpurnia to allow him to stop there then till Cæsar returned, because he had things of importance to tell him.

Moreover, a certain professor of philosophy, who was familiar with some of those who belonged to the party of Brutus, and had thus got to know most of what was going on, approached Cæsar with a small roll on which was written information of the plot. He noticed, however, that Cæsar received other such writings as he went along, and that he handed them at once to his attendants. The philosopher therefore got up as close as possible to Cæsar, and handing him the roll said, 'You alone should read this, Cæsar, and quickly too, for it is about weighty matters of the utmost concern to you.' Cæsar therefore kept the writing, but though he made several attempts to read it, the crowd of people who came in his way prevented his doing so, and he entered the senate holding the roll, still unread, in his hand.

When Cæsar came in, the senate rose to do honour to him. At once some of the accomplices placed themselves behind his chair, while others presented themselves before him, as if to support the prayer of one of their number, who besought Cæsar that his banished brother might be recalled. All these conspirators followed Cæsar and continued their entreaties till he came to his chair. When he was seated, he refused their plea, and as they continued to urge him still more strongly, he began to grow angry. Then one of them seizing Cæsar's toga with both hands pulled it down from his neck, and thus gave the signal for the attack. Casca struck the first blow, and wounded Cæsar in the neck. The wound was not mortal, nor even severe, and Cæsar turning round seized hold of Casca's sword. At the same time he cried, 'What meanest thou, villain Casca?' while Casca called to his brother in Greek, 'Help, brother!'

All the conspirators now drew their swords and

JULIUS CÆSAR

surrounded Cæsar, so that whichever way he turned he saw nothing but gleaming blades thrusting at him, and met with nothing but wounds. Thus he found every hand raised against him, and was driven about like some wild beast attacked by the hunters, for the conspirators had agreed that each should have a share in the slaying and that each weapon should taste the blood of the victim. Therefore Brutus himself dealt him one blow in the groin. Some say that Cæsar defended himself against the others, calling out and struggling, but that, when he saw the sword of Brutus drawn, he pulled his toga over his face and offered no further resistance. Either by chance or by the design of the conspirators, Cæsar had been driven to the foot of Pompey's statue. There he fell, drenching the base of the statue with his blood. It seemed as if Pompey himself were directing the vengeance against his enemy who lay prostrate at his feet, writhing in the agony of death.

It is said that Cæsar received three-and-twenty wounds, and that many of his murderers were wounded by their fellows as they crowded around their victim and aimed their blows at him.

Thus died Cæsar at the age of fifty-six, having survived his rival Pompey not much more than four years. The spirit which had attended Cæsar throughout his life followed him even after death, and as his avenger pursued and hunted his assassins across sea and land till there was not one left of all those who had either shed the blood of Cæsar or consented to his death.

Signs from heaven marked his death. A great

THE MURDER OF CÆSAR

comet blazed in the skies for seven nights after his murder, and then disappeared. The sun's lustre faded and its orb looked pale all that year; it rose without its usual radiance and did not give forth its usual heat. The air was dark and heavy by reason of the feebleness of the sun, and the fruits withered and fell half-ripened from the trees.

BRUTUS

PLUTARCH evidently regarded Brutus with especial admiration, and would scarcely admit any flaw in the character or conduct of his hero. It is probably through his influence that Brutus has long been regarded by many as the very embodiment of patriotism.

It is no doubt true that Brutus regarded the murder of Cæsar as an act of political justice and necessity, and it would certainly not be right to judge his action entirely by the standard of our times, in which political murder is looked upon with abhorrence. But, even if it be allowed that murder for political purposes can sometimes be justified, it is impossible to acquit Brutus of base ingratitude in sharing in the murder of the man who had pardoned him when an enemy, and who had loaded him with favours and honours as a friend. The character of Brutus in this respect gains a lustre, not its by right, because his motives, though misguided, were at any rate far nobler than the base envy and malice of Cassius. Brutus seems in truth to have been an austere, hard man, by no means so free from fault as Plutarch represents, but with the avarice and love of money so often found in men of his character. Though a man of great industry and learning, his mind was narrow in its scope. Hence he did *not see that the death of one man, however great he might be, would not avail to alter the course of events which were leading inevitably to single rule in the dominions of Rome. Julius Cæsar died, but, in a few years after his death, the young Cæsar had established himself as sole ruler and had, as the Emperor Augustus, restored order to the dominions of Rome, and was able to hand down his power to his successors.*

*Shakespeare closely follows Plutarch in his rendering of the character of Brutus in his **Julius Cæsar**, and indeed makes him the true hero of the play.*

It is said by some that Marcus Brutus was the descendant of the Junius Brutus whose statue, bearing a naked sword in its hand, was set up in the Capitol by the Romans of old time, in witness that it was he who had completely put down the line of the Tarquins, kings of Rome.

That Brutus of old time was like a sword forged of cold iron. For his temper was hard by nature, and was not made more gentle by education, so that through his hatred of tyrants he went even so far as to slay his own sons. But Marcus Brutus tempered his natural disposition by the discipline of learning and philosophy, so that he is considered as having most fully shaped himself to the pursuit of virtue. Hence it was, that even those who were the enemies of Brutus through the slaying of Cæsar credited him with whatever of good came from the dictator's death, while that which was evil they laid to the charge of Cassius, who was kinsman and friend to Brutus, but of a nature less frank and noble.

Some there are, however, who say that Marcus Brutus was not descended from Junius Brutus, the expeller of the Tarquins. It is, however, agreed that his mother Servilia was descended from that Servilius who concealed a dagger about him, and, going down to the Forum, struck down one who was aspiring to make himself a tyrant.

Of all the Romans, Brutus took Cato the philosopher most for his model. With him he was closely connected in kinship, for Cato was his uncle, being the brother of Servilia. Moreover, Brutus married Cato's daughter Porcia. As for the Greek philosophers, Brutus was well versed in all of them, but devoted himself especially to those of the school of Plato.

When the rupture between Pompey and Cæsar took place, it was expected that Brutus would side with the latter, since Pompey had put his father to death some time before. Brutus, however, placed the public affairs before his own personal feelings, and, as he considered that Pompey had more right upon his side than Cæsar, he joined his party. He acted thus even although up to that time he had refused to speak to Pompey, thinking it shame to have any converse with the murderer of his father.

Brutus was at first sent by Pompey to Sicily. He found, however, that there was nothing of importance to be done in that island. He went, therefore, as a volunteer to Macedonia, where the forces of Pompey and Cæsar were already assembled to contend for the mastery of the Roman world. It is said that Pompey, surprised and in a special degree delighted at his coming, rose from his seat as to a man of great importance and embraced him with fervour.

During the campaign Brutus spent the whole of his leisure in reading and study. This was the case even immediately before the great battle of Pharsalia. He was at this time put to much discomfort from the intense heat, for it was the height of summer, and his tent-bearers delayed in coming, so that it was almost midday before he had anointed himself and taken a little food. Nevertheless, while others slept or made arrangements for the future in view of the battle, Brutus calmly occupied himself until eventime in writing an epitome of a historical author.

It is said that Cæsar was not indifferent to the fate of Brutus, and that he gave orders to his officers not to kill him in the battle, and to suffer him to escape if he would not yield himself up. Brutus did indeed succeed in escaping from the camp after the defeat and the flight of Pompey. He stole out through a gate which led to a marshy part of the country, full of reeds and pools of water, through which he made his way to a town at no great distance. Thence he wrote to Cæsar, and was pardoned by the victor, who was glad to hear that he had survived the battle. Indeed, Cæsar kept Brutus about him and treated him with great consideration, so that by his intercession Cæsar was even induced to pardon Cassius, who had married the sister of Brutus.

It is said that, on the first occasion upon which he heard Brutus making a speech in public, Cæsar remarked: 'I know not what this youth wills, but I see that what he does will he wills with all his might.' Indeed, the earnest character of Brutus, and his determined intention of being guided by reason and reflection, gave force to his efforts to accomplish whatever he set his hand to. But he was deaf to flattery and to unreasonable requests, and was wont to express his contempt for those who are so weak that they can refuse nothing.

Now there was a certain office of great honour to which it was expected that either Brutus or Cassius would be appointed. The claims of Brutus rested upon his good fame and the esteem felt for his character, while Cassius was supported by the splendid exploits he had accomplished in the campaigns against the Parthians. Cæsar consulted with his companions about the office and the claims of Brutus and Cassius, and then announced this decision: 'Brutus must have the office, though perhaps there is more justice in the claim of Cassius.'

This was a source of anger against Cæsar on the part of Cassius, for, though he was appointed to another office, his mind was filled not with gratitude for what he had received, but with resentment on account of what had been denied him.

As for Brutus, he might, had he so pleased, have been the first of Cæsar's friends and second only to him in power. But though he was not yet reconciled to Cassius after their recent rivalry, he inclined towards him rather than to Cæsar. Moreover, many urged him not to allow himself to be won over entirely by Cæsar, whose favours, said they, were due to a wish to undermine his patriotism and his sturdy love of liberty.

But though Cæsar showed his affection for Brutus, he was not entirely without suspicion of him. For when he was told that Antony was aiming at a change in the government, Cæsar replied that he had no fear of trouble from such a plump, long-haired fellow as Antony, but from the lean and hungry ones, whereby he meant Brutus and Cassius. On another occasion, when some one hinted doubts of the faithfulness of Brutus, Cæsar touched his own body with his hand and said: 'What! do you think he cannot wait to take his turn after this poor body?' It therefore appears that Cæsar regarded Brutus as the fittest to succeed to his power. Certainly, it seems that Brutus might indeed have been the first man in the state, if he could for a time have endured to be second to Cæsar.

Cassius, however, a violent-tempered man who hated Cæsar himself rather than his rule, lost no opportunity of inflaming the mind of Brutus against the power of Cæsar. But Brutus hated the system of government, and was not moved by hatred of Cæsar as a man.

Cassius had a number of personal grievances against Cæsar. Among these, one was the fact that the dictator had seized the lions which Cassius had procured for certain public shows he intended to provide. Some say that this was the chief cause of the plot of Cassius, but they are mistaken. For from earliest youth there was in the nature of Cassius a hatred and enmity to all tyrants, as was shown when he was still a lad and went to the same school as the son of Sulla, the dictator. One day this schoolfellow began bragging among the other boys about his father's absolute power, whereupon Cassius jumped up and gave him a sound trouncing. The affair attracted some attention, and there was even talk of prosecuting young Cassius for the attack. Pompey, however, prevented this, and having had both the boys brought before him, questioned them about the quarrel. Thereupon Cassius said to his schoolfellow, 'Come now, say again before Pompey, if you dare, the words that made me angry, so that I may have the pleasure of cracking your mouth again.'

As for Brutus, he was incited to act against Cæsar, not only by many words from his friends, but also by many exhortations, both spoken and written, from the citizens. On the statue of his ancestor, that Brutus who put an end to the kings, they wrote, 'Would that you were now here, Brutus!' and 'Would that this Brutus were alive!' And every morning Brutus found his official seat full of papers bearing such writings as these: 'Art thou asleep, Brutus?' and 'Thou art not really Brutus!'

The real cause of these discontents lay in the actions of the flatterers of Cæsar, who placed crowns upon his statues by night, as if they designed to lead on the crowd to salute him as king.

When Cassius sought to induce a number of his friends to join in a plot against Cæsar, they all agreed, but only on the condition that Brutus would take the lead in it. For they said that the design required the support of his character more than it needed many hands and much daring. If he would not join them, they could not act boldly in the matter, since everybody would say that it could not be a good cause or Brutus would have been of their number. Cassius saw the force of this argument, and now began to make the first advances to Brutus since their rivalry.

When they were once more upon friendly terms, Cassius asked if Brutus intended to be present in the senate on the day when, it was said, Cæsar's friends meant to propose that he should be given the kingly power. Brutus answered that he should not attend the meeting. 'But,' said Cassius, 'what if they summon us to be present.' 'In that case,' answered Brutus, 'it would be my duty not to keep silence, but to fight and die in the cause of liberty.'

Cassius was encouraged by the words and went on 'What man amongst the Romans will suffer you to die thus? Do you not know yourself, Brutus? Do you think that it is men of no account who put those exhortations in your seat? Be assured rather that they are the best men in Rome. From others they demand gifts and displays and shows of gladiators, but from you the destruction of tyranny. With you they are ready to dare and suffer anything, if you prove yourself such a man as they think you to be.' So saying he embraced Brutus, and then each went to sound his own friends on the matter.

Among the most intimate friends of Brutus was Caius Ligarius, one of Pompey's followers. Though he had been pardoned by Cæsar, he felt no gratitude for the mercy, but rather hatred for the power which had put him in danger. He lay sick when Brutus came to visit him. 'Alas, Ligarius,' said he, 'that you should be ill at such a time.' At once the sick man raised himself on his elbow, and seizing his friend's hand, said, 'But, Brutus, I am well if you have on hand any design worthy of yourself.'

From this time the two leaders secretly spoke of the plot to those whom they trusted, and added them to the number of the conspirators, choosing such as they knew feared nothing and despised death. In addition to such men, they also gained over another Brutus, surnamed Albinus, because, although he was not a bold and courageous man, he was strengthened by a body of gladiators he kept, and also because he was in the confidence of Cæsar. He, like most of the others, was persuaded to join the plot on account of the reputation of Brutus.

The lives of the first men in Rome were now in some sense dependent upon him as their leader in the conspiracy. Hence, though in public he kept strict watch upon himself, so that there should appear no change in his manner, yet when he was at home care and anxiety lay heavy upon him, especially during the night. Sometimes he lay sleepless, often he was lost in thought and sat brooding over the difficulties of the attempt, so that he seemed an altered man. The change did not escape the notice of his wife Porcia, who loved her husband dearly. But to her affection she added something of the spirit of a philosopher, as became the daughter of Cato. She determined, therefore, that she would not seek to find the cause of her husband's anxiety before she had made full trial of her own firmness, and had proved herself strong enough to bear the weight of his secret, however heavy it might be.

Therefore she made trial of herself in this manner. She ordered all her servants out of her room, and then with a knife wounded herself deeply in the thigh. The wound bled freely and caused her such great pain that she fell into a fever. Brutus was deeply affected by her condition, and attended to her with care. Then, in the height of her pain, she spoke thus to him: 'Brutus, when you married the daughter of Cato, you did not, I imagine, look upon her as a mere companion, but as the partner of your fortunes. Never have you given me cause to repent my marriage, but how can I for my part prove my love and faith to you if I may not share your secret counsels? Even if secrecy be not a virtue of women, yet remember that I, though indeed a woman, am the daughter of Cato and the wife of Brutus. But I did not place full confidence in the strength I draw from such a parentage and such a marriage until I had tried myself and proved myself above the fear of pain. See, here is the wound by which I made the trial.'

Astounded at the strength of mind and the resolution of his wife, Brutus told her of the plot which was on foot. Then, raising his hands to heaven, he besought the favour of the gods upon the enterprise, and that he might be enabled to prove himself worthy of the love of Porcia.

The conspirators decided that the best time to carry out the plot would be at a meeting of the senate which had been called for the Ides of March, for it was only on such an occasion that they could all assemble together without giving rise to suspicion. Moreover, the hand of fate seemed to point to the spot where the meeting was to be held as the place of Cæsar's death. For it was a portico adjoining the theatre, and in it there stood a statue of Pompey; so that the death of Cæsar in that place would make it seem as though some god had led him thither that the death of Pompey might be avenged.

When the day came, Brutus armed himself with a dagger concealed about his person and went forth. The other conspirators met at the house of Cassius, and first of all conducted his son, who was that day to assume the man's toga, to the Forum. Thence in a body they went to Pompey's portico to await the coming of Cæsar. Had any onlooker been privy to their plot, he would have been astonished at their calmness. Such of them as were magistrates heard causes as coolly and decided as clearly as though nothing else were upon their minds. One of those who came before Brutus appealed from his judgment to Cæsar. 'Cæsar does not and shall not,' said Brutus, 'prevent me from acting according to the law.'

But, though they appeared calm, the conspirators were disturbed by a number of accidents. The day was far spent, but still Cæsar did not come, and their anxiety grew as the time went on. While they were thus waiting, a man came up to Casca, and, putting his hand upon him, said: 'You hid this matter from me, but Brutus has told me all.' Casca burst out with a cry of astonishment, whereupon the other, laughing, went on: 'Yes, about this office for which you are standing, how came you suddenly to be rich enough to do so?' At about the same time a certain senator saluted Brutus and Cassius and, in a whisper, said: 'You have my best wishes, but do not delay. It is no longer a secret.' He then went hurriedly away, leaving them in consternation, for they thought that everything was known.

Soon after, a messenger came running to Brutus to tell him that his wife was dying. Porcia had been in great anxiety, and consumed with care as to how events were going. After her husband had gone forth, she started up and ran to the door at every little sound and every voice she heard. She sent messenger after messenger to make inquiries, and at length, unable to bear her anxiety longer, she fainted away. Her women shrieked in alarm, neighbours ran to her assistance, and a report soon spread through the city that she was dead. In truth, however, she soon recovered through the care of those about her.

The news, not without reason, caused great distress to Brutus. His private grief, however, had to give way to his zeal for the public. He remained at his post, for by this time it was reported that Cæsar was coming, carried in a litter. He had been delayed by the predictions of the soothsayers, who declared the day to be of ill omen, and by the entreaties of his wife.

As soon as Cæsar had descended from the litter, the very senator who had wished Brutus success went up to the dictator and spoke with him for some considerable time, Cæsar all the while listening intently. The conspirators, who could not hear what was being said, suspected from what the senator had said to Brutus that he was now revealing the whole of the plot. They were much alarmed, and by looks from one to the other agreed that they would not suffer themselves to be seized, but would at once slay themselves. Indeed, Cassius and others began to draw their swords from beneath their robes with this intent. Brutus, however, was able to tell from the senator's looks and gestures that he was only presenting a petition. He reassured his fellow-conspirators by smiling upon them, for, as strangers stood mingled with them, he dared not express his relief in words. Soon afterwards the senator kissed Cæsar's hand and withdrew, so that it was plain that he had only been speaking about his own affairs.

The senate was already seated, and the conspirators placed themselves so as to be near Cæsar's chair. Cassius turned his face to Pompey's statue and invoked his old leader, as though the dead stone could hear his prayers. Meanwhile another of the conspirators kept Antony, the friend of Cæsar, in conversation outside the court.

Now Cæsar entered, and the whole senate rose to salute him. He took his seat, and the conspirators, under pretence of presenting a petition, crowded around him.

One of their number spoke to him, and begged for the recall of his brother who had been banished. All joined in the appeal, and some laid hold of Cæsar's hand and kissed it. The dictator refused their request, and when they still continued to press their suit, rose to his feet in anger. Thereupon one of them seized the robe of Cæsar and pulled it down from his shoulders, while Casca, who stood behind, struck the first blow and wounded him slightly near the shoulder. Cæsar seized the sword-hand of Casca, crying, 'Villain, what wouldst thou?' At once he was wounded by many, almost at the same instant. He looked around for some way of escape, but, when he saw the dagger of Brutus pointed against him, he ceased to make any effort for his life. Loosing his hold on Casca's hand, he covered his head with his robe and fell beneath the swords that stabbed at him so furiously that the murderers wounded one another. Brutus was stabbed in the hand; all were covered with blood.

Thus was Cæsar killed. Then Brutus stood forth in order to speak, and called upon the senators with reassuring words to stay and hear him. They fled, however, in panic, thronging and jostling at the door. None pursued them, for the conspirators had firmly resolved that Cæsar alone should die, and that all others should be called to enjoy the blessings of freedom. True, all of them except Brutus were of opinion, when they were discussing the deed, that Mark Antony should be slain at the same time. For Antony was an ambitious and violent man, and was strong in his popularity with the army. Hence the conspirators feared him, especially as he also held the office of consul at the time.

Brutus, however, was strongly opposed to the slaying of Antony. At first he based his opposition on the grounds of justice, and afterwards on the hope of a change in the disposition of Antony. He trusted that, when Cæsar was once out of the way, Antony would display his generous nature and his love of fame and honour by joining his countrymen in welcoming the coming of freedom. Thus Antony was saved by the efforts of Brutus, and, in the general confusion which followed the death of Cæsar, he escaped disguised in plebeian dress.

Brutus and his comrades then, their hands still all bloody, went to the Capitol, waving their naked swords and calling the citizens to liberty. At first, however, all was confusion; shouts were raised on all sides, and men ran aimlessly hither and thither. But, when it was found that there was no more killing and no plundering, both the senators and many of the people took courage and went up to the conspirators in the Capitol. Brutus then spoke to them in such a manner as to pacify the people and calm their fears. They applauded and praised him, and called upon Brutus and his companions to come down. The conspirators therefore left the Capitol and went down to the Forum, most of the rest of the people following. Some of those of high rank, however, mingled with the slayers of Cæsar, and surrounding Brutus, conducted him with great honour from the Capitol to the place whence speeches were delivered in the Forum.

BRUTUS

At the sight of Brutus and his comrades thus supported, the mob which had assembled in the Forum, though it was divided in opinion and inclined to raise a tumult, was afraid to do so. The people, therefore, listened in silence to what Brutus had to say when he stood forth. Nevertheless it was plain that they did not all agree with the murder of Cæsar, for when the conspirator Cinna began to speak and to bring accusations against the dead man, they broke out into disorder and abused the speaker. The conspirators therefore withdrew again to the Capitol, and Brutus, fearing that the mob would blockade them there, sent away those who had accompanied them but had not taken part in the murder, for he deemed it not right that they should share the danger.

However, when the senate met on the following day, Antony and several on both sides spoke in favour of letting bygones be forgotten, and in favour of peace. In the end it was resolved that the conspirators should not only escape punishment, but that the consuls should bring forward a measure for conferring honours upon them. Antony also sent his son to the Capitol as a hostage. Brutus and his comrades now came down from their place of refuge and greetings and handshakings were exchanged between them and Cæsar's friends. Indeed, Antony entertained and feasted Cassius, Lepidus received Brutus, and the rest of the conspirators were in like manner entertained by others of the opposite party.

At daybreak of the following day the senate met again. Honours were first conferred on Antony, for having prevented the outbreak of civil war, and afterwards on Brutus and those of his friends who were present. Moreover, provinces were distributed among them, Crete being decreed to Brutus and Libya to Cassius.

There next arose a discussion about the will of Cæsar and about his funeral. Antony demanded that the body should be borne forth, not in a secret manner, but with the honours due to so great a man, and that his will should be read in public. Cassius was strongly opposed to these proposals, but Brutus gave way. Herein Brutus is considered to have made a second great mistake; his first having been the sparing of the life of Antony. For, in the first place, the will left to every Roman the sum of seventy-five drachmæ, and, moreover, Cæsar's gardens beyond the river were bequeathed to the people. When they heard these things the citizens were filled with affection for Cæsar and regret for his death. And, in the second place, the people were deeply stirred when the body of Cæsar was carried into the Forum, and Antony, according to custom, made a funeral oration in his honour. For, seeing that the citizens were affected by his speech, Antony played upon their feelings of pity, and, holding up the blood-stained garment of Cæsar, he unfolded it and showed the rents made by the swords of the murderers and the number of the wounds under which Cæsar fell. Then the mob burst out into furious disorder; some clamoured for the blood of the assassins, and some tore down benches and tables from the workshops, and with them built a vast funeral pyre upon which they placed the body of

Cæsar and burnt it. When the pile was blazing, some plucked out burning brands and ran to the houses of the conspirators, intending to set fire to them. This danger was, however, repelled, for the conspirators had guarded against such an attack.

The mob was now in a ferocious mood, as was shown by their murder of Cinna the poet, who was in no wise concerned in the plot against Cæsar, whose friend indeed he was. It chanced that during the previous night he had been troubled with terrifying dreams about Cæsar, and that afterwards he had fallen into a fever. Nevertheless, when morning came, he thought it shame not to be present at Cæsar's funeral. There he was seen, and it being known that his name was Cinna, the mob took him to be Cinna the conspirator, who had recently reviled Cæsar before the people. They set upon the unfortunate poet and tore him to pieces.

The change in Antony's conduct and the fear of the mob, now suddenly raised to fury, made Brutus and his friends fly from the city. At first they stayed at no great distance from Rome, for they expected that the violence of the people would soon wear itself out, and that they would then be able to return. They were encouraged in this belief by the fact that the senate favoured them, and had punished those who sought to fire the houses of the conspirators. They learnt, too, that the people were murmuring at the power of Antony, and were beginning to turn towards Brutus, whom they expected to return to the city to superintend the public spectacles, according to the duties of the office which he held. Brutus indeed bought a great number of wild beasts for the shows, and gave orders that all should be killed and none sold or kept over, but because he heard that friends of Cæsar had formed plots against him and were quietly entering the city, a few at a time, he did not venture to return to Rome.

The arrival of the young Cæsar brought about another change in the state of affairs in the city. He was the son of Cæsar's niece, and by the dictator's will was left his son and heir. At the time of the murder he was studying at the town of Apollonia, but as soon as the news reached him he came to Rome. He assumed the name of Cæsar as a first step towards gaining the favour of the people, whom he further gratified by distributing the money left them by the will. He also gathered round him by rewards many of those who had served Cæsar. By these means he made himself a powerful party against Antony.

Now, when the people of Rome were thus found to be separating themselves into two parties, one for Cæsar and one for Antony, and the armies showed themselves so corrupt as almost openly to sell themselves to the highest bidder, Brutus altogether despaired of the state of affairs. He resolved to leave Italy, and, setting out by sea, made his way to Athens. There he was well received by the people.

At Athens he attended the lectures of certain philosophers, but at the same time, though no one suspected it, he was making preparations for war. He was able to obtain possession of a large sum of money and stores of arms, and the old soldiers of Pompey, who were still wandering about the country, gladly flocked to his standard. Moreover, the governor of Macedonia surrendered that district to him, and the rulers and kings all round about began to come over to his side. He was thus strong enough to defeat Caius, the brother of Antony, who was sent against him.

Brutus was about to set out for Asia, when news came of events at Rome. The young Cæsar, with the support of the senate, had made himself too strong for Antony and had driven him out of Italy. His power was now formidable, and he began to seek to be made consul contrary to the law. Moreover, he maintained large armies which were not required for the public service. When, however, Cæsar saw that the senate were displeased at these things, and that the minds of the senators began to turn towards Brutus, he became alarmed. He therefore sent to Antony, and became reconciled with him. Next he surrounded the city with his soldiers, and thus got the consulship, although he had hardly reached the age of manhood, for he was only in his twentieth year. He then began a prosecution of Brutus and his accomplices on a charge of murder, in having put to death without trial the first man in the state. The judges being compelled to give their votes, the accused were condemned in their absence. It is said that the whole body of people gave a groan when the crier, in accordance with custom, summoned Brutus to appear before the court, while the nobles bent their eyes to the ground in silence. One of them, indeed, was seen to shed tears, and for that reason his name was shortly afterwards put on the list of those who were to be killed.

Then three men, Cæsar, Antony, and Lepidus, divided the empire among themselves, and they prosecuted and put to death two hundred men, one of whom was Cicero.

Brutus having taken his army, which was now a considerable force, over into Asia, set about fitting out a fleet. He also sent to Cassius, urging that they should meet and that they should hold their forces at no great distance from Italy, since their object was not conquest and dominion, but the deliverance of their country. Cassius agreed, and the two friends met at Smyrna. They could not but feel pleased at the contrast between their present fortunes and their circumstances when they last parted in the harbour of Athens. For they had hurried from Italy as miserable fugitives without arms and without money; without a single ship or soldier or stronghold; yet after no long interval they met as the leaders of armies and the commanders of navies, strong enough to fight for the mastery of Rome.

Now that they had joined their forces, Cassius wished that each should have equal rank and honour. Brutus, however, generally went to Cassius as being his superior in age and less strong in body. The general opinion concerning Cassius was that he possessed considerable military skill, but that he was violent in temper and disposed to rule by fear; while Brutus had the esteem of most men, the love of his friends, and the admiration of all. Even by his enemies he was not hated, for he was of a moderate and high-minded temper, unswayed by anger, pleasure or rank, upright in judgment and unswerving in honour. Most of all, his good repute sprang from the faith which men had in his motives.

While the two were at Smyrna, Brutus applied to Cassius for a share in the large amount of money which the latter had collected, because his own resources were exhausted in building a fleet. The friends of Cassius were opposed to letting Brutus have the money, but, nevertheless, Cassius gave him the third part. Some time after they separated again in order to carry on the undertakings they had in view. As for Brutus, he made a demand upon the Lycians for men and money. They refused to supply him, however, and, revolting against him, occupied certain steep passes to prevent the passage of his army. Brutus attacked them with his cavalry, killed six hundred of them, and then captured the positions and forts which they had occupied. He set free without ransom all the prisoners whom he took, hoping by kind treatment to win over the nation. The Lycians, however, continued obstinate, until at last Brutus drove the most warlike of them into the town of Xanthus, and there besieged them. Some of those who were thus shut up endeavoured to get away by swimming under the water of the river which flowed by the city. These, however, were caught in nets which were stretched down to the bottom of the river by weights, and on the top of which bells were fixed, so that an alarm was given whenever a swimmer was entangled in the net.

One night the besieged made a sally and set fire to certain engines. The Romans, however, saw them and drove them back to the town, but meanwhile a strong wind blew the flames against the battlements and the houses near by began to take fire. Brutus, therefore, fearing that the city would be destroyed, ordered his soldiers to help to put out the fire. But the Lycians all at once became seized with a kind of madness, a frenzy of despair in which they welcomed death. Men, women and children, freemen and slaves, young and old joined in hurling missiles from the walls upon the Romans who were trying to put out the flames. They brought wood and reeds and all manner of combustible things to feed the fire, and to make it spread to the whole city. Hence the flames rushed onward, and blazing furiously, girdled the whole city with a ring of fire. Meanwhile Brutus, in distress at the horror of the sight, rode round the walls and besought the Xanthians to save themselves and their city from the fire. None heeded him. In all kinds of ways they sought death; men and women and even little children. Some with shouts and cries leapt into the flames, others broke their necks by jumping from the wall, while some bared their throats to their father's knives and bade them strike. After the city was destroyed, one woman was found hanging by a rope, a dead child slung about her neck, and in her hand a torch to fire the house. Brutus could not bear to see this dreadful sight. He wept on hearing about it, and offered a reward to every soldier who should save the life of one of the Lycians. But, in spite of this offer, it is said that only one hundred and fifty were prevented from finding death. It seemed as if the Xanthians in their despair were reproducing one of the scenes of their earlier history, for their forefathers had in like manner set fire to their city and destroyed themselves in the time of the Persian wars.

Brutus now found that another Lycian city which he approached was preparing to resist his entry. He hardly knew what to do, being unwilling to attack it, because he feared that the horrors of the siege of Xanthus would be repeated. However, as he happened to hold some of the women of the town captives, he let them go without ransom. They spread such a good report of Brutus, and praised his justice and moderation so highly, that they persuaded the citizens to give up the place. Upon this all the rest of the Lycians surrendered. They found that Brutus was indeed just and merciful beyond their expectation. For he demanded from them only one hundred and fifty talents, and then, without doing them any injury, departed.

After some time Brutus invited Cassius to join him at Sardis, and met him upon his approach, the whole of the armed forces saluting both of them as generals. Now, as often happens between commanders in the stress of great affairs, causes of difference and feelings of suspicion had arisen between Brutus and Cassius. Hence, directly they came to Sardis and were within doors, they entered a room by themselves, and having closed the door began to blame one another, and to bring forward charges and accusations. This led on to tears and unrestrained anger, so that their friends outside wondered at their violent language, and feared lest they should do one another an injury. But, as the generals had forbidden any one to enter the room, they could do nothing. However, at length one of them, a senator whose character and freedom of speech led to his rough speeches being often taken as jests, forced his way into the room, although the slaves at the door tried to stop him. With mock solemnity he addressed the angry men in words taken from the poet Homer to this effect, 'Obey me! for both of you are much younger than I.' Thereupon Cassius laughed, but Brutus turned him out with some harsh words. However, the upshot of the interruption was that the friends became reconciled, and their difference was ended for a time. Cassius gave an entertainment to which Brutus came with his friends, and they all made merry over the feast.

On the following day Lucius Pella, who had been in the confidence of Brutus, was accused by the people of Sardis of taking money unlawfully. He was publicly condemned by Brutus, and his name declared infamous, whereat Cassius was much vexed. For only a few days before he had, after blaming them in private, publicly acquitted two of his friends guilty of the same offence. He now blamed Brutus for being too strict in keeping to the exact letter of the law, at a time when they should do their best to please and gratify their supporters. Brutus, however, bade him remember the Ides of March, and how they had slain Cæsar, not because he himself plundered the people, but because he supported others who did so. He declared that, if justice can be rightly overlooked upon occasion, it would have been better to bear the wrongs inflicted by Cæsar's friends than to allow injustice to be wrought by their own party.

It is said that when Brutus and Cassius were about to pass over from Asia into Europe, a wonderful sign came to Brutus. He was by nature wakeful, and by his temperate life and strength of will he had reduced the time he gave to sleep to a very small space. He never lay down during the day, and only slept for such a time at night as could not be employed in business. Now that the war was going on and he had the care of so many great matters, he was accustomed to give even less time than usual to sleep, and to employ the rest of the night on pressing affairs, or in reading, until the time when the officers of the army came to wait upon him for his orders. Now on the occasion in question, it being the dead of night and the lamp burning dimly in his tent, Brutus sat thinking and reflecting, while deep silence lay upon the whole camp. Suddenly it seemed to him that some one entered the tent, and, looking towards the entrance, he had a strange vision of a huge and terrible form standing by him in silence. Brutus, however, found courage to ask the phantom, 'What god or man art thou, and why comest thou hither?' Thereupon the form replied, 'I am thy evil spirit, Brutus. Thou shalt see me again at Philippi.' Then the apparition disappeared. Brutus called his slaves, but they one and all declared that they had neither seen nor heard anything.

Another strange occurrence happened when the soldiers were embarking. Two eagles appeared and perched upon the foremost standards of the army. The soldiers fed them, and the birds were carried along with them until they came to Philippi. But there, the day before the battle, the winged visitors flew away.

When Brutus and Cassius had crossed into Europe, they nearly succeeded in capturing a force of the enemy which had been sent on in advance. Antony, however, saved them by a march of wonderful rapidity. Some days later Cæsar joined him, and the two armies were then drawn up against one another on the plains of Philippi, Cæsar being over against Brutus and Antony opposed to Cassius. The forces were the largest Roman armies that were ever engaged one against the other. In numbers Cæsar had a considerable superiority, but the troops of Brutus outshone their foes in the splendour of their arms. Although Brutus made his officers in other respects adopt a simple and hard mode of life, yet much of their armour was of gold, and silver was used lavishly. Their leader believed that the value and the splendour of their military dress would raise the spirits of the soldiers and increase their courage. Before the battle there were some signs and omens which disturbed the soldiers of Brutus and Cassius. For when Cassius was conducting a solemn ceremony, his attendant officer brought him the garland reversed. On a previous occasion, too, a golden statue of Victory which belonged to Cassius fell down, through its bearer slipping while it was being carried in a procession. Moreover, great numbers of birds of prey appeared daily in the camp, and swarms of bees collected at a certain spot within the lines of the army.

The soldiers were much cast down by these omens, which were not without some effect even upon their general himself. On account of this Cassius was not anxious for immediate battle, but was in favour of drawing out the war, especially as Brutus and he were stronger in resources than the enemy, but weaker in numbers. Brutus, however, had all along been anxious to bring matters to an issue as soon as possible, in order that the country might, at any rate, be relieved from the burden of war. Moreover, he was encouraged by the success of his cavalry in some skirmishes and affairs of outposts. The matter was debated at length among the chief officers, and it was finally decided to fight the next day.

Brutus retired to rest after spending the evening in high spirits and in talk about philosophy. Cassius, however, passed the evening with only a few of his most intimate friends, and appeared unusually thoughtful and quiet. After supper he took aside one of his companions, and pressing his hand, said, 'I call you to witness that, like Pompey the Great, I am forced to hazard the safety of my country upon the chances of a single battle. However, let us be of good heart and trust in fortune, although we may have decided badly.'

Next morning at daybreak a purple garment was hung out as the signal of battle in the lines of Brutus and of Cassius, and the two leaders met between the camps of their armies. Then Cassius addressed his fellow-general in these words: 'Brutus, I trust that we may win the victory and live long happily together. But if the battle ends otherwise than as we expect, it will not be a simple matter for us to see one another again. I therefore beg you to tell me now what you intend to do in regard to flight or death, if fortune goes against us.' Brutus answered that it had formerly been his opinion that it was not right for a man to kill himself, but that he had now changed his views, and that he did not intend to survive defeat. 'In that event,' he went on, 'I shall withdraw from life satisfied because on the Ides of March I dedicated my life to my country, and have since then lived in freedom and honour for her sake.' Cassius smiled approval at these words, and embraced his friend. 'Let us go into battle with such thoughts,' said he, 'for then we shall either be victors, or, at the worst, be undismayed by defeat.'

They now arranged the order of battle. Brutus asked Cassius to be allowed to command the right wing, and his request was granted, though Cassius, by reason of his greater age and experience, was considered more fitted to command in that part of the field. Brutus at once led forth his splendidly equipped cavalry and also rapidly brought up the infantry.

At the time the soldiers of Antony were engaged in cutting trenches in the marshes near which they were encamped. Meanwhile Cæsar was on the watch, but was not actually on the spot because of sickness, while his soldiers did not expect any serious battle. They supposed that the enemy intended merely to make sallies upon the works and to disturb their comrades who were making the trenches by showers of missiles and by threats and shoutings. Hence they paid but little attention to those who were opposed to them, and did not understand the meaning of the loud but confused clamour which came from the direction of the trenches.

In the meantime the command to attack came from Brutus to his officers, and he himself advanced on horseback in front of the legions, and encouraged them to fight bravely. Some few of the soldiers heard the word of command as it was passed along, but the greater part rushed shouting upon the enemy without awaiting the order. Hence there arose some irregularity and some gaps in the line of battle, and as a result some of the legions completely outflanked Cæsar's left. There was some fighting with those soldiers of Cæsar who were stationed on the extreme left, and some few of them were killed. Some of the troops of Brutus, however, passed right round this flank and fell upon the camp of the enemy. There Cæsar had a narrow escape, for he had but just been carried out of the camp when the soldiers of Brutus burst into it. Indeed, they pierced his empty litter with darts and spears, and for a time it was supposed that he had been killed. The prisoners who were taken in the camp were slaughtered, and with them two thousand Greeks who had lately come in as allies.

Those troops of Brutus who had not thus outflanked the enemy, but had been engaged in a frontal attack upon them, easily put their opponents, who were in disorder, to flight. In hand-to-hand fighting they broke up and destroyed three legions, and following up their success rushed, with Brutus amongst them, into the camp in pursuit of the fugitives.

But meanwhile the attack of Cassius on the other wing had been beaten back, and the enemy had in turn captured his camp. Thus it came about that while Brutus thought their troops completely victorious, Cassius believed that they were totally defeated. This mistake ruined their cause, for on the one hand Brutus did not come to the aid of Cassius, since he believed that his fellow-general was victorious, while on the other Cassius did not await Brutus, for he thought that his friend had perished.

When Brutus retired after destroying Cæsar's camp, he was surprised to find that he could not see the tent of Cassius standing out plainly as usual in its place. Nor indeed were the other tents of Cassius's army to be seen, for they had been torn down and destroyed when the soldiers of Antony burst into the camp. Those followers of Brutus who were gifted with the keenest eyesight now told their general that they could see the glitter of many helmets and the gleam of many silver shields moving about in the camp of Cassius. Neither the number of these nor the style of armour seemed to them to agree with the idea that the soldiers moving about were the men left by Cassius to guard his camp, but, on the other hand, there did not appear to be so many dead bodies lying about as might be expected, if so large a force as that of Cassius had been defeated. These observations first gave Brutus some inkling of the misfortune which had overtaken his fellow-general. He at once set a guard over the camp of the enemy, and recalling his men from the pursuit, got together a force to go to the aid of his fellow-general.

The affairs of Cassius had fared in this manner. He had been displeased to see the soldiers of Brutus make their onset without the word of command and in disorder, and still further displeased to see them rush to plunder the camp for their own profit, instead of striving to encircle the enemy and attack them in the rear. For his own part, Cassius conducted his operations too slowly and without sufficient vigour and judgment. Hence he was surrounded by the right wing of his opponents. His cavalry broke and fled towards the sea, and he soon found his infantry wavering, though he strove desperately to rally them. He seized a standard from a flying standard-bearer, and with his own hands stuck it in the ground before his feet. But his efforts were in vain. Even those who were close about him lost heart and courage. Hence, being hard pressed, Cassius was forced to give way and to fly with but a few followers to a hill which commanded a view of the plain.

From the hill Cassius himself could see nothing of what was going on in the plain, and could but dimly perceive the plundering of the camp, for he was weak of sight. The horsemen who accompanied him, however, saw a good many soldiers approaching across the plain. These were in reality messengers whom Brutus had sent to announce his victory. Cassius, however, feared that they were enemies in pursuit of him, and in order to make sure, sent one of his followers, Titinius, to reconnoitre.

When the cavalry of Brutus saw the messenger approach, and recognised him as a friend, they shouted for joy. Some who knew him leapt from their horses and embraced him, while the rest rode their horses in circles round him with clashing of arms and cries of triumph. The commotion fatally deceived Cassius. He took it for granted that Titinius was taken prisoner by the enemy, and lamented aloud that he, through too great a love of life, had caused his friend to fall into the hands of the foe. Then, in despair, he withdrew into an empty tent, taking with him only one freedman, whom he had long ago instructed how to act in such an extremity. Wrapping his robe about his face, he laid bare his neck and commanded his freedman to strike. The blow fell, and the head of Cassius was afterwards found severed from the body.

It was soon discovered that the approaching cavalry were friends, and presently Titinius, crowned with garlands, rode up to the place where he had left Cassius. The laments and mournings of his friends informed him of the unhappy fate of his general. His rejoicings were immediately changed to bitter grief, and deeply reproaching himself for his delay when speed in returning might have prevented the tragic end of his friend, he resolved to accompany him in death, and falling upon his sword made an end of himself.

When Brutus had certain information of the defeat of Cassius, he made all haste to come to his relief, but he knew nothing of the death of his fellow-general until he came up to his camp. Then he mourned over the dead body and lamented his friend, whom he called the 'Last of the Romans.'

Brutus then set himself to gather together the scattered and dispirited soldiers of Cassius, and as they had been stripped of everything they possessed by the enemy, he promised to each of them the sum of two thousand drachmæ. The soldiers were both surprised and encouraged by this generosity. They loudly acclaimed him, and praised him as the only general of the four who had not been beaten. He had indeed, with but a few legions, overcome all those who were opposed to him, and if most of his soldiers had not passed beyond the enemy in quest of the plunder of the camp, he would have won a decisive victory.

As for the forces of Cæsar and Antony, they were at first much more discouraged than their opponents. But, during the evening, one of the servants of Cassius came over to Antony with the news of the death of his master, and in proof thereof brought with him the robe and sword of Cassius, which he had taken from the dead body. This news so emboldened them that by daybreak they were drawn up in order of battle.

Brutus found each of the two camps which his army occupied a source of difficulty. His own was full of prisoners, and therefore required a strong guard, while in the camp of Cassius there was some murmuring at the change of masters, and some jealousy, on the part of the beaten troops, of the victorious soldiers of Brutus. The general therefore, though he drew up his army, thought it well to avoid fighting.

As the slaves who had been taken prisoners were found to be tampering with the soldiers, they were all put to the sword. Most of the freemen and citizens, however, were set free. Brutus, indeed, told them that they were more truly prisoners while in the hostile ranks than when they had fallen into his hand. 'With Cæsar and Antony,' said he, 'you were indeed slaves, but with me you are freemen and citizens of Rome.' He was obliged, however, to dismiss them secretly, for some of his own officers were their implacable foes.

Brutus now gave his soldiers the promised rewards. He rebuked them mildly for beginning the attack without waiting for the order, and promised that if they satisfied him by their conduct in the next engagement he would give up to them certain cities to be plundered. This is the only circumstance in the life of Brutus that admits of no defence. It is true that Antony and Cæsar afterwards acted with more unbounded cruelty in rewarding their soldiers. But such conduct from them was only in agreement with the motives by which they were inspired, while it was not expected that even the hope of victory would tempt Brutus from the straightest path of honour and justice. He had, however, as sole head of the army, to make use of such advisers as he had, and generally followed the advice of those who proposed any measures which would keep the soldiers of Cassius in a good humour. These troops he found very difficult to manage, for they were insolent in the camp and cowardly in the field.

Cæsar and Antony found themselves also in a position of difficulty. They had but a scanty supply of food, and the marshy nature of the land upon which they were encamped made them dread the approaching winter. Already, indeed, they had experienced a foretaste of its hardships, for heavy autumn rains fell after the battle, and filled their tents with mire and water, which the cold weather immediately froze. While they were enduring these hardships, they received news of a great disaster which had befallen their cause at sea. Their fleet, which was on its way from Italy with a large number of soldiers, had been met by the ships of Brutus, and defeated so utterly that the few men who escaped with their lives were reduced by famine to devour the tackle of the ships. The news determined those on Cæsar's side to fight before Brutus and his army were encouraged by news of the victory.

This sea-fight, it appears, took place on the same day as the land-battle, yet by some accident Brutus received no news of the victory of his fleet till too late. Had he known in time, he would certainly not have risked a second battle. He had provisions sufficient to last for a long time, and his army was posted so advantageously that he had no need to dread either the hardships of the weather nor the attacks of the enemy. Moreover, had he known that he was wholly master by sea as well as partly victorious by land, he would have had every inducement not to throw away his great advantages over the enemy by any hasty action.

But it would seem that Providence had decreed that the Republic of Rome should no longer exist, and that, in order to remove the only man who could resist the destined master of the state, Fate kept the knowledge of the victory from Brutus till it was too late to avail to save him. Yet how near he was to receiving the intelligence! For, on the very evening before the battle, a deserter came over from the enemy to tell him that Cæsar was eager for battle because his fleet had been destroyed. But his information was scouted as being either treacherous or merely idle babble, and he was not even brought into the presence of Brutus.

That night, it is said, the spectre again appeared to Brutus in its former shape, but vanished without saying a word. Yet a writer well versed in philosophy who bore arms with Brutus throughout this war makes no mention of the apparition. He tells, however, of a number of omens; among which was the appearance of two eagles, who immediately before the battle were seen in the heavens between the two armies, fighting in the upper air. The soldiers watched the fight with eagerness, and an incredible silence fell upon the field until the eagle which fought on the side of Brutus was beaten and driven away.

After Brutus had drawn up his army in order of battle, some time passed before he gave the word for the attack. As he passed among the ranks, he could not help suspecting some of the soldiers, and accusations were made to him concerning others. He found that his cavalry showed little eagerness for the battle, and that they seemed inclined to wait and see what success might attend the infantry. Moreover, a certain soldier, famous for his courage, rode close by Brutus, and in full sight of his general deserted to the enemy.

This desertion was unspeakably mortifying to Brutus, and either out of anger or because he feared that the treason might be followed by other desertions, he at once, about three o'clock in the afternoon, led his army against the enemy.

Where Brutus fought in person he was, as in the previous battle, successful. He charged the enemy's left wing with his infantry, and broke it. Then his cavalry, following up the impression which the infantry had made, routed that wing. But meanwhile the soldiers in the other wing of his army, when ordered to advance, were afraid that the enemy, who had the advantage in numbers, would surround them. Moved by this fear, they extended their line so much that it was made fatally weak. The centre of Brutus's left wing, therefore, could not sustain the shock of the enemy's charge, but was almost immediately broken and put to flight. So thoroughly were they swept from the field that the enemy surrounded Brutus. In this desperate situation he did everything that the bravest and most skilful general could do to restore the battle. His conduct at least deserved victory. But the soldiers of Cassius, dispirited by their former defeat, were a great source of weakness. They fought feebly, and the terror and confusion in their ranks infected the greater part of the army.

There were, however, many who fought most bravely for their cause and general. Marcus, the son of Cato, was slain fighting among the bravest of the young nobles. He disdained flight or surrender, and calling out his name as the son of Cato continued to ply his sword until he fell upon a heap of slaughtered foes. At the same time fell many others who fearlessly exposed themselves in order to preserve their general.

Lucilius, a man of virtue and a close friend of Brutus, saw a body of barbarian horse in the service of Antony riding at full speed with the special object of attacking and killing the general. He determined to stop them, though at the hazard of his life. He therefore shouted to them that he was Brutus, and they believed him, because at the same time he implored them to take him before Antony and pretended to be afraid of being carried to Cæsar. The horsemen rejoiced at this capture, and, esteeming themselves especially fortunate, sent word to Antony of their success. Their general was greatly pleased at the news, and went forth to meet them as they returned with their prisoner. Many others, when the news spread that Brutus was captured, went forth to see him; some pitying his misfortunes, others blaming him for baseness in allowing himself to fall alive into the hands of barbarians.

When at last the captive and his captors approached, and Antony was considering in what manner he should receive his conquered foe, Lucilius boldly addressed him. 'Be assured, Antony,' said he, 'that Brutus neither is nor will be taken alive by an enemy. Dead or alive, his state will not be unworthy of him. As for myself, I deceived your soldiers, and am prepared to suffer the worst penalty which you can inflict upon me.'

Thus spoke Lucilius, to the amazement of those who stood by. Then Antony addressed himself to the captors. 'I see, fellow-soldiers,' said he, 'that you are angry at the deceit which has been practised upon you. But you have really brought me richer booty than you thought. You sought an enemy; you have brought me a friend. How I should have treated Brutus I know not, but this I know, that I would rather have such a man as this for a friend than for an enemy.' So saying, he embraced Lucilius and handed him over to the honourable care of one of his friends. Ever afterwards Antony found Lucilius faithful to his interests.

Meanwhile Brutus, flying from the battlefield with a few of his officers and friends, passed a brook overhung by cliffs and shaded by trees. There they rested in a hollow under a great rock, for darkness had fallen. Casting his eyes upwards to the heavens, bright with many stars, Brutus repeated the words of the Greek poet, 'Forgive not, Jove, the cause of this distress.' Then sadly he went over the names of those of his friends who had fallen in the battle, sighing deeply at the mention of those whom he most loved.

Meanwhile, one of his attendants being thirsty and seeing that his general was in like case, took his helmet and went down to the brook to get water. At the same time a sound was heard on the opposite bank, and two of the little band went to find out the cause. On their return they asked for water. 'All has been drunk,' said Brutus, with a smile, 'but another helmetful shall be brought.' The attendant, therefore, was again sent down to the brook, but in going he was wounded by the enemy, and with difficulty made his way back.

It was therefore evident that parties of the enemy were very near the hiding-place. Nevertheless, Brutus was not without hope that his affairs might yet be restored, for he thought that his losses in the battle had not been very heavy. One of his followers, Statilius, therefore volunteered to try to make his way through the enemy, in order to find in what condition their camp was. It was arranged that if he got there safely, he should hold up a lighted torch in the camp as a signal, and then return with his intelligence.

Statilius arrived in safety at the camp, for the torch was held up as had been arranged. But his companions waited in vain for a long time for his return. 'If Statilius were alive,' said Brutus at length, 'he would be here by this time.' In truth, as the messenger was making his way back to his friends, he fell into the hands of the enemy and was slain.

When the night was far spent, Brutus whispered some words to one of his servants, who made no answer but burst into tears. After this, the general took his armour-bearer on one side and said something to him privately. Next he spoke in Greek to another friend, whom he besought by the memory of their studies and deeds together to help him by putting his hand to the sword, so that he might give himself the fatal thrust. His friend, as well as several others whom Brutus addressed, refused, and one of them remarked that it was time that they should fly.

'We must indeed fly,' said Brutus, rising hastily, 'but with our hands, not our feet!' Then, taking each of two of his friends by the hand, he spoke very cheerfully to this effect: 'It is to me a source of great gladness that my friends have been faithful. And if I have any resentment against fortune, it is for my country's sake and not my own. For I count myself more happy than my conquerors in the unsullied reputation I shall leave behind me.' He then besought his followers to provide

BRUTUS AND HIS COMPANIONS
AFTER THE BATTLE OF PHILIPPI

each for his own safety, and withdrew with only two or three of his closest friends.

One of these friends was Strato, who had been his friend since the time when the two studied rhetoric together. Brutus placed this friend next to him, and then, laying hold of the hilt of his sword with both hands, fell upon the point and died. By some it is said that Strato, at the request of Brutus, turned aside his friend's head and held the sword, and that Brutus threw himself upon it with such violence that the point, entering at his breast, passed right through his body, so that he died immediately.

When Antony found the body he caused it to be covered with the richest of his robes, and he afterwards sent the ashes of Brutus to his mother Servilia. As for Porcia, the wife of Brutus, some writers tell us that she was for a time prevented from finding the death she sought by the watchfulness of her friends. But at length she eluded their care, and killed herself by swallowing coals of fire which she snatched from the hearth.

www.ingramcontent.com/pod-product-compliance
Lightning Source LLC
Chambersburg PA
CBHW020345170426
43200CB00005B/58